Men, Masculinities and Honour-Based Abuse

This book explores the largely neglected relationship between men, masculinities and honour-based abuse (HBA). There is a common misconception that HBA – whether physical violence, emotional abuse or so-called honour killings – occurs only against women.

This book addresses the gap in the current literature concerning the relationship between men, masculinities and HBA. With contributions from an international and interdisciplinary range of both academics and professionals, the book examines HBA and forced marriages from specifically male-victim perspectives, both in the UK and internationally. Providing a clear understanding of the main theoretical and sociological explanations of HBA against male victims, the book demonstrates that, although men are indeed the main perpetrators of HBA, state agencies must address the fact that many men are also victims.

This book is essential reading for students, academics and practitioners alike.

Mohammad Mazher Idriss, PhD, is Senior Lecturer in Law at Manchester Metropolitan University.

This is book is dedicated to all victims of HBA and forced marriages, male and female. No one should be denied access to support and intervention, whoever they may be.

Men, Masculinities and Honour-Based Abuse

Edited by
Dr. Mohammad Mazher Idriss

Routledge
Taylor & Francis Group
a GlassHouse Book

First published 2020
by Routledge
2 Park Square, Milton Park, Abingdon, Oxon OX14 4RN

and by Routledge
52 Vanderbilt Avenue, New York, NY 10017

A Glasshouse Book

Routledge is an imprint of the Taylor & Francis Group, an informa business

First issued in paperback 2021

British Library Cataloguing-in-Publication Data
A catalogue record for this book is available from the British Library

Library of Congress Cataloging-in-Publication Data
A catalog record for this book has been requested

ISBN: 978-0-367-20444-0 (hbk)
ISBN: 978-1-03-208256-1 (pbk)
ISBN: 978-0-429-27772-6 (ebk)

Typeset in Galliard
by Apex CoVantage, LLC

Contents

Foreword

I must first thank Manchester Metropolitan University for asking me to write this foreword. When I joined the Metropolitan Police in May 1979, I had a clear picture in my mind of the type of crimes I would be asked to investigate and police. Men running around in striped jumpers with masks and a bag marked 'swag' on their back. Drug dealers in big cars and menacing clothing, and also football fans who could not behave even if the team they supported won. I joined and spent my first 20 weeks at Hendon, and most of the training focused on the crimes I have just mentioned. Section 1 of the Theft Act 1968. Section 8 Robbery. Section 12 Burglary. The Offences Against the Persons Act 1861, giving a whole range of assaults. Parking on yellow lines, zebra crossings and civil disputes. 'Domestics are not the responsibility of the police', I was told. 'Get in and get out quickly'. But my mentor was a fictional character from TV. 'Evenin' all'. From the moment the crackling black-and-white image of Jack Warner delivered those words on a Saturday night, until he wrapped up thirty minutes later with his regular sign-off, 'Evenin' all', you could hear a pin drop in our house. Everything stopped for TV's first police drama, *Dixon of Dock Green.*

If there's been a greater influence on me outside my own family, then I can't place it. Sgt. George Dixon, the kindly old gent with the downward-pointing triple arrows on his epaulette, fascinated me. He was so twinkly eyed and friendly, but he struck fear into the hearts of the low-level criminals in the Dock Green area. Bike thieves, blackmailers, bank robbers – you name it – every wannabe Big Time Charlie in Dixon's vicinity knew they'd met their match with the Sarge. A mob doing over a bakery before the early crusts had risen? There was George to save the village's buns. On the hunt for a missing child – no one was better at getting information from witnesses, because who didn't want to speak to Dixon of Dock Green? He didn't carry a gun; he didn't drive a fast car – in fact he wheeled around on a pushbike most the time, his cape flapping in the breeze. But what George Dixon *did* have was a sense of community, of putting people first, of knowing what was right and wrong. Some people he brushed up against – officers and criminals alike – were a bit flash, a bit full of themselves or smug. But George was never like that. He was fair. He was kind. He had a way with him that put you at ease, even from the other side of the TV set. 'And, in 1979, I wished I'd never set eyes on him'. This is a quote from a book I wrote in 2014. I wasn't exactly thinking of old George when I got on the tube at Morden more than forty years ago. Nor was he specifically in my thoughts when I emerged, a little bit lost, an hour later at Colindale. But since Dixon was the inspiration for me applying to join the police force, the reason I was lugging a suitcase along Aerodrome Road towards the Metropolitan Police Training College and the reason I was about to start seventeen grueling weeks away from home, at least part of the sense of dread in the pit of my stomach could be pinned on him. That was only fair; he'd have to see that. The Peel Centre they call it now, named after the Met's founding father, Lord Robert Peel, although most coppers just refer to it as 'Hendon'. Whatever its name, I knew I was close when I saw the three dark tower blocks looming towards me, about as welcoming as something from *Hammer Horror*. All they needed was a lightning storm around the top and a bit of howling. To this day, I still break out in a cold sweat whenever I have to go there. Back then, I almost turned on my heels. I certainly stopped and asked myself the same question I'd been anguishing over throughout the long trip north. The Met has sold most of it now and it is not the place it used to be.

Come on, Driscoll, I thought. *It can't be as bad as it looks.* Actually, it could – and it was. In the entrance hall, sitting behind a table that looked like it had been put there as a temporary desk many years earlier, a roly-poly geezer in a blue police sweater was thumbing through a paperback. I wasn't expecting anyone to rush over with open arms, but I did think the man might actually acknowledge my presence. He didn't. Not till I gave one of those coughs that civilisations have decided are more polite than just saying 'oi' but mean the same thing. Without looking up, the desk dweller said, 'Name?' 'Driscoll, Clive', I said. This was my first day of a thirty-four year career that saw so many changes in the police and the attitude of the public. I often ask myself what is normal and the answer always comes back the same: 'It's what my mother said was normal'. I remember an incident when I was 16. A young girl was having problems at home. Problems that would be called domestic abuse now, but in 1966 it was just called 'problems at home'. She and a friend had told one of the lads in my group that they could not go home and would be staying out sleeping in a slip road behind Wandsworth Park. I didn't know this girl; she wasn't my girlfriend and nor did I think she ever might be, but something in me said, 'Hang on, you can't let two girls stay out on their own'. So me and another one of the crowd said we'd hang around as well. Not being the brightest, we didn't tell any adults, not that they would have let us stay out all night if we had, but when, at about two in the morning, the big Shell garage opposite the park was broken into, I wished we had. Suddenly the park was swarming with the police and an officer with a dog saw us four, in a side road by the park in the middle of the night, and put two and two together. The first thing the copper did was smack me round the head. Then he asked if we'd robbed the place. That wasn't the way to do things, I was sure of that. Worse occurred when we were all spirited to Wandsworth Police Station. I was okay with Grandad being called, but when the desk sergeant went to phone the girl's house I said, 'You can't do that. Her old man is the reason she's got a black eye in the first place'. But they did and, sure enough, her father gave her a wallop as soon as he saw her. It made the ticking off I got from Grandad seem a bit mild. If this had been an honour-based abuse (HBA) case, the consequences for the girl or boy could have been more severe. It's a lesson I learnt at an early age and one that I carried into my police career. I said back then to the desk sergeant, 'You're meant to protect victims, not help them get hurt'. It fell on deaf ears. 'Just as well', Grandad said, or I could have got worse than a ticking off.

My first experience of HBA was not as a police officer – it was when I became an ambulance man in 1975. I don't really know where the inspiration came from, other than it being another emergency service where I got to help people. My plan was to do a couple of years working for the London Ambulance Service and then move on into the police, but that went straight out the window the second I joined. I loved everything about the Ambulance Service. I did the statutory six weeks' training at Waterloo, which was essentially a pumped-up first aid course. Intubation, infusion, cardiac massage – we ticked off all the big life-savers. Then, about halfway through that, I started to go out on call with a real ambulance man. My very first call was to the Union Jack Club. If you visit that address today, you'll find a fairly salubrious place. Back then, it was a doss house, so going to treat a vagrant who'd collapsed was no surprise. However it was my first death and honestly, I could have had a year's training and still not have been prepared for that. I wasn't scared or sick. My overwhelming thought was, *You don't look any different.* And that is how I would describe my first encounter with HBA. A family living on the Francis Chichester Estate in Battersea, SW11. I was posted at Battersea, which was a very busy station. From 7 a.m. to 3 p.m., there were two ambulances on shift, so that was all right; but from 11 p.m. to 7 a.m., you had only one. 'Battersea 3-1' was my call sign for the dispatcher, and some shifts, I was hearing it non-stop. Nights were quite perky, Battersea Rise being just down the road from some inner London addresses, and there were some tasty assaults especially towards the weekend. On the plus side, there was no time to think about what you were doing. Get in, do your stuff, get them to a hospital. A young girl with a fractured arm had presented herself to the casualty department at St. Thomas Hospital. The police had been called, but it was just 'problems at home'. She was begging the nurses not to call her family but at the age of 14, hospital procedure said they must. A man about sixty years old came, her granddad, just like mine had come for me all those years ago. He was very respectful and thanked the hospital staff for helping his granddaughter. The difference was the girl's reaction – she was terrified. I had known I was going to get a telling off and maybe a clip round the ear, but this girl's face suggested the punishment would be far more severe. But when I looked at her grandfather and thought of mine, I thought, *You don't look any different.* The family had arrived in England from India in 1947, just after the partition between India and Pakistan. Her granddad had been in the British Army, so had mine; her great-granddad had fought in the First World War, so had mine; her grandfather had fought in the Second World War, so had mine. Yet her 'normal' was different from mine.

I never condemned or ridiculed any culture or religion in my time as an ambulance man or as a police officer. I have formed the opinion that no one can say his or her culture or religion is all good, and nobody can say it's all bad. In fact, the overwhelming majority of people I have met in all religions and cultures have been charming. However the brutal fact remains that we have bad people in our society, and we have old traditions that do not fit in with the modern world and human rights. It is with regret that I cannot say what happened to that girl after she left the hospital or where she is today. I can only say the nursing staff some months later informed me that she had returned to India, according to the information they had received from the police. Which brings me to why I have been asked to write the foreword to this book and how I became involved as a police officer. The murder of Surjit Athwal. The bravery of Mrs Sarbjit Athwal and Mr Jagdeesh Singh.

It was a DI over at Barnes who contacted me. I was at the time the Detective Chief Inspector of a unit called the South Asian Crime Squad. It had been the Racial and Violent Crime Task Force, Emerging Threats in New Communities and other names, but it was the South Asian Crime Squad, and now SCD 2 (2). DI McKellen was his name. 'Is that the South Asian Crime Squad?' 'That doesn't technically exist anymore', I said. 'But go on'. 'I've got a case involving an honour killing that's been mothballed since 1998. New information has come in. Do you want it?' I cannot say I remembered my ambulance case, but I soon realised this was serious. The team – despite the name changes and constant upheaval from outside – was on an upward curve. Of course, I said yes. The only hitch was, not everyone wanted us to have it. I'm not saying it was personal because I have no proof of that, but I can say that my team was being squeezed out of existence. There was to be a restructuring, a bi-annual occurrence with the Met, and when the music stopped there would be one chair missing. All I cared about – all I still care about – is the victim. Did they or did they not get justice? In the honour killing of Surjit Athwal, she most definitely had not. The honour killing in question was that of a young Sikh woman, Surjit Athwal. Surjit had married Sukhdave Athwal then moved in with him, his mother, his brother and his brother's wife. In 1998 she had gone missing. Some people said she had been murdered. Sukhdave and the family said she had run off with her boyfriend. An investigation got precisely nowhere, with officers spending months working on it as a missing person case, then switching focus, arguably after the horse had bolted, to a murder enquiry months later. But now, six years after Surjit's disappearance, a new witness had come forward. What he had to say, I didn't yet know. First I needed to get up to speed on the case. I went over to Barnes and said to the sergeant in CID, 'I've come over to pick up Operation Yewlands'. He scratched his chin. 'Sorry, Guv. I've been here years, and we've never had an Operation Yewlands'. I was about to ask to speak to McKellen when I looked up and saw twelve boxes on a high shelf with *Operation Yewlands* written on the front. I said, 'Humour me for a minute, will you? I'm a bit of the detective – do you think those boxes might be relevant?' He looked up and said, 'Blimey, that shelf hasn't been touched for years'. That was obvious from the inch of dust on each of the boxes. By the time I got everything back to my house where I planned to read the lot that night, I was as grey and powdery as the boxes. I sat with those twelve crates on either side of me and by the time I finished, I knew less about the murder than when I started. It was so complicated. For starters, the names were so alien to me – Sukhdave, Hardave, Surjit, Sarbjit and Bachan – and the crisscrossing of leads and dead ends was mindboggling, and for once I don't think dyslexia had anything to do with it. For some reason the previous Senior Investigating Officer – SIO – had logged everything on the card system. For a case as big and complex as this, it needed to be computerised. So that was my first decision: get it all typed into the mighty Met machine; then at least we'd know what we had.

The new evidence was from a gentleman called Mr Seva Singh. He was the father of Sarbjit Athwal – sister-in-law to the missing Surjit. When I visited his house in West London, I must have been in the living room a couple of minutes before I spotted another person there. Cowering – or, at the very least, trying not to be noticed under her traditional cloth head covering – was a young woman. 'Excuse me, ma'am, I didn't see you there. My name's DCI Driscoll'. 'Detective, let me introduce you to my daughter, Sarbjit', Mr Singh said. 'It is her story that I am telling you'. Now we were cooking. Mr Singh told me how Sarbjit had been at a family meeting in Willow Tree Lane, where she lived with the Athwals, where the matriarch of the family, Mrs Bachan Kaur Athwal, had announced, 'She has to go'. She'd been talking about Surjit, Sukhdave's wife. Surjit, they felt, was straying too far from the path chosen for her by her mother-in-law. She wanted to wear western clothes, she wore makeup and she had started to go to parties with colleagues at Heathrow Airport, where she worked. These parties had involved alcohol and the company of both women and men. To you and me, she was a woman in her early twenties enjoying her life. The 14-year-old girl from Battersea entered my mind. But to Bachan Kaur, she was bringing shame on the family – and she had to die. A plan was hatched to send her to India on the pretence of attending a family wedding. There she would be murdered and her body disposed of in the Ravi River. Her children would be informed she'd abandoned them to be with another man – and that was the end of the matter. As I listened to the story, I thought Mr Singh had to be holding something back. You don't just kill your daughter-in-law because she's drinking the odd sherbet and wearing a skirt. No one in the world would think that was justifiable. 'You have to understand she was destroying the honour of the family', Mr Singh replied. 'You'll have to help me out here', I said. 'That is enough to put out a contract on her?' He nodded. 'For some people, yes'. *What is normal is what your mother said was normal, Clive*, I thought.

Throughout the entire meeting Sarbjit didn't speak once. She didn't even look at me, as if she felt I might see her. But I had to ask: 'Why come to us now? Why didn't you tell the police when she first when missing? We could have done something'. 'Please don't point a finger at my daughter', Mr Singh said very calmly. 'You see, Sarbjit did report it – *before* the murder took place'. And she had, on several occasions. 'Your officers had the chance to prevent the murder of Surjit Athwal and they did nothing'. I believe implicitly in collective responsibility. I'm a member of the Met and proud to be so. We're all brothers and sisters in arms, and as far as the public is concerned we are all the same animal. So I never distance myself from somebody else's mistakes, however bad they are. When you do that it riles everyone outside the force. I still accept that responsibility, and that is why I am honored to write this foreword. Manchester Metropolitan University and others are trying to right the wrong. We must all learn and share our successes and failures so the younger generation benefit. I say 'successes', but solving a murder has never seemed successful to me. Preventing one is 'light up a cigar and large whiskey time' – even though smoking is harmful and we all must drink responsibly. And so, as hard as it was considering the events that took place six years before I joined the team, I apologised as though I'd committed the error myself. And then I asked for the details.

Having been witness to the plan to kill her sister-in-law, Sarbjit's first thought was to get help. But who could she tell? She was living with people who would kill to protect the family name. What would they do to her if they discovered she'd spoken to the police? And so, one morning after dropping her daughter at school, Sarbjit made the bravest decision of her life and called the anonymous Crimestoppers hotline from a payphone en route home. She told the operator everything about the plan, including the flight details, hotel plans and passport names. At the end, she begged them to do something and was told it would be investigated. From that moment on, Sarbjit was living in a cocoon of fear. Her paranoia was justified. Her mother-in-law commented on the unusually long time it had taken that morning to do the school run. She had spies everywhere – people from her temple who would tell her anything by way of gossip. What if someone had seen Sarbjit enter the phone booth? Suddenly the enormity of what she had done hit her. If the police suddenly turned up to discuss the attempted murder, Bachan Kaur and Sukhdave would guess who had told them. And then what would happen? She knew the answer.

But, in a perverse way, Sarbjit got lucky and her family never found out about her betrayal – because the police did nothing about the phone call. Surjit was allowed to board the plane, attend the wedding in India, then be murdered and have her body disposed of, just as Bachan Kaur had planned. Sarbjit's life in the Athwal house after that was untenable, but she made one more attempt at getting justice. Too scared to physically enter a police station, she'd written a long letter again detailing everything and posted it to Hayes nick. Again, nothing had happened. Then months later, when Sarbjit had finally cracked and told her sister Inder everything, Inder had marched into the cop shop on The Strand in Central London and relayed the entire tale. She thought she was getting somewhere, as it took more than one meeting. But again, nothing happened. No arrests, no justice for Surjit. And here we were, years later, when finally Sarbjit was prepared to break her anonymity and go on the record. I knew what she must have been thinking: *What's the point? They won't act – and I'll be killed for nothing.* But the pain of seeing her sister-in-law not receive justice – and her poor children believing her to be a bad mother – outweighed that risk. But I knew it was the last roll of the dice for the family. After this, they would never trust the Met again. I listened to every word, and I made a promise to get right onto the job.

I met Mr Seva Singh again and this time persuaded Sarbjit to talk to me. Over the next few weeks, I met with her many times and I saw a transformation in her. From the shy, insecure mouse that I first nearly trod on, to an empowered woman – she is a lesson for all put-upon women. Ten years later, I am proud to call her a friend. But back in 2005, she still had a treacherous journey before her.

Another remarkable person in this story is Mr Jagdeesh Singh, the brother of Surjit. Together with his father, Mr Dhillon, there was not one day when they did not campaign for action into Surjit's disappearance. Jagdeesh remains one of the most honourable people I have ever met. His relentless pursuit of the truth on his sister's behalf is commendable. There is honour, and Mr Singh has shown what true honour can do. But it was when I travelled to India that I realised the size of the problem when a police officer from the Punjab asked me: 'Why is the London Met worried about this girl? It is family business'. 'Excuse me, I think that girl was murdered', I said. 'For bringing shame on her family', he replied. I couldn't believe it. In fact, I was told quite openly that Surjit wouldn't have been chucked in the River Ravi. 'It happens', one bloke said. 'And the best thing about the Ravi is it runs into Pakistan – so they get our trash'. I don't want to play the big white chief, but how had I arrived in a place where murder was okay if it was committed by a family member? England and every other country have problems. In fact, at the time of writing, London is in the middle of a knife crime epidemic. But the attitude of the Indian police officer and some members of the community showed why we all have to be vigilant and work hard to eradicate HBA, forced marriages and all forms of violence.

The court date soon whizzed round. I wasn't allowed to speak to Sarbjit during the trial as she was a witness, but our barrister, the icon that is Michael Worsley, shepherded her through it all as best he could. Then finally, after three-and-a-half long weeks, during which time my physical evidence from Pathankot shot the defence's lies to pieces, the jury retired. DS Goodley called to let me know, and I made my way over to the court. The jury could be out for five minutes or five days, but I wasn't going to visit them. The investigation ends for me when the jury retires. Up to that point, I am still scrabbling around for any evidence I can possibly find. When the twelve good men and women adjourn to their room, that's the finish line for me. That's when I like to thank all the clerks and the court staff for all their help – from the people who help you with photocopying down to the ushers. The ones I couldn't find I emailed, along with everyone else who had contributed to getting the case to court.

You never know for sure which way a dozen strangers are going to go, but I did know that I had faith in them. I have complete respect for our jury system. If they sit through all our evidence and decide the accused are not guilty, then justice has been served. I might not like it, but I can't blame them. I can only blame myself for not putting the right evidence in front of them to win the verdict I want. I was in a meeting in Tintagel House when I heard the jury had reached a decision. I flew back over to the court, but I got the news while I was still in the cab. When I phoned Sarbjit a second later, I just said one word: *Guilty.* Then she hung up on me. At least that's what I thought because the line went dead. Then I realised I could barely make out the faint sob of tears. 'Oh, Clive', she whispered. 'I can't believe you've done it. You've saved my life'. The reality is that the system saved her life; the one-chance rule saved her life. Her bravery and Mr Jagdeesh Singh's bravery saved her life, all I did is what you all paid me to do. When I did reach the court to thank everyone else, I was told Sarbjit's life wasn't the only one in my 'plus' column. A respected member of the Sikh community said, 'You have drawn a line in the sand today, DCI Driscoll. You have shown the whole of Great Britain that murders in the name of honour, even conducted on foreign soil, will not be tolerated. I believe you have probably saved tens of thousands of lives'. And that is all of our challenge – we can all sit back and do nothing and watch some of our young people be murdered, or suffer forced marriage or female genital mutilation, or we can be as brave as Mrs Sarbjit Athwal and Mr Jagdesh Singh and say no, we are not putting up with this behaviour any longer.

We also cannot make the mistake that this only happens to females. Yes, I think the majority of cases are female, but it is not an exclusive club. Since Surjit's case, I have spoken with and helped at least ten male victims. Tricked into travelling and then held captive to marry a female they have never met. Tricked into entering into a debt with gang masters that they will never be able to pay due to the interest imposed and therefore becoming slaves. Slaves in 2019. I can highlight a case concerning very respectable professional Asian men. Both men were married with children, and gay. They met once a week and enjoyed each other's company and then returned to their respective families. But both were petrified that if anyone found out about their relationship, at least one or both would be killed. One thing that united them was their thinking that the police would not help them. In fact, one of the men suggested that as a white police officer, I would be both homophobic and racist towards them and that no one would really care what would happen to them. So what can the police do to support men like these? It's simple – be open, honest and work hard. It took many months of visiting and talking to the male victims, as most of the cases I eventually investigated did. Once people see you are trying and are not judgemental, they will place trust in you, which will help to bring normality to police investigations. Both victims and the police can move forward together. I cannot divulge the area or the police service that assisted me because to do so could identify the two males who placed trust in me. But what I can say now is that they are living a life together, with regular access to their children. Trust and confidence is the backbone of helping traumatised and terrified people. I spoke to them recently and they told me that India would win the 2019 Cricket World Cup. Well, at least they are now settled and happy together, which might ease the pain of seeing India on the plane back home after the semi-finals loss!

I once said at a public meeting, and was criticised by an MP for saying, that it does not make it easier or more enjoyable to be a slave when the gang master or enslaver is not white. Bad people are bad people – they come in all shapes and sizes and all different cultures and ethnic backgrounds. But I stress, in my time, the good far outweigh the bad – we just need to make sure the good wins more often. I congratulate Manchester Metropolitan University for getting the timely message out there about male victims of HBA and forced marriages.

Evenin' all.

Dr. Clive Driscoll
Retired Detective Chief Inspector, Metropolitan Police,
and Deputy Chair and Trustee, True Honour

Contributors

The editor

Dr. Mohammad Mazher Idriss LLB (Hons), LLM, Cert. Ed., PhD is Senior Lecturer in Law at Manchester Metropolitan University. He recently completed his PhD thesis in 2018 on 'Honour-Based Violence in Ethnic Communities in England and Wales', which was externally examined by Professor Lynn Welchman (of SOAS, University of London). He is author of a number of articles and his most recent publications include: *Recommendations from the National Honour-Based Violence Roadshow 2018 – Report* (Manchester Law School, Manchester Metropolitan University, Manchester: October) [2018]; 'Key Agent and Survivor Recommendations for Intervention in Honor-Based Violence in the UK' [2018] *International Journal of Comparative and Applied Criminal Justice*, 42(4), 321–339; 'The Mosques Are the Biggest Problem We've Got Right Now – Key Agent and Survivor Accounts of Engaging Mosques with Domestic and Honor-Based Violence in the United Kingdom' [2017] *Journal of Interpersonal Violence*, ONLINE FIRST; 'Not Domestic Violence or Cultural Tradition: Is Honour-Based Violence Distinct from Domestic Violence?' [2017] *Journal of Social Welfare and Family Law*, 39(1), 3–21; 'Criminalisation of the Burqa in the UK' [2016] *The Journal of Criminal Law*, 80(2), 124–137; 'Forced Marriages – The Need for Criminalisation?' [2015] *Criminal Law Review*, 663 and 'Sentencing Guidelines for HBV and Honour Killings' [2015] *Journal of Criminal Law*, 79(3), 198–210. He is also co-editor (with T. Abbas) of *Honour, Violence, Women and Islam* (Routledge-Cavendish, 2010).

The contributors (in alphabetical order)

Dr. Lis Bates is Senior Research Fellow at the Centre for Policing Research and Learning at the Open University, and Honorary Research Fellow at the Centre for Gender and Violence Research at the University of Bristol.

She completed her PhD on honour-based abuse and forced marriage in 2017, developing a typology of HBA in England and Wales based around the relationships between victims and perpetrators. Lis researches, publishes and teaches on gender-based violence, criminology and social policy. She employs both qualitative and applied quantitative methods, specialising in secondary analysis of police and criminal justice data.

Recent research projects include: an ESRC fellowship conducting international comparative policy analysis of how the UK, Denmark, Norway, Sweden and Finland respond to HBA; an ESRC-funded project on developing a victim-centred justice system for victims of domestic abuse, rape and HBA (*Justice, Inequality and Gender-Based Violence*); a pan-EU project training professionals to help refugee women experiencing sexual violence; and two RCT evaluations of behaviour change interventions with domestic abuse perpetrators (*REPROVIDE* and *Drive* studies). Prior to academia, Lis was Head of Research at national domestic abuse charity SafeLives, and held policy advisory posts for the Home Office and Cabinet Office on domestic policy, and for parliamentary select committees on Home Affairs and Education.

Jennifer Calverley is Chief Executive Officer of The Elm Foundation, which is a specialist and experienced provider of domestic abuse services. The charity was first established in 1985 when it opened its first refuge for women. It now specialises in supporting both women and men experiencing domestic abuse, including providing the sole male refuge in the Derbyshire area since 2010.

Dr. Khatidja Chantler is currently a reader in social work at the Connect Centre for International Research on Interpersonal Violence and Harm, School of Social Work, University of Central Lancashire. She previously worked at the University of Manchester. Her key areas of research expertise are gender-based violence, particularly within minoritised communities, self-harm, gender and ethnicity. She is also an expert on forced marriage research. She has published widely in national and international journals and is author of several book chapters and co-editor of three books. Her professional background is in community development, therapeutic counselling and clinical supervision. She worked for many years in local authority settings and in the voluntary sector before joining the academy.

Dr. Rachael Clawson is Assistant Professor in Social Work at the University of Nottingham. She is a qualified and registered social worker with experience working with children and adults with learning disabilities who have been abused. Rachael has been involved in researching forced marriage of people with learning disabilities for ten years and has authored a number of papers on the subject. In 2010 she authored the first UK government guidelines on the matter (Forced Marriage and Learning Disabilities: Multi-Agency Practice Guidelines). These guidelines were incorporated into statutory guidance on forced marriage in 2014. She is in the process of completing a two-year NIHR-funded project aimed at improving policy and practice in relation to forced marriage of people with learning disabilities. This research has produced vital new understandings of forced marriage and has produced a range of free resources to help practitioners adequately recognise and respond to the issue.

Dr. Bingül Durbaş holds a PhD in sociology from the University of Sussex. Her work focuses on gender, violence, activism and criminal justice responses to gender-based violence. Her interdisciplinary doctoral research project in Turkey explored domestic violence, including HBV and state responses to these crimes by examining the court's interpretations of so-called honour killings and the criminal justice system's approaches and responses to such crimes. She previously worked as a researcher and tutor for the University of Sussex and Institute of Development Studies. She is currently a research fellow at the Centre for Applied Philosophy, Politics and Ethics, University of Brighton and is in the process of preparing her thesis for book publication.

Ayurshi Dutt is a women's rights activist based in New Delhi, India. She holds a MSc degree from the University of Edinburgh and presently provides frontline support to survivors of domestic violence at the Centre for Social Research, a Delhi-based NGO. She is currently a full-time PhD researcher in the area of forced marriages and honour-based violence at Durham University. She has conducted 'Prevention of Sexual Harassment at the Workplace' training sessions at university, institutional and corporate levels. Her main research interests include forced marriages within South Asian communities, with a focus on honour, its role in influencing genuine consent and its impacts on victims' agency. She writes avidly on issues relating to violence against women for both academic and mainstream audiences. With a strong journalism background, she has also conducted research on the systematic inequalities faced by female journalists in India while reporting in the field.

Professor Rusi Jaspal is Pro Vice-Chancellor (Research) and Professor of Psychology and Sexual Health at De Montfort University, Leicester, UK and Adjunct Professor at Abo Akademi University, Turku, Finland. Professor Jaspal is a Chartered Psychologist and a Fellow of the British Psychological Society. He has written four books and over 100 journal articles and book chapters on aspects of identity, mostly among gay men from ethnic minorities. Rusi Jaspal is the author of *Enhancing Sexual Health, Self-Identity and Wellbeing among Men Who Have Sex With Men: A Guide for Practitioners* (Jessica Kingsley, 2018) and *The Social Psychology of Gay Men* (Palgrave, 2019), and co-editor with Dame Glynis Breakwell of *Identity Process Theory: Identity, Social Action and Social Change* (Cambridge University Press, 2014).

Dr. Roxanne Khan is Director of HARM: Honour Abuse Research Matrix. A chartered psychologist and scientist based at the University of Central Lancashire, she is a senior lecturer and course leader in forensic psychology. With two decades experience of working with perpetrators and victims of violence in secure and community settings, Dr. Khan is primarily an aggression researcher with a long-standing research interest in family violence, including the psychology of honour violence, which is reflected in her publication profile.

Dr. Michelle Lowe is a reader in criminological and forensic psychology and a chartered psychologist at the University of Bolton. Dr. Lowe has published over 60 academic papers and presented at over 40 conferences in topics encompassing victimology and sexuality issues. Dr. Lowe is a founding editor of the *Journal of Aggression, Conflict and Peace Research*, holds editorial board positions at two other journals and is a regular reviewer for several outlets.

Mindy Mahil is a retired Detective Police Constable, formerly at West Midlands Police. He has dealt with complex investigations and has worked for the police force for over 30 years. Since retirement, he is now a consultant and visits police forces and other relevant agencies in the UK and around the world, sharing best practice in the investigation of HBA, forced marriage and FGM cases.

Dr. Sayed Mahdi Mosawi is a research fellow at the Kulturwissenschaftliches Institut Essen (Institute for Advanced Study in the Humanities). His work draws on masculinities, gender and migration issues. He has been working in a range of research positions and contributed to conducting and writing the first-ever study on masculinities and gender inequality in a post-conflict era of Afghanistan. The findings of the research were published in the book *The Other Side of Gender Inequality: Men and Masculinities in Afghanistan*, which was published in three different languages. Dr. Mosawi holds a PhD in sociology from Hacettepe University, Turkey. As a part of his PhD research, he explored the concept of 'masculine honour' and the way that it contributes to gender inequality and violence in the Afghan context.

Acknowledgements

The editor would like to thank Colin Perrin, the team at Routledge, Renata Corbani at Apex and everyone else who has worked on this project and assisted in the publication of this book.

Chapter 1

The 'forgotten' voices

Men, masculinities and 'honour'-based abuse – an introduction

Mohammad Mazher Idriss[1]

Background and evolution of the book

This book begins by introducing the forgotten voices of so-called honour-based abuse (HBA), violence and forced marriage – men and boys as hidden and silent victims. HBA is an incident or crime committed in order to protect or defend the honour of the family (Welchman and Hossain, 2005; Reddy, 2008; Idriss and Abbas, 2010; Gill et al., 2014; Julios, 2015). It involves abuse or violence used to control (predominantly) women who are perceived to have violated cultural norms and are thereby alleged to have tarnished their family's honour (Reddy, 2008). As a social construct, it may occur when individuals perceive that a woman has shamed the family by behaving in a too Westernised way or engaging in relationships outside marriage (Gill et al., 2014). The idea of HBA is usually associated with women from ethnic communities (Reddy, 2014). More specifically, in the UK it is usually associated with women from South Asian and Muslim backgrounds (Anitha and Gill, 2015; Begikhani et al., 2015). Crimes such as assault, blackmail, coercive control, false imprisonment, forced marriage, kidnap and, in extreme cases, so-called honour killings may be committed to supposedly cleanse the family name of the perceived shame involved (Siddiqui, 2005; Gill et al., 2014). HBA thus represents a continuum of violence against women and girls (VAWG) (Kelly, 1988; Sev'er and Yurdakul, 2001; Gryzb, 2016). There is no separate criminal offence of HBA in England and Wales, and a range of legislation (e.g. the criminalisation of forced marriages) or common law offences may be used to prosecute perpetrators. This adds to the difficulty of understanding the picture on the prevalence of HBA, arguably leading it to remain largely under-reported and underestimated (Women's Aid, 2016; Myhill, 2017). In relation to statistical information concerning the prevalence of HBA, there is lack of data of any value to give an exact measurement (Hall, 2014; Julios, 2015). Neither official Home Office reports nor the Crime Survey for England and Wales (CSEW) (ONS, 2018) contains data on the extent to which HBA (and non-fatal offences) is committed. This was also confirmed by the House of Commons Home Affairs Committee Report (HCHAC, 2008), though there have been unofficial attempts to quantify it. These statistics are however, at best, speculative.

It is possible thousands of incidents of HBA go unreported, with some unofficially estimating that 17,000 women are victims of HBA in the UK each year alone (Brady, 2008). Despite these estimates, there is no certainty how many cases of HBA there are because it is a hidden crime and perpetrators attempt to conceal their crimes (Begikhani and Hague, 2013; Hall, 2014). Furthermore, there is a general risk of double counting because cases pass between various state agencies (HCHAC, 2008; Khanum, 2008). In relation to so-called honour killings, Amnesty International estimates that approximately 5,000 cases occur worldwide each year (Amnesty International, 1999; United Nations Population Fund, 2008). However, again this is considered to be an underestimate as it fails to take into account cases not reported, as well as those women taken back home to their ancestral countries and who have then disappeared (Hall, 2014). Estimates are also difficult because so-called honour killings are rarely reported to the police and families often cover their crimes by disguising deaths as accidents or suicides (Warrick, 2009). Amnesty International has not explained how it has methodologically reached its estimation, casting further doubt on the reliability of its statistics. While the London Metropolitan Police Service estimated in 2004 that there are approximately 12 to 15 so-called honour killings in the UK per annum, this is by no means certain (MPS, 2007; Brandon and Hafez, 2008; Gill, 2009; Gill, 2010). Overall, the inconsistent way in which statistical data is collected is one of the main reasons why it is difficult to determine with any accuracy the prevalence of HBA.

There are several reasons why I, as the editor, decided to embark upon a project that analyses the experiences of men. First, I wanted to produce another book as a follow-up to my 2010 co-edited book (with Tahir Abbas) entitled *Honour, Violence, Women and Islam*. That book, first conceived in 2007, had the principal aim of highlighting women's victimisation across the world in the name of so-called honour, and we wanted to highlight that HBA is not purely an Islamic phenomenon. Rather, HBA is another example or manifestation of VAWG across the world, regardless of women's ethnicity or where they live (Baker et al., 1999). Having edited and published that collection of essays in 2010, ten years ago, I thought that it was not only time to work on another book publication project, but that one was very much needed on men's experiences of HBA and forced marriage. There is a growing wealth of research and data on HBA and VAWG since the 2010 book, yet what is distinctly absent is detailed analysis and consideration of men's experiences as victims separate from women (Samad, 2010). Any discussion of male victims is either reduced to a few sentences or a short paragraph, or included within a footnote or addendum (see e.g. Gill et al., 2014: 3 and 7; Dyer, 2015: 16). As editor, I therefore wanted to work on this project to provide greater recognition of men's victimisation, not as a counter to the discussion on VAWG, but to give better recognition to the subject that male victimisation deserves (Hogan et al., 2012). Inherited gender roles and stereotypes are burdensome and unjust to both women and men and must therefore be challenged (Honderich, 1995: 528). Although there is some overlap with the causes and responses to HBA with female victims, there are enough differences to justify studying male victims as a separate and distinct sub-group within the field. This book addresses this gap in knowledge and in doing so draws upon existing theories as applied to female victims, but develops its own methodology and theoretical standpoints to ensure that male victims are treated with the same degree of seriousness and sympathy as female victims. Another reason why I embarked upon this project relates to my personal interactions with male victims of HBA and forced marriages and my commitment to support *all* victims of abuse. In 2018, at Manchester Metropolitan University I conducted a series of HBA Roadshows across the country in front of key stakeholders, professionals, members of the public and survivors. I also produced a final report on a series of recommendations that was presented to Mr Pat McFadden MP and the House of Commons on 24 January 2019 (Idriss, 2018b). During the Roadshows, several male survivors discussed their experiences and their wishes for better recognition by state agencies as well as improved support for male victims at societal and government levels. This book is dedicated to all male victims of HBA, violence and forced marriages and is a contribution to wider discussions about how we can support *all* victims. This book, with its collection of chapters, focuses on HBA and forced marriage against men, providing new evidence and highlighting important implications for laws, policies, research and gender-neutral services, with the aim of seeking to highlight, recognise and create additional spaces and funding for male victims.

Similarities with VAWG – men as an important sub-group worthy of study

New evidence and details of male victimisation are beginning to emerge with policies, research and theory-building on male victims developing and slowly being drawn to the public's attention. For example, the CSEW details long-term trends and attitudes towards domestic abuse experienced by women and men, estimating that 7.9% of women (1.3 million) and 4.2% of men (695,000) have experienced domestic abuse between March 2017 and March 2018 (ONS, 2018). A very recent high-profile case concerns Alex Skeel, who was abused for over three years by his girlfriend. A documentary about his abuse called *Abused by My Girlfriend* (BBC, 2019) appeared on the BBC, and his girlfriend was convicted of coercive and controlling behaviour and grievous bodily harm – she was sentenced to seven-and-a-half years in prison in April 2018 (Ritschel, 2019). However, though male victims of domestic abuse are beginning to be recognised in public policy and at the national level, research illustrates that many male victims are also perpetrators and that women experience a greater amount and more severe abuse from male partners (Hester, 2009). This can sometimes blur the line between male victims/male perpetrators in comparison to female victims, many of whom may use violent resistance against violent male partners, or defensive or retaliatory force rather than initiating violence themselves (Hester, 2009: 4).

However, the CSEW's estimation and Hester's (2009) study specifically relates to domestic/intimate partner abuse and does not focus on male victims of HBA or forced marriages and who have *not* initiated abuse or violence themselves. In 2005, a Council of Europe study of forced marriages highlighted that in the UK, 15% of the victims who the Home Office had supported were male (Council of Europe, 2005: 24). This figure has since increased and according to recent statistics provided by the Forced Marriage Unit (FMU) on 24 May 2019, of the 1,322 cases that it dealt with in 2018, 75% concerned women and 17% concerned men (Home Office, 2019: 9); on 16 March 2018, of the 1,196 cases that it dealt with in 2017, 77.8% of cases that the FMU supported concerned women and 21.4% concerned male victims (the remaining victims chose not to disclose their gender) (Home Office, 2018). These statistics are not intended to reflect the prevalence of forced marriage in the UK, but to highlight the existence of male victimisation in approximately one-fifth of the FMU's caseload. On 11 June 2018, the Council of Europe in another report further repeated its recognition of male victims when it said:

> Forced marriage is a form of violence against women that entails serious violations of fundamental rights, and in particular of women's and girls' rights to physical integrity, physical and mental health, sexual and reproductive health, education, private life, freedom and autonomy. Men and boys who are victims of forced marriage face many similar violations of their rights. Neither culture, custom, religion, tradition nor so-called 'honour' can justify such violations.
>
> (Council of Europe, 2018: 1)

With this growing attention to male victims across Europe, Yasmin Alibhai-Brown recently wrote a recent *Sunday Times Magazine* article on 25 November 2018 supporting the statement that it is not just women who experience HBA and forced marriages (Alibhai-Brown, 2018). She interviewed a male victim named Suhail Khan, who had been forced to marry a woman from Kashmir. Lucky Roy Singh was another male victim interviewed by Alibhai-Brown who, as a young gay Sikh man, fell in love with another gay Sikh man. His lover's parents were liberal and urged them both to marry, but the mother-in-law told Lucky to dress as a bride in order to dupe guests into believing that this was a 'normal' heterosexual wedding (Alibhai-Brown, 2018). Things deteriorated for Lucky after the marriage, where he was pressured into a life of domestic servitude by his mother-in-law and was expected to stay at home, cook, clean and generally do as he was told. He has since published a diary called *Take a Walk in My Big Indian Heels* in which he explains that he became a 'bride' for the sake of 'honour' and Sikh culture (Singh, 2017). Lucky is not the only gay Sikh man to write a book about his experiences – Manjinder Singh Sidhu published *Bollywood Gay: A Help Yourself Book to Living an Authentic Life* (Sidhu, 2016) about coming out to his mother and the abuse from his own cousins after revealing his sexuality (Razzall and Khan, 2017). These accounts of HBA and forced marriages have been recounted elsewhere. During the HBA Roadshow 2018, several male survivors discussed their abuse before a public audience. One male survivor explained his experiences of HBA and its relationship to caste-based discrimination in the UK. As an Indian national, he married a British national in what was initially a love marriage, although both belonged to different castes. His parents did not approve of the marriage because his wife had been previously divorced, was significantly older than him and had teenage children of her own from her first marriage. Sadly, his wife became abusive towards him, coercively controlling him and his finances. He explained that his abuse was related to his caste – because he belonged to a lower caste, this somehow legitimised the abuse he experienced. His wife's teenage children were also physically and verbally abusive. When he disclosed this to his parents back in India, they refused to support him because he had married outside his caste and a divorce would bring shame on the family. When the victim tried calling the police, he explained that no one came to assist him – over a period of two days, he made nine telephone calls to the police. He put his negative experiences down to social constructions that 'men can't be victims' and so the police did not help him. When they eventually came to investigate, he was subsequently arrested because his wife had made counter-allegations against him. He has since left the relationship with the help of intervention from a support organisation that he had researched online. Fearing for his own safety if he returned to India because he married outside his caste, he has since applied for permanent residency in the UK. The support organisation explained that foreign nationals with no recourse to public funds (NRPF) based on their immigration status often apply for the Destitution Domestic Violence (DDV) Concession. The organisation commented that, in its experience, applications for DDV Concessions can take longer to process for men in comparison to women because the Home Office is more cautious of cases concerning men, who may be attempting to circumvent immigration laws by falsely claiming HBA in order to remain in the UK (Idriss, 2018b).

Another male victim who attended the Roadshows, a British national, also explained his experiences of forced marriage to a cousin from Pakistan against his will. He was pressured to get married because his father had become ill in hospital. His uncles emotionally blackmailed him by claiming that his father was ill because of his refusal to get married. The victim married in Pakistan but returned to the UK without his wife, having planned on delaying the necessary immigration papers that would bring his wife to the UK. Forced marriage is often used to facilitate immigration applications and to help facilitate migration to the UK. However, his wife was able to enter the UK via other family routes and so the male victim was forced to live with his wife. To escape his ordeal, he enrolled on a university course several hundred miles away. There, he 'partied hard' in order to 'numb the pain' (his words), consuming drink and drugs and generally behaving as 'good Muslim boys' should not. The summer periods when university ended were the most dreaded for him, as he had to go back home and live as man and wife. After graduation, he remained in the city where he had studied in order to be away from the family home. It was only then after some years that his marriage ended, as his family then realised that he was never going to return home. In some respects, the male victim enjoyed some freedom, as he was able to start university education and move away from home – these circumstances are seldom made available to female victims of forced marriage. However, the male victim added that had there been more male support services available at the time some twenty-odd years ago, he would have contemplated leaving home and would have stayed in a refuge.

In other cases, men with mental learning disabilities may also be victims of forced marriages. Potential overseas female brides are not told about their future husband's disabilities – trickery, deception and dishonesty are all tactics used to lure people into marriage and invariably the female bride from overseas is often brought to the UK as unpaid help as parents seek to find long-term carers for their disabled sons (Rauf et al., 2013; Clawson, 2016: 278; Clawson and Fyson, 2017; see also Clawson in this collection). In these instances, there are then two victims – the man who lacks the mental capacity to consent to marriage, as well as the unsuspecting bride who is duped into marrying a man with disabilities (Clawson and Fyson, 2017). These examples all demonstrate the evidence now available that men can be victims of HBA and forced marriage. In recognition of this emerging evidence, the Crown Prosecution Service (CPS) has now published a public statement 'recognising the significant numbers of men and boys affected by these crimes [including domestic abuse] and the increasing number of reports being made' and their commitment towards securing justice for all victims (CPS, 2017).

Men can be victims of HBA and forced marriage for much the same reasons as women (Samad, 2010: 189). There needs to be a much deeper understanding of male victimisation and wider changes to society's understanding of male victims amongst members of the public and professional services (Hogan et al., 2012). Under-reporting of male victimisation is a problem, particularly in less-developed and rural areas, as well as in countries both inside and outside the EU (Cheung et al., 2009; Machado et al., 2017). If men are victims of HBA, the assumption is that men have tarnished the reputation of a woman and so revenge is exacted upon the male (see *R v Chomir Ali* [2011] EWCA Crim 1011). Men may experience HBA and forced marriage because the male has become involved with a woman from a different culture, caste or religion, or is perceived as having shamed a woman by dating or marrying her, or for taking part in unsuitable heterosexual relationships (Samad, 2010; Dryzb, 2016). Men may experience HBA if they refuse to take part in an arranged or forced marriage; victimised if they fail to divorce their spouses because their wives have given birth only to female children; forced into marriage because of their disabilities, with families believing that that is the best way to support them in the long term; or forced into marriage 'as an antidote for their gayness' (Samad, 2010: 199–200). HBA and ostracisation may be experienced where the sexuality or sexual orientation of a man is discovered, including bisexuality or homosexuality (Siraj, 2006; Samad, 2010; Jaspal and Siraj, 2011; Tsui, 2014; see also Jaspal, and Khan and Lowe in this collection). Due to the stigma associated with being gay in South Asian communities, young men may be forced to marry women and be emotionally blackmailed into silence for the sake of family honour. Similarly, trans identity is negated by families because of the potentially stigmatising impact of having a trans son or daughter and the need to protect 'the gender normative status of the family' and 'hegemonic masculinity' by refusing to 'accept their gender as anything than that which was assigned by birth . . . underpinned by [a] heteronormative ideology . . . [within a] . . . prevailing hegemonic framework . . . ' (Rogers, 2017: 234, 238).

Men who do not seek help from support services have reported a number of barriers to help-seeking that are broadly similar to those known for women. These include not identifying their experiences as abuse, concern about losing access to children, simply not knowing what support might be available for men and not knowing who to approach, the availability of few male support services, concern about their partner getting in trouble with the law, concerns about being stereotyped by the police to be the perpetrator rather than the victim, fear of manipulation of legal and administrative resources by perpetrators in an attempt to control or inflict emotional or financial harm and a concern that they will be stigmatised for seeking support (Merrill and Wolfe, 2000; Grady, 2002: 85–89, 94; Cook, 2009; Durfee, 2011; Hogan et al., 2012; Tsui, 2014; Berger et al., 2016; McCarrick et al., 2016). This existing research, albeit in the field of domestic abuse, reveals that men find it hard to access much-needed services (Migliaccio, 2001; Cook, 2009), and it is submitted that the same issues are present in HBA and forced marriage cases for men.

Differences with VAWG – separate and distinct problems and the evidential gap

Both female and male victims are valid subjects to research, but there must be recognition that each group has its own specific needs, problems and issues that require examination, debate and discussion, and while there are points of convergences, there are also important differences and challenges. The perception is that men are only perpetrators, not victims of HBA, violence and forced marriage (Gill et al., 2014; Tsui, 2014; Aplin, 2017; Dogan, 2018), but the accounts detailed above clearly show that men can be victimised too. The evidence and statistics emerging show that men and young boys are slowly coming forward to disclose abuse, that they experience abuse within a system that is primarily designed to support female victims and that these facts can no longer be ignored (Hines et al., 2007). This conflicting state of affairs reveals that while men are the main perpetrators in domestic, HBA and forced marriage cases, they are simultaneously a hidden and marginalised group of victims – socialisation factors reinforce myths about men – be it domestic abuse, HBA or forced marriage cases – including that only women are abused and that abuse is perpetrated by men against women (Allen-Collinson, 2009; Tsui et al., 2010; Tsui, 2014). HBA and forced marriages within an overall context of controlling behaviours demand our attention, regardless of the gender of the perpetrator or victim (Hines, 2015), but amongst male victims, it still remains an unrecognised problem, well below the radar of public concern (Samad, 2010). As there is currently a lack of research specifically on men's experiences of HBA and forced marriages, we therefore have to look at other areas to learn more about male experiences of victimisation, namely within the field of domestic and sexual abuse. There are a growing number of studies on male-victim domestic and sexual abuse in comparison to the scant number of studies on male HBA and forced marriages. As there are overlaps, it is submitted at this stage that we can draw out important similarities from these studies and apply them to male HBA and forced marriages more generally.

There is also increasing evidence that men face different challenges than women when coming forward to disclose abuse. One of the reasons why male victims of HBA and forced marriages are a hidden and overlooked group is because NGOs and domestic abuse support organisations cater to women far better than they do to men (Cook, 2009: 87). Furthermore, the lack of empirical studies identifying male victims in HBA and forced marriage cases means that we cannot contextualise the abuse that men suffer (Grady, 2002: 81). One of the main underlying causes of women's oppression is undoubtedly patriarchy (Mies, 1986; Bhopal, 1997; Geetha, 2015; Mackay, 2015), but there is a general lack of acknowledgement that men too can be harmed by patriarchy (Migliaccio, 2001; Connell, 2005: 78–81, 143–163). Fathers and uncles may coerce younger males into marriage in circumstances where younger males feel they have little or no choice – such as in cases where the patriarchal order prohibits homosexual relationships or men's rights in marriage – men too are victims of the patriarchal system, oppressed by senior men because homosexual men do not meet the expectations of 'masculinity' (Connell, 2005: 78–81, 85, 143–163). Such men may be shamed, pressured, ridiculed, experience emotional blackmail, and in some cases, threatened with physical harm for failing to take part in a forced/heterosexual marriage (Samad, 2010). Very much like the feminist argument explaining why women become victims of patriarchal violence, young boys and men may be coerced as a way of bargaining with patriarchal forces and as a means to ensure their own safety and well-being (Kandiyoti, 1988; Hunnicutt, 2009; Balzani, 2010; Aplin, 2017), although other existing research indicates that men are more likely to experience emotional, psychological abuse and blackmail in cases of forced marriage at the hands of mothers, rather than physical violence at the hands of fathers and uncles (Samad, 2010). Male victims of domestic abuse also demonstrate greater reluctance to report violence or abuse against them in comparison to women, and when they do report abuse, they are often faced with what appears to be discrimination and prejudice by state agencies, including being disbelieved, ridiculed by the police and made pathetic figures of fun (Migliaccio, 2001; Grady, 2002: 91, 96; George and Yarwood, 2004: 11, 17; Hines et al., 2007; Cook, 2009: 82; Tsui et al., 2010; Tsui, 2014; McCarrick et al., 2016). Based on these domestic abuse studies, it is safe to assume that men in HBA and forced marriage, given their similarities, are likely to share similar experiences. In a Dewar Research Survey, 20% of male victims surveyed were themselves arrested, with minimal action taken by the authorities against their (female) perpetrators, unless the male victim had a visible or significant injury (George and Yarwood, 2004: 9, 19; McCarrick et al., 2016). The poor nature and quality of treatment by the criminal justice system is already an issue for women experiencing HBA and forced marriage (HMIC, 2015; Idriss, 2018a; Mulvihill et al., 2018), and it would appear that this is also an issue for male victims, which can result in their unwillingness to come forward to report abuse (Tsui, 2014). The institutionalised nature of policy and practice can have a negative impact upon men as a direct result of entrenched and hostile social constructions and perspectives that assume women in HBA, forced marriage and domestic abuse cases are the sole victims, while men are perpetrators (Grady, 2002; Tsui, 2014; Hines, 2015). A more holistic and equitable approach is often ignored and little government funding is made available for male services. The HCHAC Reports in 2008 and 2011 on domestic violence, HBA and forced marriages did recognise the plight of male victims (including recognising the few refuge spaces that exist for male victims: HCHAC, 2008: 72, para. 214), concluding that 'the available evidence suggests that women experience more serious and more frequent violence than men' (HCHAC, 2008: 23, para. 48). The HCHAC instead preferred to 'recommend that the Government consider whether or not alternative support might be appropriate for male victims, such as means-tested grant for accommodation' (HCHAC, 2008: 74, para. 220; see also HCHAC, 2011).

Theoretical challenges faced by introducing men as victims to the debate

The recognition and reporting of HBA is vital towards supporting victims and achieving prosecutions. It is important that we break the taboo surrounding male victimisation if men are to be encouraged to come forward. Some men may feel reluctant to come forward because of fear, shame and embarrassment linked to notions surrounding masculinity and social attitudes towards male victims of domestic abuse in general (Migliaccio, 2001; Allen-Collinson, 2009; Cook, 2009; Tsui et al., 2010; Morgan et al., 2014; Tsui, 2014; Hogan, 2016). Men are therefore silenced, allowing the abuse to persist, and this further adds to feelings of embarrassment (Migliaccio, 2001; Samad, 2010). There is no one single definition of masculinity, and theorists often talk about 'masculinities' – that is that there are a number of masculinities, but there is one central concept – hegemonic masculinity – 'against which all other masculinities are measured' (Brod and Kaufman, 1994; Migliaccio, 2001: 206; MacKinnon, 2003: 9–11; Connell, 2005: 67–81, 77). Hegemony places emphasis upon the dominance of a primary masculine identity, particularly portrayed by means of the media, which Connell explains is socially constructed (Connell, 1987: 183–188; Connell,

2000: 76–80). It is constructed through the likes of television, film, advertising, physical sport, acts of violence and heterosexual activity (Connell, 2000: 76–85; MacKinnon, 2003; Haywood and Mac an Ghaill, 2003: 67). Portraying these forms of 'machoism' signifies manliness, strength and a strong sex drive, characteristics that every man should possess (Haywood and Mac an Ghaill, 2003: 69). Hegemonic masculinity forces men to comply with such expectations, but men from lower classes, gay men and those from minority groups are all measured against it, and are thus labelled as inferior, placed outside the mainstream order and accorded a lower status in the social hierarchy (Stanko and Hobdell, 1993; Migliaccio, 2001: 206–207; MacKinnon, 2003: 10; Allen-Collinson, 2009; Dunn, 2012). 'Masculinity . . . is [also] defined less by what it *is* and more by what is it *not*' – and it exists in contrast to femininity (Migliaccio, 2001: 205–206; MacKinnon, 2003: 7; Connell, 2005: 67–81, 77). In Western society, one of the primary roles of a man is not to behave like or resemble a woman, and an association with femininity can emasculate men (Migliaccio, 2001). The fear of being classed as feminine can force men to avoid situations of disclosing personal information or instances that could classify them as feminine, such as admitting their sexuality or their experiences of domestic abuse, HBA or forced marriages, which calls into question their masculine identity and one which reflects upon them personally (Migliaccio, 2001; Allen-Collinson, 2009; McCarrick et al., 2016). This goes some way towards explaining why homosexual, bisexual and/or transgender men avoid coming out about their sexual orientation, or feign heterosexuality, for fear of being labelled with characteristics that are regarded as effeminate or unmanly or having their personal identity threatened (Jaspal and Siraj, 2011; Rogers, 2017). Men and young boys are socialised to appreciate certain masculine gender roles, which contributes towards being marginalised in a hegemonic society (Hogan et al., 2012; Tsui, 2014). Masculine notions dictate that men should deny pain, refuse assistance and dominate others, and crossing the gender (feminine) boundary can lead to stigmatisation for men (Migliaccio, 2001; Cook, 2009: 92–93).

HBA committed against men may not be perceived as grave or as serious as HBA committed against women, and so perceptions about HBA and how male victims are understood also needs to be addressed (McCarrick et al., 2016). Similar comparisons can be made here with male victims of sexual violence, including rape, and the associated barriers to disclosure (Javaid, 2016, 2017). Some men may think that their victimisation contradicts essential ideas surrounding the gendered expectations of men, especially if the authorities that they are reporting to are themselves institutionally male (Javaid, 2016, 2017). Some may feel that HBA cannot be associated with male victims because it is an issue that predominantly affects women because media accounts present HBA as gendered (Reddy, 2008, 2014). This links in with stereotypes and constructions that domestic abuse 'is male violence against female victims' (Migliaccio, 2001; Grady, 2002: 80; Machado et al., 2017). However, existing social constructions mean that men are not labelled as victims, resulting in their 'significant under-representation in the official statistics and in studies based on samples drawn from police records' (Grady, 2002: 77), men's invisibility, and their experiences trivialised, normalised or misunderstood (Migliaccio, 2001; CPS, 2017; c.f. CSEW (ONS, 2018) and Hester (2009)). In the ideas of 'social interactionism' by George Herbert Mead (1934), the social and personal identities of individuals are created and judged by the people with whom they interact. Based on the consideration of the self, a value is placed upon the self in relation to how one will be judged by others – through the verbal, symbolic and the embodied actions of others, where others will be considered to be (or consider themselves to be) socially and/or morally superior to the individual whose behaviour is being judged (Allen-Collinson, 2009; Rogers, 2017). Behaviour and interactions that are viewed positively will be met with love, acceptance and respect, so that one is able to create a positive sense of oneself (Rogers, 2017). On the other hand, behaviour and interactions perceived as deviant or shameful create a less positive sense of oneself, including feelings of inadequacy, unattractiveness and inferiority (Rogers, 2017). This can include those behaviours and identities that are considered criminal, deviant or inappropriate, or as in the present context of this book, feminine (either through publicly coming out about one's sexual orientation, or admitting to being victimised) (Migliaccio, 2001; Dunn, 2012). Here, men fail to meet the socially approved norms of male expression and behaviour (Rogers, 2017). Thus, some men may choose not to disclose their abuse because of the stigma attached to speaking about one's own feelings or fears of being perceived as a failure because they have deviated from what is expected of men (Migliaccio, 2001; Allen-Collinson, 2009; Tsui et al., 2010). Some men might feel emasculated because subtle messages through the media (e.g. films and advertising) or cautionary tales and constructions demonstrate that men are expected to fight back and are ridiculed for not fighting back or allowing abuse to continue (MacKinnon, 2003: 87–100; Allen-Collinson, 2009; Tsui et al., 2010; Moore, 2014; Entilli and Cipolletta, 2017). Research on men's sexual victimisation suggests that male victims of assault tend to view their victimisation as a sign of being weak and helpless, that they 'need to man up', illustrated by the infamous saying that 'big boys don't cry' (Stanko and Hobdell, 1993; Javaid, 2016; Javaid, 2017). Men are expected to be in control, supress their emotions and hide their weaknesses (Javaid, 2016, 2017). The ability of men to admit to HBA and forced marriage and to seek intervention may thus be hindered by their impassiveness to tolerate abuse and to play down or deny their injuries (Migliaccio, 2001). Social constructs of masculinity prevents men from showing any weakness, and action films like *Rambo*, *Commando*, *Die Hard*, and *Mission Impossible*; 'manly' characters like James Bond; classical country and western films; war films, as well as Bollywood heroes, all reinforce these images that men are macho, strong, brave and powerful and can singlehandedly defeat those who seek to harm them (Hogan et al., 2012). The emphasis in these movies is on the physical size, strength and the ability of men to use violence effectively, meaning that masculine identity is linked with the use of the body as an instrument of power and control – and filmgoers approve of such representations (MacKinnon, 2003: 37, 37–63). In contrast, to be abused is to be 'not masculine' (Migliaccio, 2001: 218). It then becomes hard for men to exhibit traditional masculine characteristics once they are labelled as victims because they are then feminised – to be labelled 'abused' is to be labelled as 'female', as domestic abuse is framed as a women's issue, contradicting the masculine ideal (Migliaccio, 2001: 208; Hines, 2007: 66). This may lead not only to the non-reporting of abuse, but also a denial by men that they are victims; if they do report abuse, they then run into further problems of having their masculinity publicly questioned by state agencies and are thus relegated to marginalized positions (Migliaccio, 2001: 208).

Male victims of HBA and forced marriage may also feel unwilling to engage with state agencies and other service providers for fear of negative treatment or hostility. Some may feel that they will not get appropriate responses because of the occupational culture of some institutions and how it can shape their responses to victims, including those relating to sexual abuse (Allen-Collinson, 2009; Javaid, 2016, 2017). The police might be a good example of this, where the occupational 'cop culture' of police forces constructs men as being dominant, strong, powerful and non-victimised (Migliaccio, 2001; Javaid, 2016, 2017). As a result of this occupational culture, male victims may feel isolated in terms of their own experiences out of fear that they will be doubted or disbelieved because 'the cultural stereotype of women as victims . . . is firmly entrenched within the psyche of the police officer 'on the ground'' (Grady, 2002: 83; Hines et al., 2007; Cook, 2009: 88; Tsui et al., 2010; Tsui, 2014; McCarrick et al., 2016). These considerations can impact negatively on men's overall experiences with state agencies, leading some to claim that men too can experience double victimisation, where they experience abuse by perpetrators and discrimination by state agencies who do not acknowledge them as victims, thus leading to feelings of frustration, uncertainty and a sense of working against a system (Migliaccio, 2001; Hogan et al., 2012: 50; see also Razack, 1998; Gill, 2004; Thiara and Gill, 2010). Women who experience HBA are constructed as the 'ideal' victims, but not men (Migliaccio, 2001). The police may therefore view women as more deserving of intervention and support than men because of the creation of powerful stereotypes to the extent that the police 'are almost blind to [and overlook] the existence of male victims' (Grady, 2002: 71, 77, 82, 85). Further problems may arise if a male victim is only able to speak to a male police officer – having been abused, a male victim may find it difficult to reveal intimate details to a male police officer (Hogan et al., 2012). Problems may exacerbate if male victims are unable to choose whether their specially trained police officer or support worker is either male or female, heterosexual or gay – the point is that a restriction in the diversity of state agencies may affect disclosure and the reporting of abuse and there is a need to design services so that men's unique needs can be met (Yarrow and Churchill, 2009; Tsui et al., 2010; Javaid, 2016; Javaid, 2017).

The ways forward – legal and policy perspectives

A gender-neutral approach to strategy and policy development should be adopted in order to address male victimisation of HBA and forced marriage. Social policies should incorporate and address the problem from multiple perspectives and not solely from feminist perspectives designed solely around the needs of women and girls with a 'one size fits all' approach. A gender-neutral approach would still recognise the fact that women are disproportionately affected by violence in all of its manifestations and that we should continue to support feminist frameworks and the promotion of single-sex services where appropriate (e.g. rape crisis centres where women are the victims of rape). However, a gender-neutral approach would also recognise the growing numbers of male victims and that the needs of men must also be met, whether it concerns domestic abuse, HBA or forced marriages (Tsui, 2014). All victims of violence and abuse deserve compassion, support and intervention. There is an urgent need to provide unbiased, gender-neutral and culturally sensitive training for all state agencies who work on the front line and who come into contact with male victims. This will also help to dispel the myths surrounding male victimisation (Tsui et al., 2010; Tsui, 2014; Hines, 2015). Healthcare institutions must also be ready to screen male patients for signs of HBA and forced marriage, something that is largely undertaken in domestic abuse cases and with only women in mind (Taket et al., 2003; Morgan et al., 2014). In some domestic abuse studies, men have reported negative experiences when seeking help or consulting with healthcare professionals (Migliaccio, 2001; Tsui, 2014). Other studies are beginning to show the importance of screening men for signs of victimisation – high blood pressure, asthma, STDs, depression and PTSDs as well as physical injuries are all health indicators that men may need intervention (Hines and Douglas, 2015). All patients should be screened for signs of abuse, regardless of the sex of the victim, and medical practitioners should be trained in this area (Morgan et al., 2014; Hines and Douglas, 2015; Williamson et al., 2015; Entilli and Cipolletta, 2017).

The needs of men who are victims should be met alongside and parallel to that of women (and not be oppositional or confrontational to female victims). This chapter does not in any way intend to minimise or reduce the appalling violence women and girls experience, nor does it seek to degender HBA, forced marriage and so-called honour killings (Allen-Collinson, 2009: 24). The positive way I view the issue is to appreciate that male victims are a neglected and under-researched group and that there are enough differences to justify studying male victims as a separate and distinct sub-group within this important area. Any opposition to the creation of strategies and policies that support male victims may be opposition to the idea of gender-neutral services or gender-neutral analyses of the problems. Some may be opposed to gender-neutral approaches for ideological reasons as well as for practical reasons, which may include the ability to apply for funding or the fear that funding will be withdrawn from women's organisations. However, advocating gender-neutral approaches should not be construed as a disingenuous attempt to undermine feminism or women's organisations, nor should it be construed as an attempt to deny VAWG or men as primary perpetrators. There needs to be *separate* discussions about male victims, within a different space and as an issue on its own terms, not relational, reactive or responsive to discussions about VAWG. Discussions about HBA and forced marriages need to go further. One unintended consequence of a gendered analysis is that we could begin to define HBA and forced marriages as being a gendered crime, when FMU statistics clearly demonstrate that a sizeable number of victims they support are male (see also Clawson and Fyson (2017), who state in their study that men and women with learning disabilities are equally likely to be forced into marriage). Thus, placing HBA and forced marriages under a gendered analysis runs the risk that men will not be recognised as victims and will therefore receive inadequate protection (Hines, 2015).

More resources and changes are needed to cater for male victims of HBA and forced marriages. It is vital to begin recording data on male victimisation in domestic abuse, HBA and forced marriage cases in order for support organisations to demonstrate demand and to apply for funding to establish more gender-neutral services. Additional funding from central government and a substantial drive to support men experiencing domestic abuse in general is also needed. In December 2016, the Home Office published the 'Violence Against Women and Girls Service Transformation Fund' prospectus (Home Office, 2016). In its prospectus, the government explained that it recognises the gendered nature of VAWG and how the bulk of funding is designated for women. However, the fact remains that male services remain under-resourced and under-funded (Lowe, 2018). It is not clear how far VAWG initiatives actually target male victims or whether such initiatives under the specific VAWG title can actually deter or discourage male victims from accessing support (Parity, 2018: 6). Currently, male victims of HBA and forced marriages are classed within the VAWG strategy. This is not only factually incorrect, but could lead to the minimisation, trivialisation or marginalisation of male experiences and could contribute towards their vulnerability. As support for men is currently provided through a small segment of the Violence Against Women and Girls Transformation Fund, there has been increasing pressure on the government to support the stance on creating an Ending Intimate Violence Against Men and Boys Strategy. At the moment, there seems to be no intention to create a separate strategy for men. This author calls for: (a) the creation of a separate Ending Intimate Violence Against Men and Boys Strategy and (b) the creation of a separate (and parallel) Violence Against Men and Young Boys Transformation Fund. Strategies are required to recognise and validate the experiences of male victims, and gender-neutral approaches to support and funding are the way forward because existing research shows that men are often not the recipients of outreach materials and services concerning domestic abuse (Tsui et al., 2010; Tsui, 2014; Hines, 2015). Male victimisation in general lacks recognition in the public domain, and there appears to be lack of policy initiatives specifically relating to men (Samad, 2010: 202–203). Although this may be partly because of the smaller estimated numbers in comparison to women, the problem is also due to men's unwillingness and inability to admit that they are experiencing abuse in the first place (Samad, 2010: 202). Thus, men have not helped themselves by remaining silent – as Samad states, 'Men have not formed self-help groups or third sector organizations to engage with the issue' (Samad, 2010: 202). Nor are they helped by the fact that HBA and forced marriages remain inextricably linked with the moral panic over the ethnic 'Other', immigration controls and Islamophobia, and the perception that HBA is primarily a South Asian/Muslim problem and an example of their cultural practices (Cohen, 2002; Reimers, 2007; Anitha and Gill, 2015). Misleading and demonising narratives act to silence *all* victims, men and women, and complicates intervention by preventing victims from coming forward because they do not want to contribute to the demonisation process by confirming their abuse to state agencies (Siddiqui, 2016).

By having a parallel Male Victims and Survivors Service Transformation Fund, this author believes that separate funding should be provided for men to help establish services that allow men to talk; furthermore, the government should make it a priority to fund research on male domestic abuse, HBA and forced marriage in order to better understand its potential consequences, including physical and mental health issues (McCarrick et al., 2016). Some studies have suggested that studies into male victimisation in general are somewhat 50 years behind the parallel research on female victims (Hines, 2015: 70). The government should look to increase the pool of funding available (i.e. 'making the cake bigger', as opposed to reducing the size of the cake or reduce funding for women's services) so that resources can be provided for both Female and Male Transformation Funds. This does not mean that funding has to be equal under each Transformation Fund – that is not the argument. Women disproportionately experience abuse more than men, and so the VAWG Transformation Fund should rightly be larger than the Male Transformation Fund. However, the government will need to uplift their overall budget on violence against both sets of victims in order to cater to both sets of Funds. In principle, it should not be a problem for a generic service to apply for funding under both the VAWG and the Male Transformation Funds either, if, for example, a generic organisation wanted to provide services for both women and men. A separate Male Transformation Fund would also help to create training programmes for state agencies and to provide more funding for accommodation, housing and support services (Tsui, 2014). Ways to improve public awareness and education should be explored, including how the media can improve addressing socially constructed gender stereotypes through awareness campaigns; designing gender-neutral public service announcements; inviting celebrity speakers to discuss male victimisation; and creating an online presence and information-sharing websites for men, where men can find information to access support (Tsui et al., 2010). However, in January 2019, the government report 'Transforming the Response to Domestic Abuse – Consultation Response and Draft Bill' stated that they have earmarked £500,000 'to improve support to male victims of domestic abuse' (HM Government, 2019: 47). Presumably, this would also include HBA and forced marriage. The report was drafted in response to widely publicised reforms in the area of domestic abuse. While there are many positive proposals contained within the consultation response (time and space in this book does not permit me to discuss these), it is submitted that the £500,000 pledge does not go far enough and indicates the government's under-representation, under-estimation and under-analysis of male victimisation in general. Furthermore, there was no discussion of a separate Male Strategy or Transformation Fund (see Her Majesty's Government, 2019: 46–48) since the response is largely focused on VAWG. This author believes that this represents a missed opportunity to really focus on male victims as a distinct and separate category.

The issues addressed in this introduction demonstrate a need to reformulate policies and the way in which male victims can be supported. First and foremost, we must improve our awareness of the existence of male victimisation at societal level and recognise that it is a problem that requires addressing (Hogan et al., 2012). If we improve our knowledge and awareness of male victimisation, including how male victims are socially constructed (whether at organisational, institutional or societal levels), this can help encourage men to come forward (Tsui, 2014). We must also resocialise men and boys with a new perspective by reframing and redefining masculinity 'in a more positive and healthy way' (Tsui, 2014), by emphasising the point that one is not less of a man simply because he is being abused. Creating more spaces for men to disclose abuse, including opening up the possibility of more women's organisations supporting men, is another option (Lowe, 2018). The creation of more male refuges for men to escape violent relationships is another option, although some studies demonstrate that some men may prefer to have non-face-to-face intervention in the first instance, or to have access to support services after hours of work (e.g. via email, social media and the Internet due to flexibility and anonymity: Tsui et al., 2010; Tsui, 2014). Male victims may also prefer seeking help from informal networks such as friends and relatives – studies have shown that friends and relatives are often the preferred helpers because of trust, and accessing friends, relatives and online services may be perceived as 'less threatening to [men's] masculine self-image and ego while still maintaining their autonomy' (Tsui, 2014: 128; Hogan, 2016). Nor should advocating a gender-neutral approach to social policies be construed as an attempt to undermine the running of women's organisations. The Elm Foundation (of which this author was previously a Trustee) was primarily set up to support women, and this still forms part of its core operation today. However, in terms of its approach to equality and respect for human rights, support and intervention is provided to all, irrespective of the gender of the victim. The Elm Foundation is one charity that advocates the expansion of government funding to cater to both women and men. Rather than reducing the 'size of the cake' so that there is less funding for women's organisations, what is recommended is an 'enlargement of the cake' – increasing the availability of funds so that both male and female victims can be supported under separate policies that validate *both groups as victims.* The government must begin to appreciate the different narratives that exist within this field of research – it needs to recognise that men and women can both be victims of domestic abuse, HBA and forced marriages.

Thus, the chapters selected and contained within this edited book provide new and emerging evidence on men's experiences of HBA and forced marriages – research that is very much needed. One of the strengths of this book is the presentation of new empirical evidence, both quantitative and qualitative, demonstrating the existence of male victims of HBA and forced marriage and the particular challenges that such men face. Chapter 2 by Ayurshi Dutt builds upon some of the debates discussed within this chapter by highlighting the specific contexts where men can become victims of HBA and/or forced marriage, calling for better attention towards male victims in order to allow men to obtain appropriate intervention. Chapter 3 by Lis Bates discusses her statistical research emanating from her PhD on police case files and files from the voluntary sector about male victims and 'who does what to whom – and why' in HBA and forced marriage cases. In her chapter, Lis discusses the lack of empirical data on male victims and presents her own new data on male victims in order to help develop an evidence base that can inform intervention, including law and social policy. In Chapter 4, Khatidja Chantler discusses men's experiences of forced marriage based on her narrative study of five men with experiences of forced marriage. Her chapter represents one of the first in-depth studies on male victims, where she talked directly to male victims of forced marriage. Her rationale for conducting the study is that relatively little is known about forced marriages for male victims, including the impact of forced marriage and men's different coping mechanisms – her study thus fills an important gap in our knowledge and understanding of male victims in this area. Chapter 5 by Rachael Clawson discusses the impact of learning disabilities on men, highlighting the risks such men face and the reasons why such men may be forced into marriage. She also discusses improved responses and strategies to protect such vulnerable men from abuse. Chapter 6 (by Roxanne Khan and Michelle Lowe) and Chapter 7 (by Rusi Jaspal) both discuss the experiences of South Asian gay men and how coming out can result in the infliction of HBA and forced marriage by their families; furthermore, Rusi's chapter focuses on the psychological impact of (negative) parental reactions towards coming out and how this can negatively impact the identity and experiences of British South Asians who come out as gay. Chapter 8 (by Sayed Mahdi Mosawi) and Chapter 9 (by Bingül Durbaş) provide a different perspective of the discussions in the book thus far by offering analysis on HBA and forced marriages in countries other than the UK, namely Afghanistan and Turkey respectively, and how men across the world can be victimised in the name of honour. In particular, building on the literature on VAWG in Turkey and poor protection, Bingul discusses her court case files and how the Turkish criminal courts, in effect, legitimise the so-called honour killings of men who are alleged to have dishonoured other men. Finally, Chapter 10 (by Mindy Mahil) and Chapter 11 (by myself and Jennifer Calverley) offer detailed consideration of case studies by West Midlands Police Force and The Elm Foundation respectively, where men have been victims of HBA and forced marriages and who have sought intervention from the police and third sector voluntary services. These two chapters provide further evidence demonstrating the existence of male victims from state and voluntary agency perspectives, whilst offering some recommendations on how intervention can be improved for male victims.

We, as contributors, hope that readers find this book very informative and that it helps to improve knowledge of the different experiences of men. More importantly, we hope that it sparks further debates and research into male victimisation of HBA and forced marriages, with the view towards improving awareness, recognition and intervention for male victims as a separate and distinct group.

Note

1 The views expressed in this chapter are my own and may not necessarily be shared by the other contributors.

References

Alibhai-Brown, Yasmin (2018) 'To Have and To Hold: Against His Will', *The Sunday Times Magazine*, 25 November.

Allen-Collinson, Jacquelyn (2009) 'A Marked Man: Female-Perpetrated Intimate Partner Abuse', *International Journal of Men's Health*, Vol. 8, No. 1, 22.

Amnesty International, Pakistan (1999) *Violence Against Women in the Name of Honour*, AI Index: ASA 33/17/99, 22 September.

Anitha, Sundari and Aisha K. Gill (2015) 'A Moral Panic? The Problematization of Forced Marriage in British Newspapers', *Violence Against Women*, Vol. 21, No. 9, 1123.

Aplin, Rachael (2017) 'Exploring the Role of Mothers in "Honour" Based Abuse Perpetration and the Impact on the Policing Response', *Women's Studies International Forum*, Vol. 60, 1.

Baker, Nancy V., Peter R. Gregware. and Margery A. Cassidy (1999) 'Family Killing Fields: Honour Rationales in the Murder of Women', *Violence Against Women*, Vol. 5, No. 2, 164–184.

Balzani, Marzia (2010) 'Masculinities and Violence against Women in South Asian Communities: Transnational Perspectives', in Ravi K. Thiara and Aisha K. Gill (eds.), *Violence against Women in South Asian Communities: Issues for Policy and Practice*, London: Jessica Kingsley, pp. 80–101.

BBC (2019) *Abused By My Girlfriend*. Available at YouTube: www.youtube.com/watch?v=FK5VFSxmetc (last accessed 1 March 2019).

Begikhani, Nazand, Aisha K. Gill and Gill Hague (2015) *Honour-Based Violence: Experiences and Counter-Strategies in Iraqi Kurdistan and the UK Kurdish Diaspora*, London: Ashgate.

Begikhani, Nazand and Gill Hague (2013) '"Honour"-Based Violence: Moving Towards Action in Iraqi Kurdistan', *The Copernicus Journal of Political Studies*, Vol. 2, No. 4, 211.

Berger, Joshua L., Emily M. Douglas and Denise A. Hines (2016) 'The Mental Health of Male Victims and Their Children Affected by Legal and Administrative Partner Aggression', *Aggressive Behavior*, Vol. 42, 346.

Bhopal, Kalwant (1997) *Gender, 'Race' and Patriarchy: A Study of South Asian Women*, Aldershot: Ashgate.

Brady, Brian (2008) 'A Question of Honour: Police Say 17,000 Women Are Victims Every Year', *The Independent*. Available at: www.independent.co.uk/news/uk/home-news/a-question-of-honour-police-say-17000-women-are-victims-every-year-780522.html (last accessed 8 February 2019).

Brandon, James and Salam Hafez (2008) *Crimes of the Community: Honour-Based Violence in the UK*, London: Centre for Social Cohesion. A Civitas Project.

Brod, Harry and Michael Kaufman (eds.) (1994) *Theorizing Masculinities*, London: Sage Publications.

Cheung, Monit, Patrick Leung and Venus Tsui (2009) 'Asian Male Domestic Violence Victims: Services Exclusive for Men', *Journal of Family Violence*, Vol. 24, 447.

Clawson, Rachel (2016) 'Safeguarding People with Learning Disabilities from Forced Marriage: The Role of Safeguarding Boards', *The Journal of Adult Protection*, Vol. 18, No. 5, 277.

Clawson, Rachel and Rachel Fyson (2017) 'Forced Marriage of People with Learning Disabilities: A Human Rights Issue', *Disability and Society*, Vol. 32, No. 6, 810.

Cohen, Stanley (2002) *Folk Devils and Moral Panics*, London: Routledge, 3rd Edition.

Connell, R.W. (1987) *Gender and Power*, Cambridge: Polity Press.

Connell, R.W. (2000) *The Men and the Boys*, Maryborough: Allen and Unwin.

Connell, R.W. (2005) *Masculinities*, Los Angles: University of California Press, 2nd Edition.

Cook, Phillip W. (2009) *Abused Men: The Hidden Side of Domestic Violence*, Westport:, CT: Praeger, 2nd Edition.

Council of Europe (2005) (Prepared by Dr. Edwige Rude-Antione, *Forced Marriages in Council of Europe Member States: A Comparative Study of Legislation and Political Initiatives*, Directorate General of Human Rights, Strasbourg, CDEG (2005) 1.

Council of Europe (2018) *Parliament Assembly: Forced Marriage in Europe*, Doc. 14574 (11 June 2018).

Crown Prosecution Service (CPS) (2017) *Public Statement on Male Victims for Crimes Covered by the CPS Violence against Women and Girls (VAWG) Strategy* (September 2017).

Dogan, Recep (2018) 'Do Women Kill for Honor? Conceptualizing Women's Involvement in Honor Killings', *Deviant Behavior*, Vol. 39, No. 10, 1247.

Dunn, Peter (2012) 'Men as Victims: "Victim" Identities, Gay Identities, and Masculinities', *Journal of Interpersonal Violence*, Vol. 27, No. 17, 3442.

Durfee, Alesha (2011) 'I'm Not a Victim, She's an Abuser: Masculinity, Victimization, and Protection Orders', *Gender and Society*, Vol. 25, No. 3, 316.

Dyer, Emily (2015) *'Honour' Killings in the UK*, London: The Henry Jackson Society.

Entilli, Lorenza and Sabrina Cipolletta (2017) 'When the Woman Gets Violent: The Construction of Domestic Abuse Experience from Heterosexual Men's Perspective', *Journal of Clinical Nursing*, Vol. 26, Nos. 15–16, 2328.

Geetha, V. (2015) *Patriarchy*, Kolkata: Mandira Sen for STREE.

George, Malcolm J. and David J. Yarwood (2004) *Male Domestic Violence Victims Survey 2001: Main Findings*, October. Dewar Research, Ascot.

Gill, Aisha K. (2004) 'Voicing the Silent Fear: South Asian Women's Experiences of Domestic Violence', *Howard Journal of Criminal Justice*, Vol. 43, No. 5, 465.

Gill, Aisha K. (2009) 'Honor Killings and the Quest for Justice in Black and Minority Ethnic Communities in the United Kingdom', *Criminal Justice Policy Review*, Vol. 20, 475.

Gill, Aisha K. (2010) 'Reconfiguring Honour-Based Violence as a Form of Gendered Violence', in Mohammad Mazher Idriss and Tahir Abbas (eds.), *Honour, Violence, Women and Islam*, London: Routledge-Cavendish, pp. 218–231.

Gill, Aisha K., Caroline Strange and Karl Roberts (eds.) (2014) *Honour Killing and Violence: Theory, Policy and Practice*, Hampshire: Palgrave MacMillan.

Grady, Ann (2002) 'Female-on-Male Domestic Violence: Uncommon or Ignored?', in Carolyn Hoyle and Richard Young (eds.), *New Visions of Crime Victims*, Oxford: Hart Publishing, pp. 71–96.

Gryzb, Magdalena A. (2016) 'An Explanation of Honour-Related Killings of Women in Europe Through Bourdieu's Concept of Symbolic Violence and Masculine Domination', *Current Sociology*, Vol. 64, No. 7, 1036.

Hall, Alexandra (2014) '"Honour" Crimes', in Pamela Davies, Peter Francis and Tanya Wyatt (eds.), *Invisible Crimes and Social Harms*, Basingstoke, Hampshire Palgrave MacMillan, pp. 81–101.

Haywood, Chris and Mairtin Mac an Ghaill (2003) *Men and Masculinities: Theory, Research and Social Practice*, Buckingham: Open University Press.

Her Majesty's Government (2019) *Transforming the Response to Domestic Abuse: Consultation Response and Draft Bill*, CP 15, January.

Her Majesty's Inspectorate of Constabulary (HMIC) (2015) *The Depths of Dishonour: Hidden Voices and Shameful Crimes.* Report (8 December 2015).

Hester, Marianne (2009) *Who Does What to Whom? Gender and Domestic Violence Perpetrators*, Violence against Women Research Group, School for Policy Studies, University of Bristol, June 2009, in association with the Northern Rock Foundation.

Hines, Denise (2015) 'Overlooked Victims of Domestic Violence: Men', *International Journal for Family Research and Policy*, Vol. 1, No. 1, 57.

Hines, Denise A., Jan Brown and Edward Dunning (2007) 'Characteristics of Callers to the Domestic Abuse Helpline For Men', *Journal of Family Violence*, No. 22, Vol. 2, 63.

Hines, Denise A. and Emily M. Douglas (2015) 'Health Problems of Partner Violence Victims: Comparing Help-Seeking Men to a Population Sample', *American Journal of Preventative Medicine*, Vol. 48, No. 2, 136.

Hogan, Kevin (2016) *Men's Experiences of Female-Perpetrated Intimate Partner Violence: A Qualitative Exploration*, Professional Doctorate Thesis, University of the West of England. Available at: http://eprints.uwe.ac.uk/28618/ (last accessed 8 February 2019).

Hogan, Kevin F., John R. Hegarty, Tony Ward and Lorna J. Dodd (2012) 'Counsellor's Experiences of Working with Male Victims of Female Perpetrated Domestic Abuse', *Counselling and Psychotherapy Research*, Vol. 12, No. 1, 44.

Home Office (2016) *Violence against Women and Girls Service Transformation Fund: Prospectus* (December 2016).

Home Office (2018) *Forced Marriage Unit Statistics 2017* (16 March 2018).

Home Office (2019) *Forced Marriage Unit Statistics 2018* (24 May 2019).

Honderich, Ted (1995) *The Oxford Companion to Philosophy*, Oxford: Oxford University Press.

House of Commons Home Affairs Committee (2008) 'Domestic Violence, Forced Marriage and "Honour"-Based Violence', *Sixth Report of Session 2007–08*, Vol. 1, 13 June, HC 263-I.

House of Commons Home Affairs Committee (2011) *Forced Marriage* (Eighth Report of Session 2010–12, 17 May 2011, HC 880).

Hunnicutt, Gwen (2009) 'Varieties of Patriarchy and Violence against Women: Resurrecting "Patriarchy" as a Theoretical Tool', *Violence against Women*, Vol. 15, No. 5, 553.

Idriss, Mohammad Mazher (2018a) 'Key Agent and Survivor Recommendations for Intervention in Honour-Based Violence in the UK', *International Journal of Comparative and Applied Criminal Justice*, Vol. 42, No. 4, 321.

Idriss, Mohammad Mazher (2018b) *Recommendations from the National Honour-Based Violence Roadshow 2018*, October. Available at: www2.mmu.ac.uk/business-school/research/research-centres/national-hbv/ (last accessed 8 February 2019).

Idriss, Mohammad Mazher and Tahir Abbas (eds.) (2010) *Honour, Violence, Women and Islam*, London: Routledge-Cavendish.

Jaspal, Rusi and Asifa Siraj (2011) 'Perceptions of "Coming Out" Among British Muslim Gay Men', *Psychology and Sexuality*, Vol. 2, No. 3, 183.

Javaid, Aliraza (2016) 'Giving a Voice to the Voiceless: Police Responses to Male Rape', *Policing*, Vol. 11, No. 2, 146.

Javaid, Aliraza (2017) '"Walking on Egg Shells": Policing Sexual Offences against Men', *Police Journal*, Vol. 90, No. 3, 228.

Julios, Christina (2015) *Forced Marriage and 'Honour' Killings in Britain: Private Lives, Community Crimes and Public Policy Perspectives*, Surrey: Ashgate.

Kandiyoti, Deniz (1988) 'Bargaining with Patriarchy', *Gender and Society*, Vol. 2, No. 3, 274.

Kelly, Liz (1988) *Surviving Sexual Violence*, Oxford: Polity Press.

Khanum, Nazia (2008) *Forced Marriage, Family Cohesion and Community Engagement: National Learning Through a Case Study of Luton*, Watford: Bartham Press Ltd.

Lowe, Michelle (2018) 'Male Sexual Assault Survivors: Lessons for UK Services', *Journal of Aggression, Conflict and Peace Reconciliation*, Vol. 10, No. 3, 181.

Machado, Andreia, Anita Santos, Nicola Graham-Kevan and Marlene Matos (2017) 'Exploring Help Seeking Experiences of Male Victims of Female Perpetrators of IPV', *Journal of Family Violence*, Vol. 32, 513.

Mackay, Finn (2015) *Radical Feminism: Feminist Activism in Movement*, London: Palgrave Macmillan.

MacKinnon, Kenneth (2003) *Representing Men: Maleness and Masculinity in the Media*, London: Arnold.

McCarrick, Jessica, Catriona Davis-McCabe and Sarah Hirst-Winthrop (2016) 'Men's Experiences of the Criminal Justice System Following Female Perpetrated Intimate Partner Violence', *Journal of Family Violence*, Vol. 31, No. 2, 203.

Mead, George H. (1934) *Mind, Self and Society*, Chicago: Chicago University Press.

Merrill, Gregory S. and Valerie A. Wolfe (2000) 'Battered Gay Men: An Exploration of Abuse, Help Seeking, and Why They Stay', *Journal of Homosexuality*, Vol. 39, No. 2, 1.

Metropolitan Police Service (2007) *Honor-Based Violence Action Plan and MPS Strategy*. London.

Mies, M. (1986) *Patriarchy and Accumulation on a World Scale: Women in the International Division of Labour*, London: Zed Books.

Migliaccio, Todd A. (2001) 'Marginalizing the Battered Male', *Journal of Men's Studies*, Vol. 9, No. 2, 205.

Moore, Sarah E.H. (2014) *Crime and the Media*, Hampshire: Palgrave Macmillan.

Morgan, Karen, Emma Williamson, Marianne Hester, Susan Jones and Gene Feder (2014) 'Asking Men about Domestic Violence and Abuse in a Family Medicine Context: Help Seeking and Views on the General Practitioner Role', *Aggression and Violent Behavior*, Vol. 19, No. 6, 637.

Mulvihill, Natasha, Geetanjali Gangoli, Aisha K. Gill and Marianne Hester (2018) 'The Experience If Interactional Justice for Victims of "Honour"-Based Violence and Abuse Reporting to the Police in England and Wales', *Policing and Society*, 1 [ONLINE FIRST].

Myhill, A. (2017) 'Measuring Domestic Violence Context Is Everything', *Journal of Gender-Based Violence*, Vol. 1, No. 1, 33.

Office for National Statistics (ONS) (2018) *Domestic Abuse: Findings from the Crime Survey for England and Wales: Year Ending March 2018* (22 November 2018).

Parity (2018) *Equality Services for All? Domestic Violence/Abuse Services in London: Enquiry into DVA Services Provided by London Boroughs in 2016/17: General Results* (March 2018).

Rauf, Bushra, Nadia Saleem, Rachel Clawson, Mandy Sanghera and Geoff Marston (2013) 'Forced Marriage: Implications for Mental Health and Intellectual Disability Services', *Advances in Psychiatric Treatment*, Vol. 19, 135.

Razack, Sherene H. (1998) 'What Is to Be Gained By Looking White People in the Eye? Race in Sexual Violence Cases', in S. Razack (ed.), *Looking White People in the Eye: Gender, Race, and Culture in Courtrooms and Classrooms*, Toronto: University of Toronto Press, pp. 56–87.

Razzall, Katie and Yasminara Khan (2017) 'Charities Sound the Alarm on Male Honour Abuse', *BBC News*. Available at: www.bbc.co.uk/news/uk-39485348 (last accessed 8 February 2019).

Reddy, Rupa (2008) 'Gender, Culture and the Law: Approaches to Honour Crimes in the UK', *Feminist Legal Studies*, Vol. 16, No. 3, 305.

Reddy, Rupa (2014) 'Domestic Violence or Cultural Tradition? Approaches to "Honour Killing" as Species and Subspecies in English Legal Practice', in Aisha K. Gill, Caroline Strange and K. Roberts (eds.), *Honour Killing and Violence: Theory, Policy and Practice*, Hampshire: Palgrave MacMillan, pp. 27–45.

Reimers, Eva (2007) 'Representations of an Honor Killing: Intersections of Discourses on Culture, Gender, Equality, Social Class and Nationality', *Feminist Media Studies*, Vol. 7, No. 3, 239.

Ritschel, Catherine (2019) 'Man Burnt and Cut by Ex-Girlfriend in Horrific Domestic Abuse Case was "Waiting to Die"', *The Independent*, 21 February. Available at: www.independent.co.uk/news/uk/home-news/alex-skeel-domestic-abuse-girlfriend-man-documentary-violence-good-morning-britain-a8790671.html (last accessed 1 March 2019).

Rogers, Michaela (2017) 'Transphobic "Honour"-Based Abuse: A Conceptual Tool,' *Sociology*, Vol. 51, No. 2, 225.

R v Chomir Ali [2011] EWCA Crim 1011.

Samad, Yunas (2010) 'Forced Marriage among Men: An Unrecognized Problem', *Critical Social Policy*, Vol. 30, No. 2, 189.

Sev'er, Aysan and Gokcecicek Yurdakul (2001) 'Culture of Honor, Culture of Change', *Violence Against Women*, Vol. 7, No. 9, 964.

Siddiqui, Hananna (2005) 'There Is No "Honour" in Domestic Violence, Only Shame! Women's Struggles Against "Honour" Crimes in the UK', in Lynn Welchman and Sara Hossain (eds.), *'Honour': Crimes, Paradigms, and Violence Against Women*, London: Zed Books, pp. 263–281.

Siddiqui, Hannana (2016) 'What Will It Take to End Honour Based Violence in the UK?', *Open Democracy*, 28 November. Available at: www.opendemocracy.net/5050/hannana-siddiqui/lasting-change-to-end-honour-based-violen (last accessed 8 February 2019).

Singh, Lucky Roy (2017) *Take a Walk in My Big Indian Heels*, Serialised Diary, Kindle Edition.

Sidhu, Manjinder Singh (2016) *Bollywood Gay: A Help Yourself Book to Living an Authentic Life, My Spiritual Soul*, 1st Edition.

Siraj, Asifa (2006) 'On Being Homosexual and Muslim: Conflicts and Challenges', in Lahoucine Ouzgane (ed.), *Islamic Masculinities*, London: Zed Books, pp. 202–216.

Stanko, Elizabeth A. and Kathy Hobdell (1993) 'Assault on Men: Masculinity and Male Victimization', *The British Journal of Criminology*, Vol. 33, No. 3, 400.

Taket, Ann, Jo Nurse, Katrina Smith, Judy Watson, Judy Shakespeare, Vicky Lavis, Katie Cosgrove, Kate Mulley and Gene Feder (2003) 'Routinely Asking Women about Domestic Violence in Health Settings', *British Medical Journal*, Vol. 327, No. 7416, 673.

Thiara, Ravi K. and Aisha K. Gill (2010) 'Understanding Violence against South Asian Women', in Ravi K. Thiara and Aisha K. Gill (eds.), *Violence against Women in South Asian Communities*, London: Jessica Kingsley, pp. 29–54.

Tsui, Venus (2014) 'Male Victims of Intimate Partner Abuse: Use and Helpfulness of Services', *Social Work*, Vol. 59, No. 2, 121.

Tsui, Venus, Monit Cheung and Patrick Leung (2010) 'Help-Seeking among Male Victims of Partner Abuse: Men's Hard Times', *Journal of Community Psychology*, Vol. 38, No. 6, 769.

United Nations Population Fund (2008) *State of World Population 2008: Reaching Common Ground: Culture, Gender and Human Rights*, UNPF.

Warrick, Catherine (2009) *Law in the Service of Legitimacy: Gender and Politics in Jordan*, Surrey: Ashgate.

Welchman, Lynn and Sara Hossain (eds.) (2005) *'Honour': Crimes, Paradigms and Violence Against Women*, London: Zed Books.

Williamson, Emma, Sue K. Jones, Giulia Ferrari, Thangam Debbonaire, Gene Feder and Marianne Hester (2015) 'Health Professionals Responding to Men for Safety (HERMES): Feasibility of a General Practice Training Intervention to Improve the Response to Male Patients Who Have Experienced or Perpetrated Domestic Violence and Abuse', *Primary Health Care Research and Development*, Vol. 16, 281.

Women's Aid (2016) *Annual Survey*, Bristol: Women's Aid. Available at: www.womensaid.org.uk/research-and-publications/annual-survey-2016/ (Last accessed 8 February 2019).

Yarrow, Chris and Suzy Churchill (2009) 'Counsellors' and Psychologists' Experience of Working with Male Survivors of Sexual Trauma: A Pilot Study', *Counselling Psychology Quarterly*, Vol. 22, No. 2, 267.

Chapter 2

'Seeing the unseen'

Male victims of forced marriages

Ayurshi Dutt

Introduction

The year 2018 proved to be a pivotal year that saw two consecutive forced marriage convictions within a week – in the first, a mother was found guilty on two counts of forcing her daughter to marry in Pakistan and in the second, a Bangladeshi couple was convicted for tricking their daughter into visiting Bangladesh with the underlying motive of her marriage (Summers, 2018; Taylor, 2018). During the same time, a young man from South Yorkshire was the first male victim of forced marriage to be issued a Forced Marriage Protection Order (Parveen, 2018). This chapter aims to intersperse debates about female victims of forced marriages with those of male victims, identifying the similarities and differences in perception, understanding and experience of forced marriage between the two groups. Against the backdrop of socio-cultural expectations and masculinities, this chapter demonstrates the specific contexts in which men become victims of forced marriage. In doing so, it contributes to the research lacuna of the nature and pattern of forced marriages that men face, the impact that it has on them and in particular how men themselves understand their experiences. This chapter utilises the wider literature on male victimisation to frame a better understanding of the issue of forced marriage of men, highlighting the similarities that men face during and after victimisation in a variety of contexts. It calls for serious attention towards male victims of forced marriage and cautions against the ridicule, disbelief and trivialisation that they may face. It is important that men's overall experiences of forced marriage is recorded and mobilised adequately so that they are not treated as a minority and are able to obtain appropriate intervention.

Forced marriage – culture or gender-based violence: positioning men

Forced marriage is universally recognised as a human rights abuse and occurs in the absence of free, full and informed consent. It is a case of forced marriage when either one or both parties do not (or in cases of adults with learning disabilities, cannot) consent to marriage, or feel like they do not have much choice in terms of whether to marry, when to marry and whom to marry (Home Office, 2012; Lott, 2018). Additionally, individuals almost always experience varying forms of duress to enter a marriage union. The issue of forced marriages has gained significant prominence wherein both academic and legal perspectives ratify the controversial nature of 'force' employed (Gill and Anitha, 2009b; Eshareturi, Lyle and Morgan, 2014; Brandon and Hafez, 2008; Sowey, 2017). Duress, force or abuse can range from subtle manifestations in the form of emotional pressure, psychological abuse, isolation, incarceration, withdrawal from schools/universities, confiscation of legal documents to more drastic and dramatic ones constituting physical abuse, violent assaults, threats and kidnapping. This chapter promotes an understanding that consent is meaningful only when it is equally safe to say *no* as it is to say *yes* to a marriage offer.

Often, there is a related overseas element within forced marriage cases, where individuals are taken out of the country to visit their home country, on the pretext of a family holiday or visiting ill relatives, and are later informed about their impending marriage. Cases of forced marriage are observed mainly within the UK-based Pakistani, Bangladeshi and Indian communities, which also accounts for the Forced Marriage Unit's classification of Pakistan, Bangladesh and India as 'focus countries' (PTI, 2017), with 439 cases linked to Pakistan, 129 to Bangladesh, and 82 to India in 2018 alone (Foreign and Commonwealth Office, 2018). However, there is ample literature which asserts that forced marriages and other crimes of so-called honour should not be perceived as a byproduct of 'cultural backwardness' unique to South Asian communities in the UK (Wilson, 2007; Gill, 2006; Phillips and Dustin, 2008).

> Associating honour-based violence with 'uncivilized minorities' takes on different implications that have more to do with racism and the 'other' rather than the act of honour-based violence itself.
>
> (Gill and Brah, 2014: 73)

It runs the risk of creating an alienated and scrutinised feeling among minority groups, causing them to distance themselves from the Western majority and their assumed 'moral superiority' (Sen, 2005: 43), 'turn further inwards' and subsequently reinforce the practice of forced marriage as a hostile response to their challenged survival and culture (An-Na'im, 2000). It can be surmised that after the suspicious atmosphere generated towards these communities, male victims may find it harder to come out and report abuse, thus contributing to the hidden nature of so-called honour-based abuse.

In some cases, Western societies may choose not to intervene in order to not offend the cultural sentiments of minority groups. This, according to them, is in accordance with practicing multiculturalism so as to promote diverse cultural practices for an integrated, tolerant and egalitarian society (Patel, 2000: 6). However, a negative consequence of this perspective is that problematic cultural norms and traditions and the idiosyncratic harm they cause (Honig, 1999: 36), even when it is in direct conflict with fundamental human rights, inevitably go unaddressed by policymakers who are concerned about maintaining cultural sensitivity. It has been noted that with the rise of 'crimes of honour' and their closeness to one's culture, their overall understanding is compounded by 'state ignorance and indifference by law enforcement agencies or courts' (Smartt, 2006: 6). Many times, even forced marriage service providers, safeguarding officials and practitioners face 'race anxiety' (Chantler et al., 2001; Chantler et al., 2017: 30), which affects their understanding of the underlying causes of forced marriages concerning South Asian victims, thereby preventing proper interventionist responses. Male victims form a 'minority within a minority' and while they may seek external (formal or informal) support after one point, there is merit in exploring the capacities of practitioners, service providers and frontline workers in handling cases involving male victims (Office of Justice Programs' NCJRS, 2018), as they are predominantly trained for female forced marriage cases.

Aside from culture, there is another issue concerning gender-based violence and forced marriages which indicates a form of 'discrimination that seriously inhibits women's ability to enjoy rights and freedom on a basis of equality with men' (CEDAW, 1992). The primary rationale of incorporating cultural and gender-based violence debates in this chapter is to explicate the logical theoretical gap which does not take male victims of forced marriages into consideration. There are accounts which succinctly mention that so-called honour crimes are not exclusive to women (Welchman and Hossain, 2005: 9), and even authors struggling with the culture versus gender-based violence friction have cautioned that 'a major difficulty with the framing of honour-related violence as a gendered abuse is the issue of male victims of such violence' (Reddy, 2008: 307). However, in the same line of discussion, academic experts have argued that male victimisation too, in essence, revolves around men's attempts to control women, which ultimately makes it a gender-based violence (Reddy, 2008: 308). In this chapter, I attempt to move away from such stances which at first recognise male victims, but then rapidly attribute their victimisation to their perceived role in maintaining gender hierarchies, i.e. controlling women. By engaging with historical and contemporary literature specific to male victims, this chapter demonstrates: (a) the cultural expectations, pressurisations, emotional duress and sometimes even physical coercion men face to enter a forced marriage; and (b) how their consent can be assumed, constructed or co-opted by immediate family members. While feminists have employed a postcolonial lens to reject victimhood and the 'repressed third world women' narrative which merely sees women as a disempowered means of fulfilling cultural obligations and kinship relations (Pande, 2014), there is a wide research gap in even recognising men as victims. This gap is indicative of: (a) the remarkable extent to which forced marriage research on female victims has been developed and evolved; and (b) the unfortunate but clear lack of contextualisation of men's experiences of forced marriages which can be potentially challenging to study given the absence of basic knowledge (and acceptance) about it in the public eye.

Literature review

There are abundant links between the literature on forced marriage and that on so-called honour-based abuse wherein forced marriage is recognised as a constituent of honour-based violence (Julios, 2015; Dyer, 2015; Welchman and Hossain, 2005; Siddiqui, 2016; Siddiqui, 2005) . For example, in cases where individuals refuse to get married, they are most likely to be victims of so-called honour-based abuse before eventually being forced into marriage, as corroborated by forced marriage survivors and safeguarding practitioners alike (Sanghera, 2009; Dyer, 2015: 27). Another common feature is that most literature on both so-called honour-based abuse and forced marriages centres around the gendered nature of such crimes and succinctly addresses the issue from female victims perspectives. Honour-based societies symbolise bodies and behaviour of women, which directly influence the family's reputation and even community ratings. Honour (*izzat*) is strongly dictated by traditional family ideology and is potent in making private matters public because it commonly involves publicly articulated *justification* (author emphasis) to execute a social order which preserves male (family/conjugal) control over women's social, physical and sexual conduct – whether it is actual, suspected or potential (Welchman and Hossain, 2005: 6). Shame (*sharam*), a sentiment directly related to social standing, results in mostly negative feelings of humiliation, embarrassment, failure to maintain the status quo, and disgust and thus an ideological campaign to 'rectify sullied honour' is prioritised (Welden, 2010: 382). The onus of controlling women's transgressive behaviour is on men, as women's role in this honour system reduces them to enhancers or defaulters.

The emanating discourse of men as 'honour protectors' and women as 'honour holders' is a determinant of masculinity which is strongly identified by men's ability to keep women in check, including their mobility and autonomy. Sen (2005: 48) argues that 'codes of honour serve to construct not only what it means to be a woman, but also what it means to be a man, and hence central to social meanings of gender'. In the same vein, 'honour' is inextricably linked to masculinity (Spierenburg, 1998). Men's action or inaction can come under scrutiny for being aberrant as per traditional family/cultural norms when: (a) men are unable to control/aid in controlling women's transgressive behaviour; and (b) men themselves become transgressive in exhibiting masculinity (e.g. homosexuality, expressing 'soft' emotions like vulnerability). While Welchman and Hossain (2005) in their co-edited book *'Honour': Crimes, Paradigms and Violence Against Women*' strongly examine the practice (and manifestations) of honour-based abuse from a violence against women perspective to explicate the 'entanglement of paradigms of honour', their attention to male victims of honour-based abuse by citing real-world examples from Pakistan and Colombia (Welchman and Hossein, 2005: 9) demonstrates how the authors have addressed this lacuna in a forthcoming manner. In relation to recognising the other victims of so-called honour-based abuse, this chapter supports an understanding that views the notion of honour as not specific to women:

> Recovering or reclaiming the notion of 'honour' would reformulate it as attaching to women as well as to men, designating qualities of respect, tolerance and inclusivity.
>
> (Welchman and Hossain, 2005: 10)

In 2017, the Forced Marriage Unit handled 930 cases involving women and 256 cases involving men (Foreign and Commonwealth Office, 2018). Out of these 256 male cases (i.e. 20% of the total cases), 92 men were linked to Pakistan, 37 men to Bangladesh, 29 males to India and 26 males to Somalia, which, in sum is only 184 male cases. There is a significant statistical discrepancy here as the remaining 72 cases involving male victims are unaccounted for. Not only does this slippery data show inconsistent connection to countries where men too are victims of the prevalent practice of forced marriages, it even exacerbates the overall lack of representation of male victims. There is a broader consensus among academics, practitioners and policymakers alike that women are the most common victims of forced marriages. Forced marriages are enabled through multiple circumstances, over a period of time, and hence are process-based occurrences. Forced marriage may be considered a justifiable recourse to curb unwanted relationships of women largely disapproved by the family, women's *westernised* behaviour or their sexual promiscuity. According to a Bangladeshi woman from Gangoli, Razak and McCarry's (2006) study group, 'forced marriages happen when a daughter is misbehaving, or gets caught doing something wrong, like with a boyfriend or smoking or doing drugs or alcohol, anything wrong'. This is closely linked to a family's attempt at redressing any rumors about the girls and putting those to rest on a long-term basis in an *honourable* manner. It is also usual for women to get married just because the family has decided and she is inevitably expected to go along with their decisions. The notion of 'honour' and its proxies like respectability, duty and obedience can be implicitly or explicitly used to force women into marriage. At times, women bear the cost of poverty as they are forced into marriage for economic gains (Otoo-Oyortey and Pobi, 2003). Forced marriage is commonly linked with child marriages as well because children are not in the position to understand what marriage entails and encompasses before the age of 18 (Gill, 2015). To strengthen family ties and to be able to bring family from their 'home' country to the UK, links of forced marriages can also be found with immigration for 'a better life' (Hester et al., 2007). Due to the number and degrees of varying motivators for women which can lead them to be faced or threatened with a forced marriage, it is rightly said that it is a gendered practice which has a disproportionate impact on women. There has been progressive research on the concerns surrounding women's expectations of marriage and experiences of forced marriage which is a genuine contribution to the literature. Gill and Anitha (2009b: 258) illustrate how women are disproportionately positioned within familial pressures and constraints in marriage-related matters which influences their consent formation mechanism:

> The fact [is that] consent itself is constructed in the context of power imbalances and gendered norms, and – crucially – often in the absence of explicit threats; simply put, many coercive forces often go undetected.
>
> (Gill and Anitha, 2009a: 171)

Central to this understanding is the socio-cultural norm of honour which not only impacts how consent is framed, constructed, or sometimes even co-opted, but also how coercion is applied in implicit but palpable manner. Specific manifestations of honour-inspired parental fears and subsequent coercion has been actively discussed, emanating a theoretical understanding that the urge to uphold family honour overrides free and full consent. For example:

> The link between independent behaviour and sexuality was usually evidenced by young women desiring to go to university and work. Parents assumed that such behaviour would eventually result in an unacceptable relationship. Forcing them into a marriage of their parents' choice was seen as a way of pre-empting such an eventuality.
>
> (Samad and Eade, 2003: 56)

Furthermore, the need to agree to marriages *finalised by* parents can be especially felt by women because their socialisation with gender norms begins at a young age where they are sensitised about the significance of family honour, inevitability of marriage and are even made to internalise the limited freedom in the decision-making process. "It never occurred to me to have an opinion or a wish in the matter. . . . My parents met his parents and decided everything. No one consulted me" (Gangoli, Razak and McCarry, 2006: 10).

The underlying social expectation of agreeing to parents' decisions can also be linked to an understanding that the notion of consent can be divorced from the pressure to fulfill expected gender roles (Simmons and Burn, 2013). The notion of consent thus becomes further problematic because 'it is embedded within power relations rather than an act of pure individual agency' (Chantler, 2012: 177; Gill and Anitha, 2009a; Chantler, Gangoli and Hester, 2009). In an analysis of fraudulent or tactical practices used to inform consent, Scutt (2014: 95–96) concludes that filial duty becomes a serious obligation for women to agree to parental wishes.

While consent and coercion, and the problems associated with their conceptualisation, form an essential part of defining, recognising and assessing forced marriages, there is a wider academic consensus against a binary understanding as these two are in fact dynamic in nature, and co-exist as a continuum (Gill and Anitha, 2009a; Gill and Anitha, 2009b; Sowey, 2017). This conceptual understanding also gives merit to the dominant research on forced marriages being made in the context of arranged marriages. Arranged marriage, an acceptable and widely practiced form of getting married, sees active involvement from parents in selection of the spouse. However, the final decision is completely dependent upon the bride and groom. With this distinction between consent and coercion being hazy owing to degrees of socio-cultural expectations, control, persuasion, pressure and threats, the fact that arranged marriages entail no coercion is actively questioned and thus attention is drawn to the 'grey area' between arranged and forced marriage. In relation to the contested nature of consent and undistinguishable nature of coercion, it has been argued that:

> There is a spectrum of forced marriage from physical force or fear of injury or death in their most literal form, through to the undue imposition of emotional pressure which is at the other end of the forced marriage range, and that a grey area then separates unacceptable forced marriage from marriages arranged traditionally which are in no way to be condemned, but rather supported as a conventional concept in many societies. Social expectations can of themselves impose emotional pressure and the grey area to which I have referred is where one may slip into the other: arranged may become forced but forced is always different from arranged.
>
> (SK, 2004: para 7)

As this grey area or 'slippage' characterises the cultural and contextual nature of consent, its difference in relation to coercion, and the primary role of persuasion and emotional 'talk' in this coercion, questions about how victims distinguish between persuasion and abuse are subsequently raised. It is currently unknown how victims differentiate between legitimate coercion, parental wisdom and parental dominance, thus further making it difficult for them to associate with parental guidance and the 'it's for the best' doctrine (An-Na'im, 2000). Sometimes, aside from contextual reasons, women may agree to forced marriages due to fear of the consequences of saying no. This fear of consequence has a direct link with women's response to such situations because women's disagreement and protest to a marriage offer is considerably 'dishonourable' for the family's social standing (Phillips and Dustin, 2004: 540). Family stronghold and consensus, and the fact that family interests overrule individual choice and autonomy, is also strongly felt in these situations (Sharif, 2012). Female victims may also find themselves in the 'grey area' and consciously aware of it. According to a focus group participant from Chantler, Gangoli and Hester's sample: 'They will arrange the marriage and if you reject the person they will force you to marry the person' (2009: 597).

This quick transition from arranged to forced marriage and the pouncing journey exclusive of the 'grey area' indicates that *disagreeing* to an arranged marriage is a strong enough reason for consent to be simply eliminated. In the following section, I employ the theoretical reflections illustrated above to draw a comparison between the forced marriage literature on women and the available literature on men.

Shifting the gaze on males

Comparing perspectives and experiences of forced marriage

So far, this chapter has engaged with the broader literature on forced marriages to acknowledge that women are more likely to be victims and to present the underlying dynamics of family and socio-cultural relations and consequent expectations from women which lead to a forced marriage. Delineating this spectrum is particularly important for this chapter to conclusively reflect on the similarities and differences that men face in relation to forced marriage, how they respond to these and the overall impact it has on their experience as a 'victim'. Just as an African Caribbean survivor of forced marriage in Chantler, Gangoli and Hester's (2009: 601) study explicates that conceptualising forced marriage as 'a South Asian thing' obscures similar (sometimes severe) experiences within other ethno-religious groups, this chapter uses this underlying argument and logic to warn against the marginalisation of male victims who face forced marriages at a time when most research concerns female victims. There has been scarce research on the nature of victimisation men suffer, the impact that it has on them and in particularly how men themselves understand their experience of forced marriage. This chapter by no means attempts to denigrate the existing wealth of forced marriage research which contextualises female victims, but instead seeks to revise this research imbalance by contributing to the broader debate of heterogeneity of forced marriage experiences by discussing the case of male victims.

With its sole focus on male victims of forced marriages, Samad's (2010) research is the first to bring men to the forefront. Not only does it provide a robust understanding of men's positionality in the family and their limited options in marital outcomes as a result of it, it also answers the question of why men agree to forced marriages in the first place. A combination of respect for family elders (and their decisions) and emotional pressure from them leads men to say 'yes':

> My father died at age of 79. I was in college . . . doing my 'A' levels. I went back to Pakistan for the funeral. My father actually spoke to them in the family for my marriage. Now my mother said: 'This marriage has been arranged for you by your father but he's died. What are you going to do?' My first reaction was: 'No, I wanted to complete my education, and this is true as well. Then I'll decide'. My mother said: 'That's fine, but remember if you are not going to do it, tell us now, rather than embarrass us later on because the decision they have come to' . . . 'And normally', she said, 'since your father and grandfather's word of mouth is a word of honour and if you are going to go back on that this is what is going to happen to us and what we will do'. So I said: 'Fine'. I slept over it and, by God, in the morning I said: 'I'll get married'.
>
> (Male survivor: Samad and Eade, 2003: 40; Samad, 2010: 200)

The process of upholding honour often constitutes the use of a 'we've given our word' doctrine. Opting out of this 'formal' agreement is considered highly disrespectful and affects both men and women (Samad and Eade, 2003):

> It was more like he was crying, putting his hands together, pleading with us, asking us, you know, 'you have to get married one time or another, do this for me. You know people are saying this and that'. And I was like 'no no no'. But then I thought to myself just to keep my dad happy I'd say yes.
>
> (Male survivor: Gangoli, Razak and McCarry, 2006: 18)

A key observation from the existing literature on male victims' accounts is that men are most likely to be subjected to emotional pressure, but very rarely do they experience brute use of physical force. The way men are made to enter forced marriage is different from women as the latter group generally faces different forms of coercion which can either be physical (including sexual) or emotional. The fact that there are negligible cases wherein a man was forcefully taken back home for marriage also corroborates this distinction (although see the chapter by Idriss and Calverley, later). The way that men's consent is constructed and the contested nature of their consent has not seen mention in the mainstream discourses on forced marriage.

Men also show an overwhelming disposition towards arranged marriages and essentially rely on parents for this (Gill and Harvey, 2016; Samad, 2010; Gangoli, Razak and McCarry, 2006). This can be juxtaposed with parents' perceived moral obligation to marry their children off:

> In Islam, it is a parent's duty to marry their children – this is considered to be moral act and a blessing.
>
> (Bangladeshi Elder Women in Samad and Eade, 2003: 28)

Linked with the parental guidance that men rely on for arranged marriages is an understanding where men are sometimes unable to discern coercion in their so-called arranged marriages. The following accounts from men who described their marriage to be arranged explains their indifference towards emotional duress and how it impacted their choice.

> My mum just wanted somebody from inside the family that I guess she could get on well with . . . my father said 'either you do it my way or I'm going to kick you out on the street' . . . my mum crying all the time, so it was actually very very difficult. So, you know I just . . . decided to bring it to an end so I said 'yeah, I'll do it'.
>
> I did have a choice but . . . I don't know, its emotional or whatever, but at the time mum was very poorly and basically she wanted to see me married before she passed away. So you could say there was some emotional blackmail in there I guess'.
>
> (Gangoli, Razak and McCarry, 2006: 17)

Additionally, men experience strong feelings of guilt upon not respecting parents' wishes, and blame themselves after the parent passes away without their wishes being fulfilled:

> 'I killed my mother, my beloved mother.' [In fact] she died of a heart attack soon after he refused to marry the woman she had chosen for him. He blames himself and swears he will never marry anybody else.
>
> (Alibhai-Brown, 2019)

It can be surmised that men's inability, indifference and reluctance towards naming 'family/ parental pressure' and 'emotional pressure' as force, or as a genuine form of constraint on their choice also leads to them being less aware of the arranged-forced marriage slippage. This is in contrast to Samad's (2010: 201) finding which says that some men only realise that they were coerced in hindsight. There is merit in speculating that because society does not recognise male victims, this has a direct impact on male victims as they are unable to acknowledge their own victimisation. On the other hand, women can be more reflective of the subtle forms of coercion in their 'arranged' marriage and retrospectively realise that they were in fact forced into marriage, and name it so.

> I was given a choice [about my marriage], my father did sit down with me and discuss it but I could see the pressure that he was under and I agreed. Well, I was given the choice but if I look at why I said yes, then I could say it was forced.
>
> (Gangoli, Razak and McCarry, 2006: 10)

Furthermore, the ways of coping with and exiting forced marriages are different for men and women. Women are more likely to face other related abuse such as domestic violence, marital rape, forced pregnancy, domestic servitude, endless care responsibilities and even mental harm leading to suicide attempts (Gilbert, Gilbert and Sanghera, 2004; Chantler, Gangoli and Hester, 2009). Men, on the other hand, have the ability to lead a double life out of the marriage. Men maintain a public/private dichotomy where they have a wife at home and a girlfriend outside (Samad, 2010: 202). Getting a divorce also is an option which favours men more than it does women:

> You've done it now and the family [are] all happy and that, so it's easier to try and stick with it . . . just get on with it. And like, divorce is getting lots easier now.
>
> (Gill and Harvey, 2016: 90)

Following parents' perceived obligation to get their children married, one area that is often neglected is the instance of forced marriage amongst people with learning disabilities. Parents of young children with cognitive impairments often eliminate consent and perceive marriage to be a way of securing permanent care for their child and even hoping that marriage may even 'cure' the disability (Clawson and Fyson, 2017). It has been noted that while the female-to-male ratio of forced marriage in general is 4:1, it is 1:1 in the case of people with learning disabilities, thus making it a gender-neutral phenomenon for this group (Clawson and Fyson, 2017: 821), alluding that both men and women with learning disabilities face similar risks of forced marriage. Therefore, by contextualising the intersectionality of gender and disability and the understanding of consent and disability that parents hold, it is evident that the slippage between arranged and forced marriages become further blurred. Clawson particularly discusses the case of male victims of forced marriage with learning disabilities in greater detail later in this collection.

Concerns about non-normative sexuality of men is often a strong motive for forced marriages. Gay men strongly face the cultural expectation of a heterosexual marriage (Hill and McVeigh, 2010). In such cases, men experience violence, mostly emotional and psychological, at the hands of family members who assume that a marriage will cure their 'gayness'.

> Although I am gay, I wasn't really 'out' for a long time. I felt ashamed that as a man I was being forced into a marriage, and that my family was being violent with me. It was horrible for me and the girl I was forced to marry.
>
> (Forced Marriage Unit, n.d. cited in Samad, 2010: 199)

> My family were shocked and very angry when they found out I was gay. They were violent towards me and called me names. My mother tried to calm things but couldn't. I felt guilty that I had caused them pain and let them down. They made me feel as if I owed them. They really believed that if I married who they wanted, I would stop being gay.
>
> (ibid.)

Heteronormative norms related to marriage come into play which are consequently used to make homosexuality 'invisible'. In some cases, men's homosexual behaviour may be tolerated if they contributed towards fulfilling their religious and cultural duties, including a heterosexual marriage (Murray and Roscoe, 1997; Yip, 2004). This creates a conflict between men's cultural and sexual identities (Jaspal, 2014). There have been further contributions to the scarce literature on male victims of forced marriage which shows how identities, experiences and even the well-being of British Asian gay men are impacted by the sociocultural expectation of marriage. Employing the analytical framework of Identity Processes Theory to tease out the way gay men felt about a heteronormative arranged marriage in general, Jaspal (2014: 432) opines that it propels feelings of inadequacy, embarrassment and self-disgust, poses threats to self-esteem and belonging and the non-normativity of their actions makes them feel 'left out'. The familial expectation of marriage constitutes coercion in a way that gay men, in some cases, finally capitulate and resign to the wider socio-cultural expectation often to maintain cordial family relations (Bhugra, 1997; Jaspal 2012; see further Khan and Lowe, and Jaspal in this collection). Consent can be automatically co-opted by such heteronormative pressures and men can feel an automatic loss of control as they estimate that it is a much easier mental process (and relief) to 'just go ahead and see how it pans out' (Jaspal, 2014: 440).

At this point, it is pertinent to point attention to an empirical exploratory US-based study which found that more men (9.4%) than women (5.4%) were currently living with partners they were forced to marry (Esthappan et al., 2018: 13). This study used a Google Consumer Survey wherein 752 respondents reported experiencing or facing a forced marriage, of which 58.8% were males and 41.2% were females (ibid). While this new finding can significantly help in challenging the non-normativity of recognising male victims, it should be considered that despite its attempts at selecting a nationally representative sample, the study is limited to Internet users and respondents who thoroughly completed the survey. The lack of clarity in terms of the respondents' racial and ethnic identities and religious inclinations also casts doubt on it being a representative sample and the overall results achieved. However, this study echoes earlier studies relating to help-seeking patterns of men. Notwithstanding the rate of prevalence of forced marriages among men and women, men are less likely to seek practitioner services and safeguarding help as compared to women (Office of Justice Programs' National Criminal Justice Reference Service., 2018; Love et al., 2018; Gill and Harvey, 2016). Men associate guilt with not agreeing to parental coercion, which they often justify as legitimate, and feelings of shame are strongly invoked in seeking external help. Help-seeking behaviours of men also have to do with men's interpretation of marriage as a very private matter which should be kept away from the public eye and men may thus reject public interventions in this regard (Gill and Harvey, 2016: 88). This reiterates the finding from Samad and Eade (2003) where men's ideas about masculinity and pride (self or familial) prevent them from seeking proper help. While women may experience shame for not honouring parental wisdom, men face a strong sense of shame from the 'being a man, you couldn't stop this from happening?' judgements, leading them to strongly believe that their disclosure will cause disbelief, ridicule and questioning their identity as a man.

Masculinities and perceptions about 'force'

The aim of this section is to examine the gender framework in which masculinities are (implicitly) constructed or invoked which impacts men's decision-making about marriage. The subsequent internalisation of masculine norms in the context of family has implications on the extent to which 'force' is interpreted by men. Additionally, certain masculine representations can also constrain or make men disavow their experience of victimisation: 'What kind of a man are you to be forced into marriage?' (Male interviewee, Gill and Harvey, 2016: 84). The existing empirical research focusing on men's experiences and perceptions about men being forced into marriages has directly resulted in the theoretical discourse on gender and masculinity. In a study which attempted to deconstruct the underlying gender concerns and expectations from men and women in a family setting, most female interviewees summarised men's unwillingness to report, which is very closely related to how men themselves frame their experience – 'it's hard for men because they might not expect to be taken seriously', 'the problem is the male ego, like they'd be afraid they may laugh at me', 'men aren't supposed to be pushed around like that' (Gill and Harvey, 2016: 91). Coincidentally, more women than men acknowledge the mere fact that men can be in such a situation (ibid). Men, compared to women, are more likely to be insensitive towards the victimisation of men and perpetuate the 'women as victims' myth (Chapleau et al., 2008; Javaid, 2017).

The notion of gender guides the way in which men and women behave on an individual, familial or community level, due to sharply contrasting norms and values which eventually facilitate and institutionalise the concomitant ideas of masculinity and femininity. The resulting power dynamics between men and women and the socially devised gender roles and responsibilities undergo further influence and reinforcement by key social institutions (for example, family) which impact the way individuals talk to each other, how they self-identify, how they choose work opportunities and even partners for marriage, thus making it a very gendered process (Lorber, 2011). The internalisation process within this social construction of gender then leads to what Butler (2004: 3) describes as a situation wherein 'the receiver of this internalisation is constituted by norms and dependent on them but simultaneously also endeavours to live in ways that maintain critical and transformative relation to them'. Connell (1995: 68) laid the foundational stone of the study of masculinities and argued that 'in speaking of masculinity, we are doing gender in a culturally specific way, but follow different strategies to characterize the type of person who is masculine'. The particular ideas and notions about men, resulting from the social construction of gender, such as unemotional, physically well-built, strong-minded and no constraints on autonomy and mobility then emerge, which fit the definition of 'manifesting masculinity'. Therefore, 'masculinity is an overwhelming construct in the minds of young men providing a framework to determine their self-concept and also the cultural rules relating to their actions (Verma and Mahendra, 2004: 73). For men, what constitutes masculinity co-exists with the omnipresent consciousness of how others see them and their 'masculine act' or an aberration from it. In other words, 'masculinity is viewed as a performance rather than a fixed state, an accomplishment that boys and men must achieve constantly in various contexts' (Heinrich, 2013: 105). The ideological concept of hegemonic masculinity refers to the highest regarded model of masculinity which is also described as the 'honourable' way of being a man, in contrast to subordinated masculinity where men are unable to position themselves as the 'ideal man', and instead show signs of a 'weak man' (Connell, 1995, 2005). To better contextualise the male victims of forced marriages, hegemonic masculinities form a strong theoretical framework to critically analyse how men discern 'force', what makes them *not* characterize non-physical duress as force and their dilemmas afterwards.

The journey of deeming emotional pressure and the subtleties of socio-cultural practice as a form of coercion which influences consent has been considerable (Gill and Anitha, 2009a: 168–171). Despite this being related to female forced marriage cases, similar pressures are applied to men who are less likely to compartmentalise their experiences as 'force', as outlined in earlier sections of this chapter. It is interesting to note that men reiterate community and parental perceptions that coercion does not include psychological and emotional pressure (Samad and Eade, 2003). It can be argued that non-physical forces can go undetected by men because of the strong feature of masculinity they carry, which men feel compelled to prescribe to:

> To get men is like, 'You are the man of the family, you have to', that sense of responsibility and grown-up adulthood so he feels older and responsible.
>
> It's . . . . maybe more about the honour and shame of him . . . . the duty as a man . . . that sort of thing. Playing on that macho thing, whereas with us girls I think it's more about and selfishness and letting people down.
>
> (Gill and Harvey, 2016: 92)

> Stop crying. You're a man. You're not supposed to cry.
>
> (Mother of a male victim, Office of Justice Programs' National Criminal Justice Reference Service, 2018: 11)

Hegemonic masculinity inevitably comes into play as men attempt to incorporate these invocations of masculinity in the context of family, and in doing so, sometimes accept and accommodate with duress. Men are then viewed as conduits of family 'honour' and their agreement to forced marriages is viewed as a proxy to 'honour' which primarily represents reputation and respectability. This, in turn, justifies Sen's (2005:48) argument of how honour is deeply influential in constructing 'what it means to be a man' and setting an example for the 'much appreciated' (author emphasis) masculinity. Much stronger words such as 'pride', 'responsibility' and 'internal wisdom' are associated with men while softer words like 'obedience' and 'compliance' describe women who accept forced marriages. This is indicative that the coercive intent of 'honour' is felt differently by men due to the masculine connotations associated with it. Furthermore, it can be extrapolated that men's internalisation, methods of accommodation and negotiation and self-constructed justifications based on masculinities also contribute to the arranged-forced marriage slippage. Men equate agreeing to parents and *their* choice of arranged marriage as a positive representation of manhood, which can potentially explain why many of the male participants in Gangoli, Razak and McCarry's (2006) study refused to see the grey area between arranged and forced marriages.

Men's ideas about masculinity also constrain their ability to identify themselves as victims. According to Stanko and Hobdell (1993), the term 'victim' has to do with stigma and weakness, which contrasts men's notion of hegemonic masculinity. In other contexts too where men can be victims, such as domestic violence and abuse, they prefer dismissing their victim status by naming the incident 'too trivial or not worth reporting' (Povey, 2008: 67). Even men can be victims of coercive control, which is not necessarily the use of physical force, but also 'tactics to intimidate, isolate, humiliate, exploit, regulate and micromanage' (Stark, 2007: 171). In their study of male victims of coercive control, researchers identified situations where men felt 'upset', 'anxious', 'worried', 'concerned' and 'frightened' – inevitably, they felt the need to go on with their partner's abuse behaviour and found that men would retrospectively realise their victim status only during the course of interview (Williamson et al., 2017: 61). This chapter borrows from the analysis of male sexual victims (i.e. male rape) where men struggle to come to terms with their subordinated masculinity attributed to their 'victim' status (Javaid, 2017: 9). Therefore, masculinity acts as a double-edged sword for men in a way that it compels them to prescribe to notions about an 'ideal man', entering forced marriage in this case, and also prevents them from realising the true extent of their victimised position, recognising or seeking support for the same. 'Crisis of masculinity' and 'existential angst' can be used in this context too as it places men in an unstable, uncertain and vulnerable position (Javaid, 2017: 9).

Conclusion

Research into male victims of forced marriages addresses the links between norms and values surrounding masculinity and has the potential to challenge the tolerance and normalistion of forced marriages in general and thus provide a broader and united resistance to forced marriages (Gill and Harvey, 2016: 79). Additionally, feminist scholars and criminologists can benefit from 'investigating men as gendered beings' (Peretz, 2016) – having a conscious gendered analysis while presenting the full picture of the issue of forced marriages can add nuances to the issue without undermining any understanding of forced marriages. This chapter, in its attempt to see men as victims, also discusses in detail what makes them a victim – perceived masculinity or invocation of it by the family which, if incorporated in the analytical framework of 'conducive contexts' and 'coercive control' (Chantler and McCarry, 2019), can produce well-informed theorisations of male victimisation in the context of forced marriages. In addition to illustrating the specifities of coercion (primarily non-physical in nature) directed towards men, this chapter clearly points out the underlying gendered expectations of men in their performance of masculinity. The relational, ideological and dynamically constructed notion of hegemonic masculinity plays a role in men's ability to interpret non-physical forms of force and positions their actions based on this interpretation, which prevents their ability to seek support when needed and demonstrates the dichotomous nature of masculinity in the context of forced marriages. This chapter sets the scene for other (and relatively recent) empirical studies on forced marriages and male victims to be discussed later on in this book (see further Chantler and Clawson in this collection). As a way forward, further research is required to examine the experiences of women who marry male victims of forced marriages and the level of (in)sensitivity towards male victims amongst voluntary organisations, police forces and other state agencies.

References

Alibhai-Brown, Y. (2019). Hidden torment of British MEN forced into arranged marriage [Blog]. Available at: www.dailymail.co.uk/news/article-6610763/Hidden-torment-British-MEN-forced-arranged-marriage-YASMIN-ALIBHAI-BROWN.html

An-Na'im, A. (2000). Forced marriage. [online] Available at: www.soas.ac.uk/honourcrimes/resources/file55689.pdf

Bhugra, D. (1997). Coming out by South Asian gay men in the United Kingdom. *Archives of Sexual Behaviour*, 26, pp. 547–557.

Brandon, J. and Hafez, S. (2008). Crimes of the Community honour-based violence in the UK. *Centre for Social Cohesion*. [online] Available at: http://henryjacksonsociety.org/wp-content/uploads/2013/01/crimes-of-the-community.pdf

Butler, J. (2004). *Undoing gender*. New York, NY: Routledge.

Chantler, K. (2012). Recognition of and intervention in forced marriage as a form of violence and abuse. *Trauma, Violence, & Abuse*, 13(3), pp. 176–183.

Chantler, K., Baker, V., Mackenzie, M., McCarry, M. and Mirza, N. (2017). *Understanding Forced Marriage in Scotland*. [online] Edinburgh: The Scottish Government. Available at: www.gov.scot/Resource/0051/00513514.pdf

Chantler, K., Burman, E., Batsleer, J. and Bashir, C. (2001). *Attempted Suicide and Self Harm* (South Asian Women). Manchester: MMU, Women"s Studies Research Centre.

Chantler, K., Gangoli, G. and Hester, M. (2009). Forced marriage in the UK: Religious, cultural, economic or state violence? *Critical Social Policy*, 29(4), pp. 587–612.

Chantler, K., & McCarry, M. (2019). Forced marriage, coercive control, and conducive contexts: The experiences of women in Scotland. *Violence against Women*, 107780121983023. doi: 10.1177/1077801219830234

Chapleau, K. M., Oswald, D. L. and Russell, B. L. (2008). Male rape myths: The role of gender, violence, and sexism. *Journal of Interpersonal Violence*, 23(5), pp. 600–615. doi: 10.1177/0886260507313529

Clawson, R. & Fyson, R. (2017). Forced marriage of people with learning disabilities: A human rights issue. *Disability & Society*, 32(6), pp. 810–830. doi: 10.1080/09687599.2017.1320271

Committee on the Elimination of All Forms of Discrimination against Women (CEDAW) (1992). *General Recommendation No. 19: Violence Against Women* [U.N. Doc. A/47/38].

Connell, R. W. (1995). *Masculinities*. Cambridge, UK: Polity Press.

Connell, R. W. (2005). *Masculinities* (second edition). Berkeley: University of California Press.

Dyer, E. (2015). *Honour Killings in the UK*. London: The Henry Jackson Society.

Eshareturi, C., Lyle, C. and Morgan, A. (2014). Policy responses to Honor-based violence: A cultural or national problem? *Journal of Aggression, Maltreatment & Trauma*, 23(4), pp. 369–382.

Esthappan, S., Bastomski, S., Zweig, J., Dank, M., & Love, H. (2018). Understanding forced marriage in the United States: Developing measures, examining its nature, and assessing gender disparities. *Journal Of Interpersonal Violence*, 088626051880193. doi: 10.1177/0886260518801935

Foreign & Commonwealth Office. What is Forced Marriage? London: Forced Marriage Unit (n.d.).

Foreign & Commonwealth Office. (2018). *Forced Marriage Unit Statistics 2017*. Home Office. Available at: https://assets.publishing.service.gov.uk/government/uploads/system/uploads/attachment_data/file/730155/2017_FMU_statistics_FINAL.pdf

Gangoli, G., Razak, A. and McCarry, M. (2006). Forced marriage and domestic violence among South Asian Communities in North East England. *School for Policy Studies, University of Bristol and Northern Rock Foundation*. [online] Available at: http://citeseerx.ist.psu.edu/viewdoc/download?doi=10.1.1.550.9584&rep=rep1&type=pdf

Gilbert, P., Gilbert, J. and Sanghera, J. (2004). A focus group exploration of the impact of izzat, shame, subordination and entrapment on mental health and service use in South Asian women living in Derby. *Mental Health, Religion & Culture*, 7(2), pp. 109–130.

Gill, A. (2006). Patriarchal violence in the name of 'honour'. *International Journal of Criminal Justice Science*, [online] 1(1). Available at: www.sascv.org/ijcjs/aisha.pdf

Gill, A. (2015). Criminalising forced marriage has not helped its victims. Available at: http://theconversation.com/criminalising-forced-marriage-has-not-helped-its-victims-43351

Gill, A. and Anitha, S. (2009a). Coercion, consent and the forced marriage debate in the UK. *Feminist Legal Studies*, 17(2), pp. 165–184.

Gill, A. and Anitha, S. (2009b). The illusion of protection? An analysis of forced marriage legislation and policy in the UK. *Journal of Social Welfare and Family Law*, 31(3), pp. 257–269.

Gill, A. and Brah, A. (2014). Interrogating cultural narratives about 'honour'-based violence. *European Journal of Women's Studies*, 21(1), pp. 72–86.

Gill, A., & Harvey, H. (2016). Examining the impact of gender on young people's views of forced marriage in Britain. *Feminist Criminology*, 12(1), pp. 72–100. doi: 10.1177/1557085116644774

Heinrich, J. (2013). The making of masculinities: Fighting the forces of hierarchy and hegemony in the high school setting. *The High School Journal*, 96(2), pp. 101–115. doi: 10.1353/hsj.2013.0001

Hester, M., Chantler, K., Gangoli, G., Devgon, J., Sharma, S. and Singleton, A. (2007). Forced marriage: The risk factors and the effect of raising the minimum age for a sponsor, and of leave to enter the UK as a spouse or fiancé(e). [online] Available at: http://citeseerx.ist.psu.edu/viewdoc/download?doi=10.1.1.586.2826&rep=rep1&type=pdf

Hill, A. & McVeigh, K. (2010, July 1). Gay men become victims of forced marriages. *The Guardian*. Available at: www.guardian.co.uk/world/2010/jul/01/gay-men-forced-marriage

Home Office. (2012). Guidance and instruction on forced marriage. Available at: www.ukba.homeoffice.gov.uk/sitecontent/documents/policyandlaw/IDIs/chp8-annex/forced.pdf?view=Binary

Honig, B. (1999). My culture made me do it. In S. Okin (Ed.), *Is Multiculturalism Bad for Women?* Princeton, NJ: Princeton University Press.

Jaspal, R. (2012). "I never faced up to being gay": Sexual, religious and ethnic identities among British South Asian gay men. *Culture, Health and Sexuality: An International Journal for Research, Intervention and Care*, 14(7), pp. 767–780.

Jaspal, R. (2014). Arranged marriage, identity, and well-being among British Asian gay men. *Journal of GLBT Family Studies*, 10(5), pp. 425–448. doi: 10.1080/1550428x.2013.846105

Javaid, A. (2017). The unknown victims: Hegemonic masculinity, masculinities, and male sexual victimisation. *Sociological Research Online*, 22(1), pp. 1–20. doi: 10.5153/sro.4155

Julios, C. (2015). *Forced Marriage and 'Honour' Killings in Britain: Private Lives, Community Crimes and Public Policy Perspectives*. Surrey: Ashgate.

Lorber, J. (2011). The social construction of gender. In D. Grusky & S. Szelenyi (Eds.), *The Inequality Reader: Contemporary and Foundational Readings in Race, Class and Gender David Grusky* (second edition). Boulder, CO: Westview Press.

Lott, S. (2018). how the forced marriage unit saves lives [Blog]. Available at: https://blogs.fco.gov.uk/sophielott/2018/11/29/sophie-lott-how-the-forced-marriage-unit-saves-lives/

Love, H., Dank, M., Esthappan, S. & Zweig, J. (2018). Navigating an unclear terrain: Challenges in recognizing, naming, and accessing services for 'forced marriage'. *Violence against Women*, 107780121880839. doi: 10.1177/1077801218808397

Murray, S. O. & Roscoe, W. (1997). *Islamic Homosexualities: Culture, History and Literature*. New York, NY: New York University Press.

Office of Justice Programs' National Criminal Justice Reference Service. (2018). Exploratory research into the intersection of forced marriage, intimate partner violence, and sexual violence. *Office of Justice Programs' National Criminal Justice Reference Service*. Available at: www.ncjrs.gov/pdffiles1/nij/grants/251485.pdf

Otoo-Oyortey, N. & Pobi, S. (2003). Early marriage and poverty: Exploring links and key policy issues. *Gender & Development*, 11(2), pp. 42–51. doi: 10.1080/741954315

Pande, R. (2014). 'I arranged my own marriage': Arranged marriages and post-colonial feminism. *Gender, Place & Culture*, 22(2), pp. 172–187. doi: 10.1080/0966369x.2013.855630

Parveen, N. (2018). South Yorkshire man wins protection order in forced marriage first [Blog]. Available at: www.theguardian.com/society/2018/jun/20/south-yorkshire-man-wins-protection-order-in-forced-marriage-first

Patel, P. (2000). Gender and racial discrimination: An urgent need to integrate an intersectional perspective to the examination and development of policies, strategies and remedies for gender and racial equality. Paper presented at the UNDAW Expert Group Meeting on the Gender-Related Aspects of Race Discrimination, Zagreb, Croatia, 21–24 November. Available at: www.un.org/womeneatch/daw/csw/Patel45.htm

Peretz, T. (2016). Why study men and masculinities? A theorized research review. *Graduate Journal of Social Science*, [online] 12(3), pp.30–43. Available at: http://gjss.org/sites/default/files/issues/chapters/papers/GJSS%20Vol%2012-3%20Peretz.pdf

Phillips, A. & Dustin, M. (2004). UK initiatives on forced marriage: Regulation, dialogue and exit. *Political Studies*, 52(3), pp. 531–551.

Phillips, A. & Dustin, M. (2008). Whose agenda is it? *Ethnicities*, 8(3), pp. 405–424.

Povey, D. (Ed.), Coleman, K., Kaiza, P., Hoare, J. & Jansson, K. (2008). Homicides, firearm offences and intimate violence 2006/07 (Supplementary Volume 2 to Crime in England and Wales 2006/07). *Home Office Statistical Bulletin 3/08*. Available at: www.homeoffice.gov.uk/rds/pdfs08/hosb0308.pdf

PTI. (2017). UK tackled 79 forced marriage cases in India in 2016 [Blog]. Available at: https://indianexpress.com/article/india/uk-tackled-79-forced-marriage-cases-in-india-in-2016-4563992/

Reddy, R. (2008). Gender, culture and the law: Approaches to 'honour crimes' in the UK. *Feminist Legal Studies*, 16(3), pp. 305–321. doi: 10.1007/s10691-008-9098-x

Samad, Y. (2010). Forced marriage among men: An unrecognized problem. *Critical Social Policy*, 30, pp. 189–207.

Samad, Y. & Eade, J. (2003). Community perceptions of forced marriage. *Foreign and Commonwealth Office, Community Liaison Unit*. [online] Available at: https://core.ac.uk/download/pdf/135337.pdf

Sanghera, J. (2009). *Daughters of Shame*. [ebook] London: Hodder and Stoughton. Available at: https://books.google.co.uk/books?hl=en&lr=&id=1t9gvTQlAvoC&oi=fnd&pg=PT3&dq=sanghera+shame&ots=HiUILVR_CX&sig=B0AosWOIuieWb1Xazyp5dVzemjg#v=onepage&q=sanghera%20shame&f=false

Scutt, J. (2014). Human rights, arranged marriages and family law: Should culture override or inform fraud and duress? *Denning Law Journal*, [online] 26, pp. 62–97. Available at: http://heinonline.org.ezproxy.is.ed.ac.uk/HOL/Page?public=false&handle=hein.journals/denlj26&page=62&collection=journals

Sen, P. (2005). Crimes of honour, value and meaning. In L. Welchman & S. Hossain (Eds.), *'Honour': Crimes, Paradigms and Violence against Women* (pp. 42–63). London: Zed Books.

Shariff, F. (2012). Towards a transformative paradigm in the UK response to forced marriage. *Social & Legal Studies*, 21(4), 549–565. http://dx.doi.org/10.1177/0964663912453848

Siddiqui, H. (2005). There is no 'honour' in domestic violence, only shame! Women's struggles against 'honour' crimes in the UK. In L. Welchman & S. Hossein (Eds.), *'Honour': Crimes, Paradigms, and Violence against Women* (pp. 263–281). London: Zed Books.

Siddiqui, H. (2016). What will it take to end honour based violence in the UK? *Open Democracy*, 28 November. Available at: www.opendemocracy.net/5050/hannana-siddiqui/lasting-change-to-end-honour-based-violen

Simmons, F. & Burn, J. (2013). Without consent: Forced marriage in Australia. *HeinOnline*, [online] pp. 970–1008. Available at: http://heinonline.org/HOL/Page?handle=hein.journals/mulr36&div=31&g_sent=1&casa_token=&collection=journals

SK (An Adult (Forced Marriage: Appropriate Releief), Re [2004] EWHC 3202 (Fam).

Smartt, U. (2006). Honour killings. *The Journal Dedicated to Magisterial and Local Government Law*, 4, p. 4.

Sowey, H. (2017). From an emic perspective: Exploring consent in forced marriage law. *Australian & New Zealand Journal of Criminology*, 51(2), pp.258–274.

Spierenburg, P. (1998). *Men and Violence: Gender, Honor and Rituals in Modern Europe and America*. Columbus, OH: Ohio State University Press.

Stanko, E. & Hobdell, K. (1993). Assault on men. *The British Journal Of Criminology*, 33(3), 400–415. doi: 10.1093/oxfordjournals.bjc.a048333

Stark, E. (2007). *Coercive Control: How Men Entrap Women in Personal Life*. Oxford: Oxford University Press.

Summers, H. (2018). Birmingham woman jailed for duping daughter into forced marriage. [Blog] *The Guardian*. Available at: www.theguardian.com/uk-news/2018/may/23/birmingham-woman-jailed-duping-daughter-forced-marriage

Taylor, L. (2018). Britain makes second forced marriage conviction in a week [Blog]. Available at: www.reuters.com/article/us-britain-forcedmarriage-sentence/britain-makes-second-forced-marriage-conviction-in-a-week-idUSKCN1IU2AD

Verma, R. & Mahendra, V. (2004). Construction of Masculinity in India: A gender ans sexual health perspective. *The Journal of Family Welfare*, 50.

Welchman, L. & Hossain, S. (2005). *'Honour': Crimes, Paradigms and Violence against Women*. London: Zed Books, pp. 1–21.

Welden, B. (2010). Restoring lost 'honor': Retrieving face and identity, removing shame, and controlling the familial cultural environment through 'honor' murder. *Journal of Alternative Perspectives in the Social Sciences*, [online] 2(1), pp. 380–398. Available at: www.researchgate.net/profile/Brooklynn_Welden/publication/45146296_Restoring_Lost_'Honor'_Retrieving_Face_and_Identity_Removing_Shame_and_Controlling_the_Familial_Cultural_Environment_through_'Honor'_Murder/links/551403e30cf283ee08349f4b.pdf

Williamson, E., Morgan, K. & Hester, M. (2017). Male victims: Control, coercion and fear? In N. Lombard (Ed.), *The Routledge Handbook of Gender and Violence* (pp. 53–66). London: Routledge. Available at: https://books.google.co.in/books?id=MhFFDwAAQBAJ&printsec=frontcover&source=gbs_ge_summary_r&cad=0#v=onepage&q&f=false

Wilson, A. (2007). The forced marriage debate and the British state. *Race & Class*, 49(1), pp. 25–38.

Yip, A. K. T. (2004). Negotiating space with family and kin in identity construction: The narratives of British non-heterosexual Muslims. *Sociological Review*, 52, pp. 336–350.

Chapter 3

Male victims of honour-based violence and abuse in England

Who does what to whom – and why?

Dr. Lis Bates

Introduction

An empirical evidence gap

Societies respond to abuse in three stages: recognising and defining the topic, collecting evidence to refine understandings and causation, and developing legislation, policy and intervention to address the problem (Gelles, 2010). In my PhD thesis (Bates, 2017), I observed that, with regard to honour-based violence and abuse (HBVA), we have largely bypassed the second stage – collection of evidence to understand the problem – and jumped straight to formulating policy and law responses. This is nowhere truer than with male victims, where there remains a lack of empirical data and understanding of the nature, dynamics and profile of HBVA. This book is thus timely and this chapter presents new empirical data on male victims of HBVA to help develop a solid evidence base to inform interventions, law and policy-making.

Male victims of honour-based violence and abuse (HBVA)

Previous research has shown that victims are predominantly female (HMIC, 2015), but that men also experience HBVA and forced marriage, sometimes as part of a couple, sometimes alone (Samad, 2010; Sen, 2005). Estimates of the proportion of male victims vary. Reports to voluntary sector support services aimed at helping victims of violence tend to record fewer men: for instance, male victims accounted for only 4% of domestic abuse services supporting HBVA victims (SafeLives, 2017) and only 11% of calls made to the national HBV Helpline in 2008 (Karma Nirvana, 2008). On the other hand, criminal justice agencies (police) and governmental bodies (e.g. the Forced Marriage Unit) are increasingly reporting that around one in five victims disclosing or help-seeking for HBVA and forced marriage is male. For instance, the FMU has reported 20% male victims (FMU, 2016) and the latest Crown Prosecution Service annual report found that 31% of victims in HBV cases were men, where gender was known (CPS, 2018). For comparison, the same report shows that, for domestic abuse (including both intimate partner and familial abuse), 17% of victims were men, where gender was known.

Whilst both genders experience HBVA, the literature suggests that their experiences of it, and the expectations of women's and men's behaviour as it relates to 'honour', may differ. 'Honour' as a concept is vested in the women in the family and 'defended' by the men (Brandon and Hafez, 2008). Therefore, it is reasonable to expect that women's and men's experiences of HBVA will differ from one another. We need more research analysing cases with male victims and with female victims in order to explore the specific dynamics and impacts of HBVA on both genders and to provide gender-appropriate help.

How does 'honour' dictate and constrain the activities and freedom of men? Some research has suggested that whilst men are expected to follow codes of behaviour relating to 'honour' (and shame), in reality they can 'get away with' less-strict adherence to them (for further discussion of this, see Chantler in this collection). In the Arab world, for instance, concepts relating to women's shame are passive and static – it is a commodity present at birth and possible to lose but not (re)gain – whereas the corollary, men's 'honour', is active and can be accumulated, for instance by active participation and competition in community life (Brandon and Hafez, 2008; International Campaign Against Honour Killings, www.stophonourkillings.com, no date). A differential impact of 'honour' has been found in international contexts; for instance, a recent study in Norway on 'Negative Social Control' (the term encompasses HBVA), found both males and females experienced HBVA, but there were gender differences in terms of what activities were prohibited or restricted, the severity of the punishment for violation, and the expectations of boys and girls about their own freedoms (Friberg and Bjørnset, 2019). Samad (2010) identified forced marriage against men as an under-acknowledged problem. He noted several 'motives', primarily relating to sexuality (either gay men or men in relationships with girlfriends that their families disapproved of), but also relating to criminal behaviour of the men, marriage as a means of securing care for disabled (including mentally ill) men, of preventing the breakup of family land and as a means of immigration.

This dataset

The following sections present findings from new quantitative analysis of 60 cases of male victims of HBVA known to police and voluntary sector services in England and new qualitative analysis of 22 of these case narratives. The 60 cases are a subset of all cases with male victims drawn from an overall dataset of 1,474 cases flagged HBVA and collected by the author from one English police force and 43 voluntary sector services supporting victims of domestic abuse in England and Wales.[1] Descriptive quantitative analysis of victim, perpetrator and abuse characteristics of the 60 cases was run in SPSS for frequencies and associations between variables using Pearson's chi-square statistic; these allowed cases involving male and female victims to be compared on key characteristics. In 22 of these 60 cases, qualitative case files were also available, giving richer detail of the dynamics and circumstances of the case. These 22 cases were analysed qualitatively, using grounded thematic analysis of the case narratives. It is not possible to tell how generalisable these 22 cases are to the wider population of male victims in England, since the cases are drawn from agency samples in three areas of the country; but the analysis provided in this chapter offers a good starting point for discussion which could be further tested with other data, for instance in-depth interviews with male victims.

Prevalence, reporting and identification of male victims

What does systematic examination of the 60 cases tell us about the prevalence of male victims of HBVA, which services men present to and what support they need? These cases with male victims comprised only 4% of the overall dataset of 1,474 reported cases: 96% involved female victims. We cannot draw firm conclusions on prevalence from this dataset, since it may be that females are over-represented in this sample drawn largely from domestic abuse agencies. But we can observe that the overall pattern of these reported cases is gendered, with (many) more female victims than male; and this confirms the picture in all previous studies which shows that, overall, females are more likely to be victims of HBVA than males (HMIC, 2015; CPS; 2018; FMU, 2016; Brandon and Hafez, 2008; Dyer, 2015).

An interesting difference in reporting is observable, though, between male victims reporting and help-seeking from police and from domestic abuse support agencies. Some 18% of the police HBVA cases involved male victims, compared with only 3% of the agency cases. This greater 'visibility' to police was confirmed in another variable – victims getting support from DVA agencies were asked whether they had reported the abuse to police in the preceding 12 months: 66% of male victims said they had, a very similar proportion to the 68% of female victims who were asked the same question. Whilst most of the DVA agencies accepted both male and female clients – and many did have male victims on their caseload – given they were primarily domestic abuse services (IDVA, helpline, outreach services), it is possible that men either were less aware of their services or did not wish to use them. This raises an argument that there is a need for specific services for male victims, although this does not necessarily answer where such services should be based.

Profile and demographics of male victims

Who are these male victims and how does their gender intersect with other identity characteristics? In the overall dataset of 60 cases, male victims ranged in age between 17 and 82, but most commonly were between 25 and 34 years old – a similar age profile to the female victims. Ethnicity was primarily South Asian (65%), with smaller numbers of White British or Irish (18.3%), Black African or Caribbean (5%) or Other/Not Known (12%). The large proportion of South

Asian victims was similar amongst females in the sample and is likely to reflect population demographics local to the agencies, as well as perhaps greater practitioner awareness of HBVA amongst these ethnic groups. More male victims identified as LGBT (11%) compared with female victims (1%), a statistically significant difference ($p<0.001$). This seems to confirm previous research findings that men being gay (none identified as bisexual or transgender in this sample) may be a trigger for HBVA and/or forced marriage (Jaspal and Siraj, 2011; Her Majesty's Government (HMG), 2014; see further Khan and Lowe, and Jaspal in this collection).

Surprisingly, perhaps, the proportion of male victims with insecure immigration status (and thus no recourse to public funds) was slightly higher than the females – 23% compared with 21%. Immigration insecurity has been identified as a particular issue for female HBVA victims, where husbands and families can use threats of deportation to keep the victim in an abusive relationship, and/or offer to 'send her home' when a relationship breaks down (End Violence Against Women Coalition, 2018; Hester *et al.*, 2015; Gangoli *et al.*, 2019). Yet this issue has been rarely discussed in relation to male victims. The National HBV Roadshow during 2018 identified male HBVA victims on spousal visas who had no recourse to public funds struggling to prove violence to the Home Office (Idriss, 2018b). This issue is explored further in the following sections.

The nature of HBVA against men

In exploring the dynamics of HBVA against men (as against women), it is important to consider who was doing the abuse, as well as what it involved. This section examines who the perpetrators were and what the abusive behaviours involved.

Perpetrators

In these 60 cases, male victims were more likely to have one or more family members as perpetrators (53%) than an intimate partner (47%). This is the reverse picture to female victims who were more likely to have an intimate partner perpetrator (72%) than family member(s) (28%). Examination of the 22 case files shows that family members were involved in two distinct ways. First, 9 of 22 cases involved a male victim being controlled, abused, threatened with forced marriage, intimidated or harassed by their own family members. Second, in 11 of 22 cases the victim was abused by his in-laws. In 6 of these cases the perpetrator(s) were only their in-laws – their (ex) wife was not involved; and in 5, abuse was from both their (ex) wife and in-laws. In only one case was the perpetrator an (ex) wife acting alone. This is a different picture from the female victims in the overarching dataset, a significant proportion of whom were abused by an (ex) intimate partner acting alone. This difference is underscored by the fact that 79% of the male victim cases had multiple perpetrators, compared with only 56% of the female victims, a statistically significant difference at $p<0.05$.

Whilst previous studies have identified male victims subject to abuse from wives and female family members, as well as from older male family members (e.g. Idriss, 2018a), this evidence shows that abuse of males in most cases was from relatives and in-laws, even where an (ex) wife was also involved. A similar finding was made by Dyer (2015) on 'honour' killings in the UK, where in the 7 of 22 murders involving male victims, perpetrators were predominantly the family members of his (ex) female partner.

Abuse from family members, in-laws and (ex) partners took different forms. When it was the victim's own family members, abuse tended to be led by the father or uncle, with male family members carrying out actions (e.g. physical assaults, threats), but mothers and other female relatives very much involved in emotional blackmail, harassment, trying to track the victim down and communicating threats. This is supported by previous literature (e.g. Aplin, 2017) on the roles played by mothers. For instance, in one case involving a 23-year-old British Pakistani male and 27-year-old British Pakistani female couple fleeing both families who disapproved of their relationship (C001), her uncle kept her locked up and took away her phone in another country before she was rescued by police; the male victim was shot by some male relatives in Pakistan and his brother confiscated his property. However, it was her mother who initially tempted the couple home by saying the families accepted their relationship (before they were held hostage). In another case (C007) involving a 44-year-old gay British Pakistani male fleeing from his family with his boyfriend, his aunt was trying to track him down and was harassing him, despite being issued a harassment warning by police.

Where perpetrators were in-laws only, there was less evidence of female perpetrators: rather, it tended to be fathers-in-law, brothers-in-law or uncles-in-law, and often involved threats to kill. In case C002, the 25-year-old British Pakistani victim was subjected to threats by his father-in-law (who was also his uncle) to kill him and his mother and sister for leaving his wife. In case C009, the 44-year-old British Asian victim's father-in-law and brother-in-law threatened to kill him and demanded that he pay £20,000 from his for divorcing his wife. In case C019 a 35-year-old British Pakistani man who had left his wife and moved in with his girlfriend was threatened by his brother-in-law to "sort you out", which the victim interpreted as a credible threat to kill.

Where abuse was from an (ex) female partner it usually also involved her relatives, the victim's in-laws. In the one case file involving the victim's (ex) partner only (C016), the 43-year-old male's ex-wife was harassing him and his new girlfriend by making malicious phone calls. It was not altogether clear why this case was classed as HBVA – perhaps a case of ethnic profiling rather than anything more. In the other four case files involving a female (ex) partner plus in-laws, abuse tended to be controlling, harassing and emotionally abusive behaviour from the (ex) partner, plus threats or actual physical violence primarily from her brothers and male cousins. For instance, case C003 involved a 24-year-old Pakistani national who had experienced controlling and emotionally abusive behaviour from his wife during their marriage. He left his wife and was worried about threats of reprisal violence from her brother and male cousins. In case C015 the 22-year-old British Bangladeshi victim reported being harassed and stalked by his (ex) wife, who had also made threats to harm herself; as well, her brothers and male cousins had threatened to beat him up.

Profile of abuse

In terms of the profile of abuse, the 60 male victims reported slightly lower rates of jealous, controlling or emotional abuse than the cases with female victims (76% compared with 88%), but the majority of men still reported experiencing these behaviours. Similar rates of harassment and stalking behaviours were reported for male and female victims (both 62%), and physical violence (59% to 65%). Sexual violence was much lower for men, at 8% compared with 30% for women.

In-depth examination of the 22 case files showed that abuse of male victims fell into four main behaviours: emotional abuse/blackmail, harassment and stalking, controlling behaviour and physical violence. First, emotional abuse and blackmail – for instance, case C014 in which the victim's mother and sister sent text messages to him and his friends abusing his girlfriend and threatening to disown him. His mother manipulated his 14-year-old sister to emotionally blackmail him by sending text messages about the impact of his actions for her: "it's been hell for her and he's the main cause; he has abandoned his family". In a similar case (C011), the victim's mother threatened to kill herself due to the shame of him moving in with his white girlfriend and her five-year-old child. Emotional abuse and blackmail were often carried out by female family members and/or female (ex) partners. This echoes previous findings: for instance Samad (2010) found that most male victims of forced marriage experienced emotional blackmail from mothers and sisters applying extreme 'psychological pressure'. It also mirrors what happens with female victims, where these behaviours are often carried out by female family members.

Second, harassment and stalking – for instance, case C018 in which a gay male fleeing his parents was subjected to multiple harassing phone calls in attempts to track him down. Many cases involved harassment by often multiple family members in order to try to locate the victim. Harassment and stalking of male victims was carried out by a wide range of family members and in-laws, generally with a view to trying to locate the victim's whereabouts and 'persuade' them to return home. This was somewhat different from cases with female victims, where harassment and stalking behaviour were often carried out by their male (ex) partners.

Third, controlling behaviour and even false imprisonment were evident in the dataset. For instance, case C001 in which the victim was coerced by his family to travel to Pakistan (they threatened that his girlfriend would be harmed if he did not go) and was then shot at; meanwhile his girlfriend was held prisoner in a house in another country by her uncle who removed her phone and all forms of communication. Case C021 involved the victim's parents closely controlling his movements, trying constantly to find out who he was with. Controlling and isolating behaviour tended to be carried out by parents and sometimes by an (ex) partner, and this also mirrors the female HBVA victim cases.

Fourth, physical violence was also evident – for instance case C013 in which the victim's wife's uncle and his sons assaulted him, punching him in the face, for leaving his wife. Physical violence tended to be carried out by male relatives: this is again a bit different from the female HBVA victim cases, in which physical violence came from male relatives but often also from a male (ex) partner. Samad (2010) found that physical violence carried out by male relatives tended to only occur where emotional and psychological pressure from female family members failed to produce compliance by male victims.

Emotional and psychological abuse, and physical violence, have previously been discussed in the literature on HBVA against men (e.g. Samad, 2010; Chantler, 2019). But findings about control and imprisonment and harassment and stalking seem to be new angles and are more typically associated with intimate partner violence against women, rather than HBVA against men.

The 22 cases revealed two further interesting abusive behaviours against male victims which are generally associated with female victims of intimate partner violence and not previously identified with male HBVA victims. One is financial abuse, the other immigration abuse. In three cases the victims' family members used finances to pressure them to comply with the families' wishes. In C001, the victim's brother confiscated his house after the victim fled town with his girlfriend, refusing to let the victim have the property back, but instead renting it out and keeping the money. In C014, the victim's family gave his BMW car to a friend and offered to return it if they could drop it back to his house – which would involve him disclosing his current location to them. In C020, the victim's job was as Director in the family business; his family attempted to blackmail him into ending his relationship with his girlfriend by cutting him off from the business and thus any wages.

In two cases, the male victim was a non-British national and was threatened with deportation if he reported the abuse or left his wife. In case C017, the victim was in the UK on a spousal visa; his wife and in-laws threatened to deport him if he did not do what the wife wanted or if he socialised with other people. In case C003, the victim was also on a spousal visa; his wife threatened to "send him back" to Pakistan and prevent him from seeing their children if he left her. Whilst the issue of male victims with insecure immigration status who struggled to prove they were victims of domestic abuse has been recently highlighted (Idriss, 2018b), uncovering evidence of wives and in-laws specifically using deportation as a threat against male victims is a new dimension.

Triggers and justifications given for HBVA against men

Existing literature identifies varying triggers or justifications offered for perpetration of forced marriage. Government guidance on forced marriage states that both genders can be victimized by family members in order to prevent relationships deemed 'unsuitable' and as a means of controlling unwanted sexuality, which might include LGBT relationships, but particularly relates to the sexual behaviour of women (Her Majesty's Government (HMG), 2014). Leaving a relationship is also seen as particularly dishonourable for women (HMG, 2014). As well as for the purpose of controlling sexuality or relationships deemed 'unsuitable', the literature shows that men experience forced marriage in particular circumstances, including when they are disabled (and are deemed to require a carer – see Clawson's chapter, later), have mental health issues or for immigration purposes (e.g. Samad, 2010; Hester *et al.*, 2008).

Far less has been written about the triggers and justifications for wider HBVA – other than forced marriage – against men (hence the timeliness of this collection). Idriss identified a range of reasons including having a relationship outside marriage, being too "westernised" or refusing to enter a forced marriage (Idriss, 2018a). Jaspal and Siraj (2011) identify coming out as gay as bringing shame on the family and thus being a trigger for HBVA. A closer examination of the 22 in-depth case files with male victims uncovers a range of triggers or justifications for both forced marriage and HBVA.

Forced marriages

In the overarching dataset, male victims had similar, very slightly higher, rates of forced marriage than females (30% compared to 28%). Of the 22 in-depth case files, five contained a concrete threat or plan by the victim's family to force him to marry. One case involved a report to police from a friend of the victim who reported him missing after he had expressed concern he would be forced to marry; a second male was threatened with marriage by his parents because he was gay; a third case involved a threat by the male's family to marry him off because they did not approve of his girlfriend; in a fourth, the victim's parents wanted him to marry someone in India to care for his disabled sisters; and in the fifth case, the man had refused to marry a family friend to prevent her from being deported.

These all fit with previous literature on potential circumstances for males being forced to marry. As well as forced marriage which occurs in the context of honour-based abuse, a range of other routes into forced marriage have been identified. These include poverty (Chantler *et al.*, 2009); bride price (Hester *et al.*, 2008); child marriage; 'correcting' sexuality (Gangoli *et al.*, 2011; Chantler *et al.*, 2009); a means of securing care for disabled relatives (HMG, 2014); ensuring protection for widows (HMIC, 2015); ensuring land, property and wealth remain within a family (HMG, 2014) and assisting claims for UK residence and citizenship (HMG, 2014).

However, a new element emerged in this dataset. As well as cases involving clear threats of forced marriage, there was a second type of case where the male was leaving his wife and this led to HBVA from his family or in-laws; but there was a suggestion that the original marriage may have been forced, or not fully consented to. Two cases fell into this pattern: one where the victim, after leaving his wife of ten years, explained to police that it had been 'an arranged/forced marriage in Pakistan'; in the second case, the male also left his wife of ten years – he did not say that the marriage was forced, but implied this was why his wife lived with his parents and he lived separately elsewhere.

Different conceptions of 'force' and choice in entering a marriage have been discussed in relation to female victims (e.g. Hester *et al.*, 2008; Chantler *et al.*, 2009; Dustin and Phillips, 2008). It has been argued that the notion of 'force' is complex, with many victims not recognising the language of 'force' even when they themselves had been coerced into an unwanted marriage (Hester *et al.* (2008). Research has also highlighted that conceptualisations of forced marriage should not focus solely on 'entering' marriages but also on barriers to divorce. For instance, Gangoli *et al.* (2011) show that women may be prevented from divorce or separation due to cultural pressures from 'shame' or 'dishonour', as well as practical difficulties such as poverty or immigration status. They argue that this lack of exit options should also be part of the concept of forced marriage – i.e. being forced to stay in an unwanted marriage.

Samad (2010) also identified changing understandings of force and consent amongst male victims, with many only realising 'with hindsight' that family members had coerced them into marriage. However, this issue has not been widely explored in relation to male victims, and does not tend to be discussed in policy and practice. The findings presented here suggest that the issues of (a) problems with understanding choice, consent and force when entering into a marriage and (b) needing to understand the implications for exiting unwanted marriages do apply to male victims as well as female.

Sexual orientation

For men, there was evidence of forced marriage and HBVA as a way of 'correcting' and punishing gay sexual orientation. In two cases, the victim was disowned and threatened with forced marriage by their family members for being gay. In one case (C018) the 25-year-old British Indian Sikh victim fled a forced marriage his parents were arranging for him when they found out that he was engaged to another man. His parents were trying to track him down in refuge and threatened to send him to India to be married. In a second case (C007) the 44-year-old Pakistani male had fled home with his boyfriend. His family, too, were trying to track him down, harassing him and making multiple malicious phone calls, despite having disowned and disinherited him for being gay.

'Western' behaviour

One case (P004) mirrored what is generally seen as a trigger for HBVA against females – he was rejected by his family and exposed to verbal abuse and coercion because he was 'Western' – rejecting their Islamic faith and lifestyle and drinking alcohol. In another (P006), the 23-year-old male's girlfriend's family objected to him because he 'used to drink alcohol and this was against their religion'.

Family rejects their choice of partner

A group of cases involved abuse from the male's family because they were engaged in a relationship of their own choosing of which the family disapproved. Reasons for disapproval seemed to fall into two categories: disapproving because his girlfriend was of a different religion or nationality or because the girlfriend was white and had a child from a previous relationship. In the first category, in C020 the 28-year-old British Indian victim was experiencing threats of forced marriage, threats to disinherit him and cut him off from the family business, verbal abuse and control from both his own family and the family of his British Pakistani girlfriend. Both families disapproved the match because of the different cultural backgrounds, with the male's father saying that 'marrying a Pakistani would bring shame on the family'. In C016 the 43-year-old Muslim male had a Christian girlfriend who both families disapproved of. In the second category, in case C011, the 24-year-old British Pakistani victim's parents rejected his White British girlfriend because she had a child from a previous relationship. In this instance, the victim's mother threatened to kill herself if he moved in with her. In C014, the male victim's family were very unhappy that his girlfriend had a daughter "born out of wedlock" – they tried to split the couple up and disowned their son. The parents were reported as saying that the son had 'dishonoured the family by setting up home with a Western White girl who already has a family', believing that this would 'bring shame on the family within the Asian community'.

The trigger for abuse of a victim making a love match which the family rejects is commonly written about in relation to female victims. It has been occasionally also recognised in relation to male victims – generally in relation to forced marriage (e.g. Samad and Eade (2002) recognised families' desire to end perceived unsuitable relationships as a key motivation for forcing men to marry), although more recently in relation to HBVA as well (e.g. Idriss (2018b) identifies families perceiving partners as 'unsuitable' or of the 'wrong caste' as triggers for HBVA).

These cases present new evidence of this trigger for HBVA against men. With male victims, the dynamics and reasons for families objecting seem to differ from cases with female victims who have boyfriends – in those cases, often it is just the fact that a girl has a boyfriend that is the issue, because it raises the concern that the women will be impure and not marriageable. With the males, it is more the families objecting to the class, culture, status or gender of the partners they have chosen, and sometimes also because the family have a prospective wife in mind and arrangements will have to be undone if the male chooses his own partner.

Punished for 'shame' brought by leaving wife

The biggest single group of triggers/justifications – seven cases – related to males suffering HBVA from their own family members or in-laws because they were leaving or divorcing their wives, and this was seen to bring shame on the wives and their families. In one example (C002) the victim's uncle (who was also his father-in-law) threatened to shoot him and his mother and sister as 'revenge for divorcing his daughter and bringing shame on the family'. In another case (C003), the male victim, leaving his wife after four years of abuse from her, reported threatening calls from his wife and her sister saying that if he did not go back to her, they would 'get someone to come to [town] and kill your family'. In another (C009), the victim was divorcing his wife: the police record states that the divorce had 'given dishonour to the family so they have threatened to kill him', threats which the victim believed.

Divorce or leaving as a trigger for HBVA has again been written about in relation to female victims. It is seen as particularly dishonourable for women (HMG, 2014), but clear evidence of it as a trigger for abuse of the male partner who is leaving is under-acknowledged in the literature. In the cases examined here, the male is punished for bringing shame on his (ex) wife by leaving her.

Intimate partner violence

A final group of four cases related to intimate partner violence. Two seemed to involve the male as a victim of abuse from his (ex) female partner and her relatives. In one case (C004), the 38-year-old male victim reported suffering physical violence, isolation and control from his wife: she controlled his wages, monitored his communications, did not feed him and she and her sister threatened to kill him if he left. He was reported as suffering learning disabilities and poor mental health, with suicidal thoughts. A second case (C017) involved the 32-year-old Pakistani male victim suffering sustained verbal abuse and controlling behaviour from his wife and her family members: threatening him with deportation, preventing him visiting his sister, changing the locks, shouting at him for not doing housework, threatening to chop his head off and threatening his family back in Pakistan. In both these cases, there was clearly domestic abuse from the (ex) partner and her family members, but there was not an honour element clearly identified. One possibility is that these were 'simply' domestic abuse cases classified as HBVA on the basis simply of the ethnicity of those involved and/or the fact of involvement of wider family members rather than on an examination of the nature of the abuse. Another possibility is that these cases initially involved domestic abuse but later involved elements of honour and HBVA, perhaps arising from the perceived 'shame' of the relationship breaking down and others in the family or community finding out.

The other two cases both involved a male victim of actual or threatened assault from his wife's relatives, but there was evidence also of him having been abusive towards his wife. In C013, the main incident was the male reporting being victim of a physical assault by his wife's uncle and his two sons. However the victim's wife had an injunction out against him, preventing him attending the home, and a police report on file for high-risk domestic abuse of the male against his wife. The uncle and his sons reported the victim as being the aggressor in this incident too. There is not enough information on file to be certain, but it seems possible this incident was a retaliation or punishment by his wife's family for his domestic abuse against her. She told police that there had been previous incidents, but that she had been unable to report them because family members prevented it. This could be a case of family members preferring to 'sort out' maltreatment of the wife by her husband and not wishing to go to the police, perhaps because that is seen as increasing the shame. In C015, the male had been threatened with assault by his girlfriend's cousins and brothers, but after making the police report was arrested himself for assaulting his girlfriend and was charged with two counts of common assault and one of criminal damage.

Conclusions

To focus on the greater prevalence and impact of violence against women is not a call to ignore men, and those who advocate for a gendered perspective do not make this argument. Instead, as Feder and Potter (2017) have written about domestic violence: 'recognition of the gendered nature [of abuse] is not a justification to ignore the needs of male survivors. Instead, it needs to inform how we design programmes to support these men (and their children), with the understanding that some of their experiences and needs may be similar to women survivors, but others may be different'. It is vital that we explore the needs of both men *and* women, and taking a gendered approach allows us to do just that.

With this in mind, what do the findings in this chapter allow us to conclude about HBVA and forced marriage against men? First, whilst HBVA and forced marriage affect more women overall (and the wider study from which these data are drawn confirms this), this analysis clearly shows that men are victims too. They may under-report and be overlooked, but they are not invisible, especially to some agencies – for instance, they comprised one in five HBVA reports to the police. This is cause for optimism – we can identify and work with male victims, but we need to understand better the dynamics and impacts on men in order to offer gender-appropriate help. There are substantial issues of shame and taboo which exist around male reporting, which need to be tackled to encourage victims to come forward, but it is important also to recognise that men *are* coming forward.

Second, these findings suggest that HBVA and forced marriage are more associated with male victims than intimate partner domestic abuse. Males account for up to 31% of HBVA cases reported to the CPS (2018) compared with 17% of intimate partner domestic abuse. This analysis shows that the majority of perpetrators in HBVA cases with male victims were family members (53%), whereas for female victims the majority were (ex) intimate partners (72%). Where perpetrators in male victim cases were (ex) intimate partners, the in-laws were almost always also involved, whereas in female victim cases there were more (ex) partners acting alone. Whilst there are overlaps, these findings should caution against conflating HBVA with domestic intimate partner abuse, and we must be careful in extrapolating from profiles of male victims of HBVA and forced marriage to male victims of domestic abuse more widely.

Third, these findings shed new light on the profile of abuse experienced by male HBVA victims. In some aspects, men's experiences were similar to women's: similar rates of emotional abuse and control, physical violence and harassment and stalking were reported. The dynamics of emotional abuse and blackmail and of controlling behaviour seemed similar to those in female HBVA victim cases, with the emotional abuse and blackmail being carried out by female family members and controlling behaviour by parents and sometimes an (ex) partner. In relation to harassment and stalking and physical violence, male victims' experiences diverged somewhat from female victims, with harassment and stalking against men being carried out by family members and in-laws (in contrast, often by an (ex) partner against women) and physical violence being perpetrated by male relatives against male victims (in contrast, usually by an (ex) partner against women). This analysis also uncovers new elements of abuse against men, which have previously only been associated with female victims: experiences of financial abuse and immigration abuse.

Fourth, this systematic examination of reported cases has shown that men face many of the same triggers and justifications for abuse as women, but there are some notable differences. Evidence was found in support of previous research findings on the triggers for abuse of men – because the victim was gay, to punish 'Western' behaviour, to honour family commitments around marriage alliances, to separate them from a girlfriend deemed 'unsuitable', or occasionally to secure a spousal visa for a family member or friend from overseas. The cases profiled show that, whereas families disapprove of female victims having a boyfriend at all, the objections for male victims tend to stem from them choosing a partner who is not of the right religion or status, or who is White/Western and has children already. A new element emerges prominently from these cases: namely, how significant a trigger for abuse is the perceived shame brought to wives and their family members where a man leaves or divorces her. This has been previously written about in relation to HBVA against wives, but less in terms of triggering abuse against men too. It reflects the gendered nature of honour, where very often it is the responsibility of males in the family to avenge the slighted honour of females.

This chapter has shown that whilst HBVA against men arises from a range of triggers or family justifications, as with female victims, abuse is consistently driven by rigid community expectations about masculinity and femininity, sex and gender roles. Feminist ideas about patriarchy are key to understanding this. Men are being forced to bargain with the patriarchy in a specific way – just as women negotiate their own roles and power in relation to patriarchal norms and family hierarchies relating to age and status (Gangoli and Rew, 2011; Bates, 2018). Ultimately then, we must challenge the way gender operates to constrict the freedoms and choices of both men and women. In the meantime, we must offer gender-appropriate support to all victims to escape abuse and unwanted marriages.

Note

1 Within the overall dataset of 1,474 cases, 86 case files were collected from a police force in Southern England, 29 from a domestic abuse support service in the East Midlands supporting male and female victims, and 47 from a domestic abuse support service in North West England supporting male and female victims. The remaining 1,312 were drawn from an existing dataset of HBVA cases held by national charity SafeLives and collected by 43 domestic abuse support services across England and Wales between 2010 and 2016. The 60 cases were all those in the overall dataset of 1,474 which involved male victims. The 22 cases involving male victims where qualitative case file narratives were available were from the police site (Southern England) and two agency sites (East Midlands and North West England) where case files were collected first-hand.

References

Aplin, R. (2017) Exploring the role of mothers in 'honour' based abuse perpetration and the impact on the policing response. *Women's Studies International Forum*, 60, pp. 1–10.

Bates, L. (2017) Honour-based abuse in England and Wales: Who does what to whom? A PhD thesis. Bristol: University of Bristol.

Bates, L. (2018) Females perpetrating honour-based abuse: controllers, collaborators or coerced? *Journal of Aggression, Conflict and Peace Research* 10(4), 292–303.

Brandon, J. and Hafez, S. (2008) *Crimes of the community: Honour-based violence in the UK*. London: Centre for Social Cohesion.

Chantler, K. (2019) Men's experiences of forced marriage: Ain't I a man? In M.M. Idriss and T. Abbas (Eds.) *Men, masculinities and 'honour'-based violence*. Abingdon-on-Thames: Routledge-Cavendish.

Chantler, K., Gangoli, G. and Hester, M. (2009) Forced marriage in the UK: Religious, cultural, economic or state violence? *Critical Social Policy*, 29(4), pp. 587–612.

Crown Prosecution Service (CPS) England and Wales (CPS) (2018) *Violence against Women and Girls Report 2017–18*. Available at: www.cps.gov.uk/sites/default/files/documents/publications/cps-vawg-report-2018.pdf

Dustin, M. and Phillips, A. (2008) Whose agenda is it? Abuses of women and abuses of 'culture' in Britain. *Ethnicities*, 8(3), pp. 405–424.

Dyer, E. (2015) *'Honour' killings in the UK*. London: Henry Jackson Society.

End Violence against Women Coalition (2018) *Women Living in a Hostile Environment*. Available at: www.endviolenceagainstwomen.org.uk/wp-content/uploads/FINAL-living-in-a-hostile-environment-for-Web-and-sharing-.pdf

FCO. (2016) *Forced Marriage Unit Statistics 2015*. Available at: www.gov.uk/government/uploads/system/uploads/attachment_data/file/505827/Forced_Marriage_Unit_statistics_2015.pdf (Accessed 17 January 2017).

Feder, G. and Potter, L. (2017) Why gender can't be ignored when dealing with domestic violence. *The Conversation*. 28 March. Available at: https://theconversation.com/why-gender-cant-be-ignored-when-dealing-with-domestic-violence-74137

Friberg, J. and Bjørnset, M. (2019) *Migrasjon, foreldreskap og sosial kontroll (Migration, parenting and social control)*. FAFO: Oslo. English summary available online at: www.

fafo.no/index.php/zoo-publikasjoner/summaries/item/migration-parenting-and-social-control

Gangoli, G. and Rew, M. (2011) Mothers-in-law against daughters-in-law: Domestic violence and legal discourses around mother-in-law violence against daughters-in-law in India. *Women's Studies International Forum*, 34(5), pp. 420–429.

Gangoli, G., Bates, L. and Hester, M. (2019) *What does justice mean to black and minority ethnic (BME) victims/survivors of gender-based violence?* Journal of Ethnic and Migration Studies. Eprint ahead of publication. DOI: 10.1080/1369183X.2019.1650010

Gangoli, G., Chantler, K., Hester, M. and Singleton, A. (2011) Understanding forced marriage: Definitions and realities. In A.K. Gill and S. Anitha (Eds.) *Forced marriage: Introducing a social justice and human rights perspective*. London: Zed Books Ltd.

Gelles, R. (2010) 'Addressing academic research on violence', in Ismailji, T., Callahan, M. and Mettner, J. (eds.), 'Academy on violence and abuse, highlights of proceedings from the 2009 conference: Sowing seeds of academic change-nurturing new paradigms'. *Trauma, Violence & Abuse*, 11(2), pp. 83–93.

Her Majesty's Government (HMG) (2014) *The right to choose: Multi-agency practice guidelines: Handling cases of forced marriage*. London: Cabinet Office.

Hester, M., Chantler, K., Gangoli, G., Devgon, J., Sharma, S. and Singleton, A. (2008) *Forced Marriage: The Risk Factors and the Effect of Raising the Minimum Age for a Sponsor, and of Leave to Enter the UK as a Spouse or Fiancé(e)*. Available at: www.bristol.ac.uk/media-library/sites/sps/migrated/documents/rk6612finalreport.pdf (Accessed 17 January 2017).

Hester, M., Gangoli, G., Gill, A.K., Mulvihill, N., Bates, L., Matolcsi, A., Walker, S.-J. and Yar, K. (2015) *Victim/survivor voices: A Participatory Research Project: Report for HMIC Honour-Based Violence Inspection*. Available at: www.justiceinspectorates.gov.uk/hmic/wp-content/uploads/university-of-bristol-hbv-study.pdf (Accessed 17 April 2016).

HMIC (2015) *The Depths of Dishonour: Hidden Voices and Shameful Crimes: An Inspection of the Police Response to Honour-Based Violence, Forced Marriage and Female Genital Mutilation*. Available at: www.justiceinspectorates.gov.uk/hmic (Accessed 16 April 2016).

Idriss, M.M. (2018a) The forgotten male victims of honour-based violence. *The Conversation*. 23 May. Available at: https://theconversation.com/the-forgotten-male-victims-of-honour-based-violence-96041

Idriss, M.M. (2018b) *Recommendations from the national honour-based violence roadshow 2018*. Manchester Metropolitan University. Available at: www2.mmu.ac.uk/media/mmuacuk/content/documents/law-school/HBV-Final-Report-v2.pdf

Jaspal, R. and Siraj, A. (2011) Perceptions of 'coming out' among British Muslim gay men. *Psychology & Sexuality*, 2(3), pp. 183–197.

Karma, N. (2008) *Survivors of Honour Based Violence and Forced Marriage in the UK: Sample Study Compiled by Karma Nirvana*. Available at: http://karmanirvana.org.uk/cms/wp-content/uploads/2016/02/Survivors-of-HBV-FM-Aug-2008.pdf (Accessed 17 April 2016).

SafeLives. (2017) *Spotlight Policy Report: Your Choice: 'Honour'-Based Violence, Forced Marriage and Domestic Abuse*. Available online at: http://safelives.org.uk/sites/default/files/resources/Spotlight%20on%20HBV%20and%20forced%20marriage-web.pdf

Samad, Y. (2010) Forced marriage among men: An unrecognised problem. *Critical Social Policy* 30(2), pp. 189–207.

Samad, Y. and Eade, J. (2002) *Community perceptions of forced marriage*. London: Foreign and Commonwealth Office.

Sen, P. (2005) "Crimes of honour", value and meaning. In L. Welchman and S. Hossain (Eds.) *"Honour": Crimes, paradigms and violence against women*. London: Zed Books, pp. 42–63.

Chapter 4

Men's experiences of forced marriage

Ain't I a man?

Khatidja Chantler

The vast majority of victims of early and forced marriage globally are women (UNCF, 2018). Forced marriage disproportionally affects girls and young women, and Samad (2010) argues that policy responses largely have girls and young women at the forefront of their interventions. In the UK, the Forced Marriage Unit (FMU), UK, collects data on age, gender, ethnicity, sexual orientation (where disclosed) and geographic location of all cases of forced marriage in the UK about which they have been contacted. Data is based on contacts made to the FMU by either the victim or by agencies supporting victims. It does not include data from either voluntary or statutory sector organisations that have supported a forced marriage victim independently of the FMU. This data has been collected over several years and consistently shows that most victims of forced marriage (80%) are women and 20% of victims are male. These figures are based on reported incidents and, as with other forms of domestic and gender-based abuse, are likely to be an underestimate. Determining the prevalence of forced marriage is difficult, not least because of the definitional issues of forced marriage (Chantler, 2012) and victims' perceptions of what a forced marriage is (Anitha & Gill, 2011; Chantler & McCarry, 2019).

Most research on forced marriage understandably focuses on women as victims (Hester et al., 2007; Khanum, 2008). In this chapter, I discuss men's experiences of forced marriage based on a narrative study of five men with experiences of forced marriage. The rationale for conducting the study is that relatively little is known about the process of forced marriage for male victims, the impact of forced marriage on men and men's coping mechanisms. This study therefore begins to fill a gap in our knowledge and understanding of men as victims of forced marriage. It was conducted in 2014–15. To the author's knowledge, this is the first in-depth study to talk directly with male victim/survivors of forced marriage.

The aims of the study were:

- To investigate men's experiences of forced marriage
- To explore the impact of forced marriage
- To identify coping mechanisms
- To elicit help-seeking strategies
- To explore notions of masculinity and ethnicity within the accounts

Methods

A narrative inquiry approach was utilised for the study, situating it within an interpretivist paradigm. Narrative inquiry encompasses a number of methodological considerations but has certain central characteristics. Narratives enable participants to tell their stories largely in their own way, focusing on key events, in this case forced marriage as well as family relationships and experiences before and after the key event. Narratives also involve an analysis of the way the story is told, subject positions taken up and importantly the potential to locate these accounts within a wider socio-cultural context (Riessman, 2008). The method utilised in this study was semi-structured interviews. A topic guide was created which explored men's understandings of forced marriage; their personal experiences of being forced into marriage; their relationships with their parents both before and after the forced marriage; the impact of forced marriage upon them; coping mechanisms used; whether formal or informal support was sought; their perceptions of how their identities impacted their experiences of forced marriage and their views on how support for male victims of forced marriage can be improved. A free-flowing interview style was adopted with the interviewer (KC) attending closely to the story as told by the participant. In total, five in-depth interviews were conducted, three were face-to-face, one was over the telephone and one was conducted via Skype.

Recruitment

Recruiting participants to the study was challenging despite the wide variety of approaches used. Recruitment strategies included a mailing through the Connect Centre for International Research on Interpersonal Violence list at the University of Central Lancashire, through a wide range of national and regional voluntary organisations supporting men including LGBT organisations and displaying posters around campus and in the wider locale. The difficulty of recruiting participants may indicate that there are a very limited number of male victims of forced marriage, that they are reluctant to come forward (see also Idriss, this edition) or that developing a closer relationship with some of the key voluntary sector organisations may have yielded more participants. However, most of the men's voluntary sector organisations contacted reported that forced marriage was not an issue that they had come across. Further, as with female victims, relying on support agencies only enables research with those who have contacted agencies for help. The multipronged approach to recruitment used in this study resulted in five men agreeing to participate in interviews, none of whom had used services for help with forced marriage.

Sample

Men were between 17 and 24 years old at the time of their forced marriages. At the time of interview, the age range of participants was 30–47 years. Participants were therefore recalling experiences from some time back. In four of the five cases, the marriage was contracted, of which three ended in divorce. In three of the cases where the marriage was contracted, the spouse migrated to the UK to join a British national; the remaining couple was British. Four of the five participants were from a Pakistani Muslim heritage. The fifth participant was white and British; to preserve his anonymity, further details of his ethnicity are not given. Four of the men were fathers. Of the three men where a forced marriage was contracted, one of the men also described his experiences of being a victim/survivor of domestic abuse within the relationship. Parents and grandparents were largely responsible for forced marriage. In the three cases where the forced marriage was contracted, wives also exerted pressure for the marriage to continue to 'save face', as did parents.

Data analysis

A thematic analysis was undertaken to compare salient factors across the narratives, and a more detailed case study was developed for each individual. Each case study was analysed in terms of the speaking positions of the narrator, issues of identity, masculinity and power relations, help-seeking and coping mechanisms as well as family relationships before and after the forced marriage. The chapter presents a synthesis of the two different approaches of analysis. Pseudonyms were considered, but the greater anonymity offered by numbering was chosen, hence participants are quoted as Participant 1, Participant 2, etc.

Findings

Dynamics of forced marriage: emotional pressure

The key method of gaining/forcing consent was through the use of emotional pressure. All participants spoke of the emotional pressure they were under to consent to the marriage. Emotional pressure was often applied through cultural and religious frameworks; coercive control; mother-son relationships and men's own notions of family duty. These different forms of emotional pressure are explicated below.

Religion and culture

Participant 5 came from a white, Christian heritage and when his girlfriend got pregnant, he was forced to marry her as that was considered the right thing to do. He reported that he suspected that his girlfriend had deliberately got pregnant just as the relationship was ending, in the knowledge that this would lead to marriage:

> 'my parents weren't happy at all about the whole pregnancy outside of marriage thing . . . er . . . her parents weren't happy about it either. . . . We both told our respective parents [about the pregnancy] and then there was a meeting with me, her . . . and both sets of parents and . . . what came out

> of that meeting was that we were going to get married . . . because this was the right thing to do . . . '.
>
> (Participant 5)

In sensing his reluctance to marry, '[T]he phrase I heard a lot of was "a baby brings its own love" you know', indicating that even though the relationship had been drawing to a close, the baby was seen as the glue to ensuring enduring love. He also reported being worried that if he refused to get married, his girlfriend and her family would ensure that he would never have contact with the baby. Hence, what started off as having a religious framing also took on a cultural significance. The twinning of 'baby' and 'love' responds to a universal narrative of the potency of the baby and its hoped-for qualities of bringing together the parents, and in this instance as a saviour of a relationship in trouble.

Participant 2 came from a totally different religious background. He identified as Muslim and gay and had experienced a range of coercive, homophobic and physical abuse in the process of his forced marriage, often underpinned by the use of religion:

> *And I found it quite intimidating, I felt like you know, there was a line and he'd always cross it and then any opportunity that he'd have . . . for us to be alone he would just go on and on and on at me and . . . sometimes, you know, just pushing me around and stuff and . . . you know, quite homophobic towards me as well, you know, he'd say 'oh you're disgusting, how can you do what you do? You're disgusting, you're going to burn in hell'.*
>
> (Participant 2)

The clear religious reference 'You're going to burn in hell' chimes with notions of sin and punishment for disobeying God's rules. Homosexuality is a contentious issue within many religions and the intersection of homosexuality and religion has been the subject of much debate (Hodge, 2005; Jaspal & Siraj, 2011; Lomas & Brown, 2018; see further Khan and Lowe, and Jaspal in this collection). For Participant 2, his multiple identities as Muslim and gay were used to belittle and coerce him into marriage. Whilst these attempts did not succeed, the impact on him of this experience has had a lasting impact. Participant 4 also identified as a Muslim and his religiosity influenced both his reluctant acceptance of his marriage as well as solutions to it. However, cultural influences are also apparent:

> 'it was decided ages . . . you know, way back in my childhood and her childhood, my wife's childhood . . . and so . . . that kind of thing about the relationship and marriage was in a sense predetermined by the elders, you know the grandparents.
>
> (Participant 4)

The notion of betrothals in childhood was also apparent in two other cases (P1 and P3): 'I knew from probably about the age of seven that I was either gonna marry my first cousin from my mum's side or my first cousin from my dad's side' (Participant 3).

Coercive control

Participant 1 described his father as a 'command and control' and 'a man's man' person. One of his father's strategies involved using silence and withdrawal in a powerful way to create discomfort within the household:

> Vibe . . . it was a vibe, dad stopped talking to everybody . . . so there was a big vibe in the house where dad was sitting in the other room all the time and just silent vibes, so mum was having to balance the books and everything by sitting with us in one room and then going and sitting in the other room, dad would go and eat in the other room, he would never eat with us and he started doing all that.
>
> The participant went on to say, 'The atmosphere was . . . you know, that . . . if any trauma came about it was around that time because that it [was] worse than any physical pain.' The participant later went to Pakistan due to an unforeseen situation and once he was in Pakistan, his father became more verbally aggressive:
>
> Dad got angry whilst I was there [in Pakistan] . . . and he . . . said 'it's about fucking time you got over this! Just do what he needs to do. This is bullshit, making a big issue about getting married. Get married and get on with things.' It's no Romeo and Juliet . . . and all that, so his tack changed . . . I was in Pakistan now, so I'm not in my environment, I'm out of my comfort zone as well. . . .
>
> (Participant 1)

In a similar vein, Participant 3 was also taken to Pakistan when he was 17 years old for what he thought was a family holiday:

> No, when I was seventeen there was no discussion, there was no fore-warning, it was totally . . . it was a family holiday . . . and I'd never been to Pakistan, within three weeks . . . I don't know if you understand Punjabi at all, they said . . . in our [Mirpuri language they said ____________ [00:04:58] which means 'they're going to set you a wedding date.' And I was like 'what?' I was like totally shocked and I basically started bawling my eyes out . . . I started crying my eyes out and . . . saying 'I'm not doing it, I'm not doing it, I'm not doing it' and er . . . my mum turned round to me and said to me 'well, if you don't do it, they've hidden our passports, we won't be going back to England . . . [pause] and . . . that was it, kind of, well if I want to get back to England, if I want to get back home . . . then I've got to do it. [sigh] . . . And that was it, I went through the whole ceremony, we didn't consummate the marriage, I didn't live with her, I didn't stay with her . . . and I came back to England . . . and . . . that was in between my first year of my A levels and my second year of my A levels . . . .
>
> (Participant 3)

His account clearly illustrates how coercive control is used to extract consent despite his very clear rejection of the marriage.

Mother-son relationships: ties that bind

Two of the participants discussed particularly strong bonds with their mothers, and the analysis draws on some of the complexities and ambivalences of these relationships. Participant 1 lived with his parents, is heterosexual and was forced into marriage. Akin to many other family scenarios, the role of his mother is complex. Whilst this participant's father had decided that the marriage should go ahead, it was the participant's mother who was asked by her husband to relay the news to the participant. In turn, the participant relied on his mum to act as a conduit between himself and his father, amply demonstrating the gendered dynamics within the family:

> *'I didn't want to get married and I tried to do it nicely and started saying 'maybe not yet, not yet' put it off for a while and spoke to my mum and said can you have a word with dad. My dad was . . . one of them guys that was more of a command and control type situation, you know, what he says, he's the main guy and . . . you know, it's not a negotiation or anything like that, it's a case of 'this is what's going to happen, tell them to get ready and everything' trying to say . . . mum was like that saying, you know, what do I say in this situation? Can't really say much'.*
>
> (Participant 1)

This extract illustrates where the power lies within the family and how both mother and son are relatively powerless to challenge the dominance of the patriarch of the family. Regardless of this, both attempt to challenge the father. Father utilises what could be described as 'the silent treatment' to consolidate his power. Hence emotional pressure or coercive control (discussed prior) is used to try and gain consent: 'The atmosphere was . . . you know, that . . . if any trauma came about it was around that time because that it [was] worse than any physical pain.' The participant goes on to say, 'But emotional pressure, I was soft, I was mummy's boy, always sort of like close to my mum and so I was soft and the stress and everything'. This demonstrates the softer side of the participant and his closeness to his mother. The depth and significance of the relationship is conveyed by the quotes and also by his attempts to be honest with his mother about not wanting to marry, asking her to speak with his father and his description of himself as 'mummy's boy'. Later, he makes it clear that had his mother had power within the household the marriage would not have taken place: 'I knew my mum . . . if it'd been my mum's decision she would have allowed me to do what I wanted to do . . . I do know'.

Participant 2 also had a very close relationship with his mother partly due to domestic abuse experienced by his mother and him as a child. His parents divorced, and as a young adult, Participant 2 continued to live with his mum and had financial responsibility for the mortgage. He had told his mother that he was gay, but this did not stop her or the participant's brother from pressuring him to marry. Their rationale for the marriage as reported by Participant 2, was that as his mother was getting older, she needed a younger woman in the house to perform household chores and that she had a family obligation to arrange a marriage with her family in Pakistan. In this case, it is clear that there are gendered expectations both of the participant and his potential (female) spouse. The expectation was that the newly married couple would live with the participant's mother with the daughter-in-law acting as carer and housekeeper and the participant acting as financial provider for the family. In recognition of his sexuality, Participant 2 was told that he could continue his gay relationships in the form of extramarital relationships. This also speaks to gendered 'permissions' related to sexual behaviour for men. Whilst Participant 2 had made it clear to his mother that he did not want to get married, very little notice was taken of his refusal to consent. He reported that his only option was to leave, but this presented numerous problems. Throughout his account, it is clear that Participant 2 had a very strong relationship with his mother based on his empathy for her as having a hard life. Her financial dependence on him also exacerbated matters and made leaving extremely challenging and stressful.

Family loyalty versus autonomy

A different perspective on mother-son relationships was introduced by Participant 4 who stated, 'A religious value framework which I largely operate in is that she's my mother and I only have one mother and I love her and that's all I can say really.' This appears to imply that it is the religious value framework which imposes a duty to love one's mother rather than a deeply felt sense of filial love or connection. His relationship with his mother was based on Islamic teachings of demonstrating utmost respect for one's mother: 'paradise is beneath her feet' as described in Hadith 20 (cited in Cheruvallil-Contractor, 2016). However, his relationship with his mother was reported as based on respect as well as an appreciation of all she had done for him and his siblings:

> I mean the other thing I have to say is that mum . . . she . . . we arrived in the '70s and so there's a sense of . . . erm . . . a debt to be owed as it were or appreciation of mum because mum was also . . . not educated but she went out of her way to make sure that her kids were well-fed, looked after, clean, tidy . . . you know, that they weren't messing about outside etc. etc. so she give a lot, so . . . that's probably something to say about mum as well.
>
> (Participant 4)

The conflict between loyalty to family and autonomy/self-integrity is evident in this account as both a duty to love one's mother as well as an appreciation of what his mother had done for him made it more difficult to resist the marriage. When the marriage was suggested to him, he refused, yet this marriage went ahead. Many years into the marriage, he was deeply unsatisfied as he reported having no leisure activities, intellectual or political connection with his wife. His interview emanated a deep sense of isolation and loneliness. His solution to this was to consider taking a second wife, as is permissible in Islam without divorcing his first wife. However, to do so, he was obliged to ask permission from his first wife and his mother, who both refused. His sense of loyalty and duty therefore means he is tied to his existing marriage without a way out, as he would not consider divorcing his wife – in part because of his value base.

Family loyalty is also expressed in other accounts. For example, Participant 2 displays a deep sense of empathy for his mother:

> 'Because . . . all I kept thinking was . . . 'cause . . . you know like my mum, she's had a lot of her own issues, she'd been single for a long time and she used to get down and depressed quite a lot and she used to rely on me and my brother constantly for . . . everything and you know, reassurance and stuff like that, so I felt I was tied down'.
>
> (Participant 2)

Additionally, her dependency on him and his brother for both financial and emotional support made it challenging for him to forge his own way. In another example, Participant 3 was aware of the tensions between his parents and reported that going to Pakistan was a way of improving his parents' relationship:

> 'my mother and father weren't getting on (tearful) . . . sorry, my mother and father weren't getting on at all and they used to argue all the time and my mum kind of almost . . . was trying to appease my dad that I'm going to make an effort with my mother-in-law in Pakistan and we'll get on. I went for my mum, I went purely for my mum because . . . she was . . . under a lot of pressure, she was getting harassed by my dad and my dad was always shouting at her and stuff like that and I thought, you know, I want my mum and dad to be happy, so I went when I was seventeen just as a family holiday'.
>
> (Participant 3)

Like Participant 2, Participant 3 also displays empathy, particularly for his mother and the gendered dynamics and power relations of the family are very clear in the above.

Men's accounts of sex in forced marriage

Sex featured in all five accounts. For Participant 5, it was a premarital pregnancy that precipitated his forced marriage. Both sets of parents insisted that the couple be married, as being pregnant outside of marriage was not seen as acceptable. Participant 5 was adamant that he did not want to marry, but the Christian religious background of both parties made it difficult to resist the pressure to marry. Of note is that this participant was a white Christian, so he was potentially atypical of most of the known cases of forced marriage closely associated with South Asian communities.

For two participants (P1 and P3), the marriage had been contracted without their full and free consent, and this impacted how they negotiated sexual relations within the marriage. Both men knew that they did not want the marriage to continue and resisted consummating the marriage as illustrated here:

> 'I did have a sense of decency about me . . . And I said to the girl that I married, I told her, yes I should have told her before the wedding, but I didn't, I told her after, but . . . I'd no physical relationship with her. I told her I wouldn't have and I told her that . . . her . . . the reason why that was acceptable to her because what she said was . . . 'The shame that I'm going to have here in the village will kill me, so just get me over to England and do what you want with me.' I said 'I can do that.' So there was no physical relationship and . . . that makes me feel a little bit better because I look at and read about marriages now where they go through all the physical side of it as well and that . . . I just think to myself, 'I'm going to divorce a girl' and you go out with the intention of staying with her and the physical side of it . . . is just a bit of abuse, a bit of added abuse really . . . and . . . I don't really want to.
>
> (Participants 1 and 3)

Participant 1 presents himself as having a sense of decency and not taking sexual advantage of his wife whilst also maintaining her honour (*izzat*).

Participant 3 was in a different situation as his wife had already migrated to the UK and they were sharing accommodation with his parents. At the time, the participant was still a university student (away from his hometown), so he used avoidance as a strategy to try to ensure that the marriage was not consummated. When he returned home for the summer holidays:

> 'to avoid any contact with her, so I'd make sure mum and dad and everybody was asleep, I used to watch whatever rubbish was on telly, 'til two, three o'clock in the morning . . . in the hope that she'll be asleep during those nights and that she'll leave me alone. And . . . I'd wake up in the middle of the night and basically she'd be all over me . . . and . . . you know, [name of friend] and I think this is what people understand, if you've got a naked woman next to you . . . as a man you're going to get aroused . . . and just to get that sleep I . . . did the deed, for me it was never about . . . it was just purely the . . . and I think with her . . . it was like kind of . . . she was almost brain-washed, like . . . make sure he consummates and make sure he makes you pregnant and once you're pregnant, once you've got a baby, he'll never leave you. So she kept on forcing herself upon me all the time, every time I went home.
>
> (Participant 3)

The baby is therefore again positioned as the saviour of this doomed relationship. The medium-term impact on him is described as:

> 'I was not mature enough, I didn't . . . because I'd gone through that cycle where . . . I . . . became a woman hater and I didn't want any woman to get

> close to me because of what happened to me . . . I'd gone through . . . I was very promiscuous, I was . . . I was having numerous relationships'.
>
> (Participant 3)

He also referred to his drinking as a way of dealing with his forced marriage; he missed his graduation ceremony as he did not want his parents to know that his course had ended, as he did not want to return home.

Double standards

Three of the men explicitly discussed the double standards involved in forced marriage. As men, the option of continuing relationships outside of the desired marriage was seen as permissible:

P1: It's seen as a common thing, a lot of . . . there's two ways of dealing with it, you either deal with it the way I did which is stressful and really . . . causes you a lot of internal pain and misery or you can deal with it the other way. Lots of other Asians deal with it, which is just keep them both at the side, that's the other option . . .

Interviewer: Well, that's an option for men isn't it?

P1: That's an option for men and . . . they do that, it's common as hell, you know, loads of Asians, one has a girlfriend and they try to dismiss it as being a casual thing whereas you know in the way they treat her and the way they look, that that's their relationship . . . and it's not any kind of life I wanted.

So, whilst Participant 1 was fully aware of this option, he was clear that this is not what he wanted. Equally, Participant 3 reports being upset by his friend's behaviour:

> 'I've got a best friend called [respondent's friend's name] . . . and his story still kind of haunts me to this day . . . because . . . he didn't do the right thing and I always . . . when I bump into him I say to him, 'You know, you should have done the right thing.' Basically, his wife is still . . . living with his family as their carer . . . as their concubine, as their slave, as their house servant or whatever and he went off and got married to an English girl and he's living his life and . . . you know, and it's like kind of that . . . I always used to be angry with him whenever I used to bump into this guy, but erm, yeah, he got married and then I got taken to Pakistan when I was seventeen, totally innocent . . . .'
>
> (Participant 1)

Both men are clear that whilst this type of behaviour is unacceptable to them it is widespread. The potentially more harmful impact of forced marriage for women is also indicated in Participant 3's account.

Double standards relating to sexual behaviour are also evident in Participant 2's story. As in Participant 3's account, the notion of women as carers for aging parents is evident. In return for compliance to the marriage, Participant 2 was told that a wife was needed to 'look after mum and you know, do the cooking and cleaning and no one will suspect anything about you and you do whatever you want, but just don't tell us.' *No one will suspect anything about you* relates to Participant 2's gay sexuality and indicates that community norms of heterosexual marriage can be upheld to conceal his sexuality. *You do whatever you want, but just don't tell us* as in other accounts indicates that the participant can continue with gay relationships whilst being married as long as this is done discreetly to maintain family honour. In relation to his mother, Participant 2 says:

> 'because in her view, you know . . . she want . . . she probably didn't want me to have all the discrimination from the community, she didn't want us all to be ashamed because . . . it would be horrendous, if all the community knew. And from that point of view . . . I can slightly understand maybe why she might want to put on a show, pretend everything's ok because let's be honest as much as we want gay people to be accepted into the Muslim society . . . you know, we're a long way off any of that . . . and . . . people do respond very negatively and . . . you know . . . in some ways I could understand that as well.'
>
> (Participant 2)

This quote brings an additional dimension: that forced marriage is perceived as protection against homophobia and dishonour within the community if his sexuality were known about within the community.

Impact and coping mechanisms

A variety of coping mechanisms was used to deal with the negative impact of forced marriage. These mechanisms included both positive and potentially less helpful ways of coping with forced marriage. Spirituality was key for one of the participants, and for another work provided an invaluable distraction from forced marriage. Alcohol and substance misuse was mentioned by two participants. For example, Participant 2 was worn down by the 'constant badgering' over a period of months and says:

> ' . . . and then . . . in the end . . . I remember getting really, really down to the point that . . . I started drinking quite a lot, you know, I had a professional job and stuff, but then at weekends, I'd go out with friends and I used to see everyone else drinking but then I'd sort of kind of keep away, but then I found myself drinking as well'.
>
> (Participant 2)

However, he also had positive coping strategies including immersing himself in work and progressing well. Participant 1 discussed the emotional pressure that he was under to agree to a marriage. He used a combination of alcohol and other substances as described below:

P1: So I smoked a lot of weed which was helpful.
Interviewer: So it made you feel relaxed?
P1: Put me to sleep. Relaxing all that is rubbish, it put me to sleep, I could not sleep at night time, I was tossing and turning, I was getting up, getting angry, getting agitated, knew that there were risks of a big lad getting angry outside and everything so I needed to take something off to dampen everything. So to do that was to smoke the weed and just get totally stoned and be paralytic whatever I was . . . it messed up my studies . . . Then . . . I started using a lot of drugs, you become addicted no matter what anyone says to cannabis, you get to that stage where you're looking at . . . . you're [inaudible] and you're thinking . . . [pause] . . . 'I want to . . . I just want to keep smoking this all the time'. I started drinking . . . I used to buy a bottle of Bacardi in the morning going to college, buy two cans of coke, pour half a can out on the way to the bus stop, pour my bottle of Bacardi into the coke tin and I used to sit at the back of the bus . . . we could smoke on the buses in them days . . . and so smoke on the bus, smoke weed on the bus and drink on the bus. And by the time ten o'clock came I was in college and I was totally hammered. And that was my lifestyle. I totally went away from my studies and just gave up a little bit.

The alcohol and substances were clearly being used to manage and numb the anger that was initiated by the forced marriage. The impact is clear: the difficulty of getting to sleep without cannabis, the fear of using his physical strength inappropriately and the detrimental impact on his education. Alcohol and promiscuity were used by Participant 3, and he reported that his ability to trust others had been severely compromised by his experience of forced marriage.

Participant 4 had a completely different coping mechanism and is the only one of the participants still in his forced marriage. His faith and supportive friendship network are key to his coping style, even though he is aware of support services:

> 'I've always coped through my own spirituality . . . erm and . . . I have in my drawer, which I've . . . a self-referral form to a . . . to . . . er, a counsellor, which I've never handed in yet . . . erm, largely because I think I can cope with it, but . . . the other way is to find . . . you know, find other forms of release . . . erm . . . and because they're kind of spiritual and emotional . . . it . . . again, draws back on friends and colleagues.'
>
> (Participant 4)

As a religious man, he continues to look for solutions for his predicament within a religious framework.

Masculinities and accessing support

None of the participants had accessed formal support for forced marriage. The key barriers to accessing support were perceived to be notions of masculinities and lack of availability of appropriate support, encapsulated within the following quote:

> 'As men we don't want to accept support because as men . . . you're told that you have to be strong and you have to be brave and not be a victim, it's ok for women to be a victim because you hear about that in the news and you know, you've got women's refuges, you've got women's helplines and there's a lot of women's kind of projects . . . but for . . . a man to admit . . . that there's a problem . . . I think that's a problem across the board, whether you're White, Black, Asian, whatever and the question of it is how do we shift that mindset initially'.
>
> (Participant 2)

The gendered nature of provision is highlighted, indicating that this acts as a barrier to accessing services. The conceptualisation that men have to be strong is also apparent both in this account and in Participant 1's account. In Participant 1's account, the tender relationship with his mother and his vulnerable or soft side is quickly juxtaposed with hegemonic understandings of masculinity:

> 'I was proper into my health and fitness because physically there was no way I was going to get forced or bullied into getting married. So, my parents knew that, my dad knew that as well. . . . Physical pain is not an issue for me, you know, I do a lot of boxing, I do a lot of sparring, do a lot of training. Physical training was never an issue.'
>
> (Participant 1)

Being physically strong is therefore presented as an essential aspect of masculinity for Participant 1. For Participant 3, his promiscuity (discussed above) during and following his forced marriage can also be read as the desire for virility and being a part of 'lad culture' (Phipps & Young, 2015) – relevant because he was a student at the time.

Whilst all participants had to negotiate multiple identities, the following two examples illustrate two differing sets of identity negotiation. For Participant 2, being gay was a central aspect of his identity alongside his ethnicity and religion. He is clear that there is a link between his sexuality and forced marriage:

> 'Yeah . . . well . . . when . . . when I was . . . eighteen I came out as gay to my family . . . they'd kind of always known about my sexuality but it wasn't 'til I was about eighteen that I confirmed it and there's a clear link between that and . . . being forced into a marriage'.

This participant had accessed LGBT services but reported feeling unwelcome and misunderstood:

> Yeah and I remember a brief conversation when I talked a little bit . . . that just even touched on you know, how hard it is . . . 'oh yeah . . . these Muslims, they're really barbaric aren't they? I don't even know why you're a Muslim anyway . . . ' it was that kind of response and that for me, I was like well I'm not going to abandon my religion. And then it was always that response of 'yeah, you should be whoever you want to be . . . you know, just go and tell . . . go home and tell everyone, tell everyone and say I don't give a shit, that's what we did.' And it was . . . they didn't understand the values.
>
> (Participant 2)

The gulf between the participant's experience of being gay and Muslim and the responses of the other LGBT service users were worlds apart with Islamophobia (a form of racism) evident. Hence, whilst the participant may have felt supported around his sexuality, he clearly did not feel supported or respected for his religious beliefs. In contrast, in his community setting his religious identity was respected but not his sexuality.

Participant 4 spoke of a different type of identity negotiation. Whilst he was forced into marriage, he used his experience to help prevent his siblings from being forced into marriage, as did two of the other participants. For Participant 4, this was not straightforward as he was perceived as being too acculturated:

> 'So it was that kind of negotiation, that kind of erm . . . you know, using . . . analogies that they would understand . . . but that was frought with danger because er . . . I'm seen as the English man now.'

Interviewer: Oh, so you're seen as not Pakistani enough?
P4: Yeah, yeah, not Pakistani enough.
Interviewer: Because if you were then you would condone these practices?
P4: Yeah, yeah, absolutely and . . . but from my point of view, I'm not really bothered about being Pakistani, I'm more bothered about being . . .
Interviewer: Muslim?
P4 . . . true to my values as Muslim.

In this extract, the participant prioritises his Muslim values over being of Pakistani heritage. It also sheds an interesting perspective on his family perceiving him as an 'English man', particularly given his strong adherence to his faith – Islam. The acculturation process possibly refers to class positioning, in particular, his education in England and his professional job.

Discussion

The predominance of emotional pressure is evident in the men's accounts with religious and cultural frameworks frequently used to coerce consent. Cousin marriages featured in all four Pakistani origin participants' accounts of their experiences of forced marriage. Whilst one of these marriages did not take place, the intended spouse was a cousin. The desirability of cousin marriages is argued to be a cultural practice and is widespread in Muslim communities (Bittles & Hussain, 2000; Hussain & Bittles, 1998; Bittles et al., 1993). It is influenced by ideas of consolidating wealth within the family as well as the notion of sexual purity: marrying within the extended family is assumed to ensure that young women, in particular, will not have engaged in premarital sex and will therefore be virgins at marriage. Further, cousin marriages are argued to increase family solidarity (Hammay, 2012) and ensure shared cultural values are transmitted to the next generation (Sandridge et al., 2010). Overlaying this is what Adrienne Rich calls a 'compulsory heterosexuality' (1980) which is particularly relevant to many religious communities where heterosexual marriage is the desired outcome. Religious frameworks also present problems for gay people, and Janssen and Scheeper (2018) illustrate how religiosity is involved in the rejection of homosexuality worldwide. In relation to British Muslim gay men, Jaspal and Siraj (2011) discuss the homophobia and hostility experienced by Muslim gay men within their communities, and this echoes the experiences of the only participant who was gay in this sample. Coercive control and emotional ties in mother-son relationships, as well as family loyalty, were also used to extract consent.

Double standards operate in relation to three different but interrelated domains. First, there is evidence of gendered permissions of sexual behaviour whereby men (gay or straight) can conduct extramarital affairs. Second, gendered expectations in terms of household division of labour is also apparent as wives are seen as potential carers who help with household chores which reinforces men's privileged positions within the household. The third double standard relates to the community level whereby adherence to community norms is seen as vital to uphold family honour whilst at the same time permission to engage in extramarital affairs clearly violates such norms. Further, the reputation and standing of the family is used as a method of coercion into forced marriage, albeit with an understanding that extra marital relationships (gay or heterosexual) are permitted for men. This double standard open to men enables them to lead a more fulfilled sexual life whilst also conforming to family and community expectations. Within the study sample, participants talked freely about these double standards whilst affirming their sense of integrity and decency in attempting to avoid sexual relations with the women they were forced to marry.

At a theoretical level, studies of masculinities have burgeoned, and the field is itself contested. There are two key areas of interrelated contestations that are pertinent to the data in this study (1) dominant constructions of masculinities and (2) hegemonic versus marginalised, and in particular, racialised masculinities.

Dominant constructions of western masculinities have revolved around traditional qualities such as strength, dominance and independence. As the previous accounts illustrate, these notions are not restricted to western masculinities. However, critical masculinity studies have attempted to acknowledge the heterogeneity of masculinity and its relationship with other structures of privilege such as gender, race, heteronormativity and class. Whilst engaging with the notion of multiple masculinities such research has, however, been relatively silent about racialised masculinities, particularly in the UK (Archer, 2001). The different positionalities of men structured by class, sexuality, ethnicity and disability means that they have differential access to structures of privilege. The accounts above highlight how men in this sample negotiate multiple identities including those of masculinity, class, ethnicity, sexuality and religion which impact help-seeking. These negotiations often mean that forced marriage services are not sought. However, the men in the sample were largely talking about experiences that occurred before forced marriage was recognised by the state and many non-black and minority ethnic community organisations. For the one participant who had sought help from a LGBT organisation, the response from other service users was unsympathetic, hostile and Islamophobic. Within his religious community whilst his religious identification was valorised, his sexuality was perceived negatively. An intersectional lens which can work simultaneously with both religious and cultural taboos and sexuality by recognising the complexities of different, yet connected, systems of power relations is therefore crucial. The privileging of either sexuality (in LGBT settings) or religion (in religious settings) leaves gay and religious men with nowhere to turn. Additionally, the construction of forced marriage as reliant on physical violence to extract consent and the lack of images of men as victims of forced marriage may limit men's (as well as women's) ability to access services (see Chantler & McCarry re: emotional pressure in women's accounts of forced marriage). The wider literature on men and help-seeking also identifies that men may be reluctant to access services since help-seeking does not accord with notions of hegemonic masculinities (Branney & White, 2008; Emslie et al., 2006). Some of the accounts in this sample demonstrate coping mechanisms in line with notions of hegemonic masculinity for example substance (mis)use and promiscuity. Others found solace in spirituality or in the workplace. Access to the privileges of double standards also means men have more options to negotiate living with forced marriage as compared to women. Where this is an acceptable solution to men, the need for support services may be diminished.

Limitations

The sample size might be a limitation – however the rich and in-depth narratives presented in this chapter offer an important insight into the experiences of male victims of forced marriage. A more salient limitation is that the participants were talking about events that occurred many years ago. Importantly, forced marriage legislation did not exist at the time of their forced marriages, and public and academic discourse around forced marriage was limited. Interviews with men who have more recent experience of forced marriage would have illuminated the current context of legislation and support services.

Conclusion

Emotional pressure was largely used, although one participant also experienced physical violence. Pressure was applied by fathers, mothers, brothers and wives post-marriage. Further analysis of emotional pressure illuminates the saliency of culture and religion, mother-son relationships, gender relations and notions of duty and loyalty. A wide range of coping strategies was utilised by participants: keeping busy at work, religion, friendships, and use of alcohol and other substances. Longer-term, negative, impacts included tense or loss of family relationships, a narrowing of career options and a deep-seated sense of loneliness, emptiness and bitterness for some. All participants also reported using their experiences of forced marriage in a positive way over time, including a more liberal parenting approach towards their own children than the one they had experienced. Most had also helped to prevent a forced marriage for their siblings. Four of the five men also had careers or volunteered in the care/ welfare field.

Men's notions of masculinity potentially impede accessing services and the accounts clearly demonstrate the need for appropriate support for male victims of forced marriage. None of the men had approached formal services for help, and ensuring that publicity on forced marriage appeals to men as well as to women victims is essential, as is the need to focus on the dynamics of emotional pressure. However, it should be recognised that the operation of gendered double standards offers options to men to navigate forced marriage that are not available to female victims of forced marriage.

Acknowledgements

Sincere thanks to the men who took the time to discuss their experiences of forced marriage with me. Without them, this book chapter would not have been possible.

References

Anitha, S. and Gill, A. (2011) The Social Construction of Forced Marriage and Its 'Victim' in Media Coverage and Crime Policy Discourses. In A. Gill and S. Anitha (eds.) *Forced Marriage: Introducing a Social Justice and Human Rights Perspective*. London: Zed Publications, pp. 112–136.

Archer, L. (2001) Muslim Brothers, Black Lads, Traditional Asians': British Muslim Young Men's Constructions of Race, Religion and Masculinity. *Feminism & Psychology*, 11(1), 79–105.

Bittles, A., Grant, J. and Shami, S. (1993) Consanguinity as a Determinant of Reproductive Behaviour and Mortality in Pakistan. *International Journal of Epidemiology*, June, 22(3), 463–467.

Bittles, A. and Hussain, R. (2000) An Analysis of Consanguineous Marriage in the Muslim Population of India at Regional and State Levels. *Annals of Human Biology*, March–April, 27(2), 163–171.

Branney, P. and White, A. (2008) Big Boys Don't Cry: Depression and Men. *Advances in Psychiatric Treatment*, 14, 256–262.

Chantler, K. (2012) Recognition of and Intervention in Forced Marriage as a Form of Violence and Abuse. *Trauma, Violence and Abuse*, 13(3), 176–183.

Chantler, K. and McCarry, M. (2019) Forced Marriage, Coercive Control, and Conducive Contexts: The Experiences of Women in Scotland. *Violence Against Women*, first published online March. Retrieved from https://journals.sagepub.com/doi/10.1177/1077801219830234

Cheruvallil-Contractor, S. (2016) Motherhood as constructed by *us*: Muslim Women's Negotiations from a space that is their own, *Religion & Gender* vol 6, (1): 9–28.

Emslie, C., Ridge, D., Ziebland, S. and Hunt, K. (2006) Men's Accounts of Depression: Reconstructing or Resisting Hegemonic Masculinity? *Social Science and Medicine*, 62, 2246–2257.

Hammay, H. (2012) Consanguineous Marriages: Preconception Consultation in Primary Health Care Settings *Journal of Community Genetics*, July, 3(3), 185–192.

Hester, M., Chantler, K., Gangoli, G., Devgon, J., Sharma, S. and Singleton, A. (2007) *Forced Marriage: The Risk Factors and the Effect of Raising the Minimum Age for a Sponsor, and of Leave to Enter the UK as a Spouse or Fiancé(e)*. Bristol and Manchester: School for Policy Studies, University of Bristol. Retrieved from www.bristol.ac.uk/sps/research/projects/completed/2007/rk6612/rk6612finalreport.pdf

Hodge, D. (2005) Epistemological Frameworks, Homosexuality, and Religion: How People of Faith Understand the Intersection between Homosexuality and Religion. *National Association of Social Workers*, 207–218.

Hussain, R. and Bittles, A. (1998) The Prevalence and Demographic Characteristics of Consanguineous Marriages in Pakistan. *Journal of Biosocial Science*, April, 30(2), 261–275.

Janssen, D. and Scheepers, P. (2018) How Religiosity Shapes Rejection of Homosexuality across the Globe. *Journal of Homosexuality*. Published online: 29 October 2018. https://doi.org/10.1080/00918369.2018.1522809

Jaspal, R. and Siraj, A. (2011) Perceptions of 'Coming Out' among British Muslim Gay Men. *Psychology and Sexuality*, 2(3), 183–197. http://dx.doi.org/10.1080/19419899.2010.526627

Khanum, N. (2008) *Forced Marriage, Family Cohesion and Community Engagement*. Luton: Equality in Diversity.

Lomas, E. and Brown, T. (2018) "A Whole Bunch of Love the Sinner Hate the Sin": LGBTQ Microaggressions Experienced in Religious and Spiritual Context. *Journal of Homosexuality*. Published online: 26 November 2018. https://doi.org/10.1080/00918369.2018.1542204

Phipps, A. and Young, I. (2015) Lad Culture' in Higher Education: Agency in the Sexualization Debates. *Sexualities*. First Published Online February 27, 2015. Research Article https://doi.org/10.1177/1363460714550909

Rich, A. (1980) Compulsory Heterosexuality and Lesbian Existence. *Signs*, 5(4), 631–660. Retrieved from www.jstor.org/stable/3173834

Riessman, C. (2008) *Narrative Methods for the Human Sciences*. London: Sage Publications.

Sandridge, A., Takeddin, J., Al-Kaabi, E. and Frances, Y. (2010) Consanguinity in Qatar: Knowledge, Attitude and Practice in a Population Born between 1946 and 1991. *J Biosoc Sci.*, 42, 59–82. doi: 10.1017/S002193200999023X

Samad, Y. (2010) *Forced Marriage Among Men: An Unrecognized Problem Critical Social Policy*, 30(2), 189–207

UNCF. (2018) *Child Marriage: Latest Trends and Future Prospects*. New York: UNICEF. Retrieved 17/05/2019 from https://data.unicef.org/wp-content/uploads/2018/07/Child-Marriage-Data-Brief.pdf

Chapter 5

Forced marriage of men with learning disabilities

Risks, reasons and responses

Rachael Clawson

Key points to consider

- Men with learning disabilities have the right to marry should they wish to do so, are of a legal age and have the capacity to consent.
- Men with learning disabilities also have the right to be protected from forced marriage and associated abuses.
- Men with learning disabilities are as equally at risk of being forced to marry as women with learning disabilities.
- Men with learning disabilities may be more at risk of forced marriage than men without learning disabilities.
- The most common reason men with learning disabilities are forced to marry is to obtain a carer for when parents are no longer able to provide the support they need.
- Some parents' understandings of both disability and consent may be very different from the understandings of these concepts that professionals commonly share. Forced marriage may not be recognised as such.

Case studies are included in this chapter to illustrate some of the key issues raised. They are composite case studies which reflect elements of life stories shared with us in the course of our research. Complete 'real life' case studies are not used in order to preserve anonymity.

Outline of the issue

This chapter starts from the premise that men (and women) with learning disabilities should not be discriminated against in the realm of marriage. They should be supported to enter into marriage where they are making a free choice, have the capacity to consent and are of a legal age to do so (Clawson & Fyson, 2017) and should be assisted to develop capacity to consent to marry where possible. Article 16 of the UN Declaration on Human Rights 1948 states that:

> Men and women of full age, without any limitation due to race, nationality or religion, have the right to marry and to found a family. They are entitled to equal rights as to marriage, during marriage and at its dissolution.
>
> (United Nations, 1948)

The declaration also states that free and full consent should be given by both parties. However, not all people with learning disabilities are being given the choice, or are able to make the choice, of whether to marry or not. It is well established that some people with learning disabilities are forced to marry (Clawson, 2011; UK Forced Marriage Unit statistics 2010–2018; Clawson et al., 2018) with examples of cases being heard in the Court of Protection (e.g. UK Forced Marriage Unit statistics, 2010–2014; Sandwell Metropolitan Borough Council v RG, GG, SK and SKG [2013] EWHC 2373 (COP)); XCC v AA & Anor (Rev 3) [2012] EWHC 2183 (COP) (26 July 2012)]).

In the UK *forced marriage* is defined by the government as 'a marriage without the consent of one or both parties and where duress is a factor'. With discussions frequently set within the context of violence against women, immigration control and cultural 'otherness', the practice is also widely acknowledged as an abuse of human rights (Clawson & Fyson, 2017; Chantler, 2012; Wind-Cowie et al., 2012; Gill & Mitra-Khan, 2010; Phillips & Dustin, 2004; Chantler et al., 2009). To date, most discussions have focused particularly upon non-disabled women as victims and have failed to recognise issues relating to men and, as will be discussed more specifically in this chapter, men with learning disabilities.[1]

Forced marriage happens to men with learning disabilities who may or may not have capacity to consent to marriage and who may be more at risk of being tricked, duped or coerced into marriage (Clawson, 2011; HM Government, 2014). The consequences of forced marriage often include physical, financial and sexual abuse, emotional harm and abandonment (Clawson, 2011; Clawson & Fyson, 2017), thus fitting with the definitions of abuse included in UK legislation (e.g. Care Act, 2014; Human Rights Act, 1998). Forced marriage of men with learning disabilities is, therefore, clearly a safeguarding issue, yet research tells us that the safeguarding community, including health and social care services and the police, are struggling to know how to both recognise and adequately respond to the issue on a policy and practice level (Clawson, 2013; Clawson, 2016).

In a forced marriage, one or both spouses do not, or crucially cannot, due to lacking capacity, consent to the marriage. However, we must be clear that it is not only men who lack capacity to consent who are at risk; men with learning disabilities with the capacity to consent are also being forced to marry. They may be more easily tricked or coerced into being married, may trust family members to make what they perceive as the 'right' decision for them or may simply not have the skills, knowledge or access to support to argue against a decision made for them (Clawson et al., 2018) as the following case study demonstrates.

> At 30 years old Aaden decided he wanted to get married and sought support from his father. Aaden lived semi-independently and was supported by his parents; he had the capacity to consent to marriage. His father was

happy to help him and Aaden trusted his judgement. Aaden's father told him he had arranged for him to meet four women from his home village in Somalia and organised a holiday to enable the meetings to take place. Aaden was happy about this; he met all four women and decided to pursue a potential marriage with one of them. Unfortunately his father disagreed with his choice, and Aaden was told he would have to marry a different woman, one his father considered to be a better match. Aaden told his father he wanted to marry the woman he had chosen for himself, but his father told him she was no good and that he would bring shame upon the family if he did not comply with his father's wishes. He also told Aaden he would no longer support him once home in England and that Aaden would be left on his own if he did not marry his father's choice. Aaden was forced to marry the woman and returned to England after the ceremony. His wife later decided not to apply for a visa to come to England, and the couple subsequently divorced, causing a lot of emotional pain for Aaden.

Hitherto, little attention has been paid in research and policy to the issue of men (and women) with learning disabilities being forced to marry, yet statistics from the Government Forced Marriage Unit (a joint funded Home Office/ Foreign and Commonwealth Office unit set up in 2005 to tackle the problem) demonstrate them to be an at-risk group. The exact number of people with learning disabilities being forced into marriage is not known. The UK Government's Forced Marriage Unit (FMU) is currently the only organisation in the UK (and indeed worldwide) to monitor disability in its statistics, starting to do so in 2010 at the request of this author following research which demonstrated that it was indeed a problem (Clawson, 2011). The figures for people with learning disabilities make up approximately 10% of all cases reported to them with 53 cases being reported in 2010, rising to 93 in 2018; recorded cases peaked in 2015 at 141. However, given that all types of abuse of disabled adults and young people with learning disabilities are underreported (Sobsey, 1994; NSPCC, 2003), it is possible to deduce that cases reported to the FMU merely represent the tip of the iceberg.

What little research that has been undertaken demonstrates wide-ranging differences between forced marriage of people with learning disabilities and those without, which demands changes to policy and practice if all people at risk are to be adequately safeguarded from harm (Clawson, 2011, 2016; Patterson et al., 2018). Table 5.1 highlights some of the key differences.

The human rights of disabled people to marry should be recognised and safeguarded; however disabled people also have a right to be protected from the harm and abuse associated with being forced to marry. Finding a balance between protection from abuse and defending the human right to marry is essential (Clawson & Fyson, 2017).

Table 5.1

Person without a learning disability	*Person with a learning disability*
Duress is always a factor.	Duress not necessarily a factor; may manifest itself differently or may not be present at all.
Person knows he or she a victim (at point of marriage if not before).	Person may not have the capacity to consent or may not understand he or she is a victim. May even appear happy about forthcoming marriage.
More females than males reported to be forced into marriage. Most support services for forced marriage focus on meeting needs of females.	Proportion of males and females with learning disabilities being forced into marriage is similar, and males could be at heightened risk. Services need to address needs of males and females.
Victim often reports forced marriage.	Rarely reports or may need support to report. May be reliant on others to recognise what is happening and report or take action. By far, the majority of cases come to the attention of FMU through a third party such as a social worker.
Person has capacity to give or withhold informed consent to marriage.	May lack capacity to give consent to marriage or may have capacity but not understand they are being forced into marriage. May be more easily coerced, tricked or duped into marriage.
No assessment is required to assess capacity (unless of course person experiences mental ill health that impacts upon capacity).	Assessment of capacity to consent may be required. This should be multidisciplinary to ensure fair and accurate assessment is completed.
Person forcing marriage will know this is what he or she doing.	Person forcing marriage may not understand they are organising a forced marriage, particularly where obtaining a carer is the primary motivator. Family members may have the best of intentions. Issues of capacity to consent are not fully understood.
May be able to obtain support themselves if they leave family or community (to find work, apply for benefits, housing, medical needs and so on), though they are often supported in accessing accommodation and other support services, particularly in the short term.	May be more likely to stay living within own family. Often need ongoing support from a range of professionals in order that daily living needs are met (may include personal care, helping to eat, shopping, finances, social and leisure activities, work and so on). May need specific and specialist support if placed in a refuge. Males may find it difficult to obtain place of safety given limited availability of refuges to meet their needs.

Source: adapted from Clawson (2011) and Patterson et al. (2018).

What the law says

Forcing someone to marry became a criminal offence in the UK in 2014 under the Anti-Social Behaviour, Crime and Policing Act 2014, punishable by up to seven years in prison and an unlimited fine. Prior to this, alternative available legislation was used in relation to criminal offences associated with forced marriage (for example physical or sexual assault, kidnap, false imprisonment, poisoning etc). Cases were (and still are) also dealt with using civil remedies made available under the Forced Marriage (Civil Protection) Act 2007. Under this Act Forced Marriage Protection Orders can be made to either prevent a forced marriage from occurring or to protection someone who is already a victim. The 2014 Act made breaching a Forced Marriage Protection Order a criminal offence at the same time, punishable by up to five years in prison.

The vulnerability of people with learning disabilities is recognised by the 2014 Act, s.121 makes clear that:

> (2) In relation to a victim who lacks capacity to consent to marriage, the offence under subsection (1) is capable of being committed by any conduct carried out for the purpose of causing the victim to enter into a marriage (whether or not the conduct amounts to violence, threats or any other form coercion).

So then, any marriage of a person without capacity to consent is deemed by the legislation to be forced. The issue of mental capacity is integral to safeguarding vulnerable young people and adults from harm. The Mental Capacity Act (MCA) 2005 can be used to assist practitioners in assessing individual capacity of people aged 16 and above in specific situations (the Act stipulates that capacity is situation and decision specific). It is not possible under UK law for anyone to make the decision to marry on another's behalf and, as such, causing the marriage of a person who does not have capacity to consent is against UK law. The Mental Capacity Act 2005 does allow for 'best interest' decisions to be made on behalf of a person assessed as not able to make a specific decision for themselves for example, where to live, how to manage finances etc. However, some decisions are exempt from this, the Mental Capacity Act Code of Practice stipulates:

Nothing in the Act permits a decision to be made on someone else's behalf on any of the following matters:

- consenting to marriage or a civil partnership
- consenting to have sexual relations
- consenting to a decree of divorce on the basis of two years' separation
- consenting to the dissolution of a civil partnership
- consenting to a child being placed for adoption or the making of an adoption order

- discharging parental responsibility for a child in matters not relating to the child's property, or
- giving consent under the Human Fertilisation and Embryology Act 1990.

(2007: 17)

The MCA also stipulates that where a person lacks capacity to make a specific decision, support should be provided to give that person the best possible opportunity to develop capacity. An individual's capacity to consent can change with the right support and knowledge, so a person with a learning disability may move from a position of lacking capacity to consent to marriage to having capacity to consent.

Some families believe they have the right to make decisions on behalf of their son as 'capacity to consent' in itself is not recognised as being required; parents believe they are acting in their son's 'best interest'. The issue of assessing capacity is not addressed in detail in this chapter given limits on space; however, suffice to say its subjective nature is problematic, as Groce et al. state 'Concerns about capacity assessment and prior preparation for the event [marriage] are well-founded' (2014: 7), particularly given the gravity of consequences of the assessment. Assessments should be fair, proportionate and comprehensive. Concerns have been raised by family members and professionals alike about the problems associated with obtaining a 'fair' assessment, for example the skills, knowledge and professional background of the practitioner undertaking the assessment, lack of time and adequate resources and where the assessment takes place. Concerns have also been raised regarding the use of independent experts to contest assessment outcomes and the coaching of men with learning disabilities by family members to give the 'right' answers to questions asked during an assessment (Clawson, 2011).

Some family members and health and social care practitioners struggle with the concept of capacity and, confusingly, the inclusion of the word *duress* in the definition of forced marriage (meaning physical, psychological, sexual, financial and emotional pressure is a factor), means in many cases of men with learning disabilities the marriage is not viewed as forced by the family or indeed the person with the learning disability themselves, as duress is not present. There is much confusion about the difference between arranged and forced marriage, and knowledge of legislation is (understandably) patchy. However, whatever the intent behind the marriage, distress and abuse can and does occur as the following case study demonstrates.

Vic is a 32-year-old man who has significant social care needs. He requires 24-hour support to ensure his all his needs are met, and he does not have capacity to consent to marriage. Vic lives at home with his parents who love and care for him. Vic's parents are both aging and are concerned about who will care for him when they are no longer able to. They decide to approach extended family at home in Pakistan to help them find a wife for him, and the plan is for the wife to live in England after the ceremony. The family fly out to Pakistan, where Vic is married. His parents believe he is happy about it, as he said 'yes' when they asked if he wanted to marry, and was very excited about seeing his family and having a party. After the marriage ceremony had taken place his wife's family expected Vic to have sex with her; he found this extremely distressing and did not understand what he needed to do. In attempts to educate him, his father forced him to watch pornographic films and 'coached' him in what he needed to do. Vic was traumatised by this and was subsequently taunted by his wife and her family and she refused to come to England with him. The experience left Vic highly agitated and anxious.

How 'at risk' of being forced to marry are men with learning disabilities?

Whilst a number of papers on forced marriage have been published in the UK, Chantler (2012) refers to six empirical studies which have taken place; relatively little is published about people with intellectual disabilities. Research that has been undertaken (Clawson, 2011, 2016; Patterson et al., 2018) demonstrates that men with learning disabilities are at risk, and very real differences exist between victims with and without learning disabilities and the ways they are protected from harm (or not).

Forced marriage is all too often viewed as a gendered issue, seen as affecting more women than men, and there is a belief that women experience more serious consequences as a result (Gangoli et al., 2006). In reality, forced marriage can happen to anyone, young or old, male, female or transgender, disabled or non-disabled and from any community. The UK picture demonstrates that forced marriage happens in a range of communities – the FMU has dealt with cases from over 90 focus countries since its inception in 2005 (FMU statistics, 2010–2018). Although it is clear from FMU data that forced marriage can affect anyone from any cultural or ethnic background, in the UK, most referrals made to the Unit involve Bangladesh, Pakistan, India and Somalia as the focus countries. This arguably reflects the fact that the UK has large settled communities originating from these countries where marriage and honour are both held in high regard. Within some communities the moral code of conduct is based on collective responsibilities rather than individual rights (Srinivasan & Karlan, 1997). Marriage, honour and shame are connected by complex notions surrounding the status and reputation of wider family within the community, with children being expected to obey their parents' wishes or follow an expected rite of passage in being married. The risk here is no less for men with learning disabilities. Forced marriage is not condoned by any religious group (Groce et al., 2014); it is not a cultural tradition and it differs from an arranged marriage in which the family of both spouses take a leading role in orchestrating the marriage, but the decision to accept the arrangement remains with both prospective spouses (although one might argue there is a continuum along which arranged and forced marriage sit rather than a clear delineation between the two).

The often portrayed picture of a 'typical' victim being a young South Asian woman can be unhelpful as it leads to forced marriage being unrecognised in other victims, particularly men, with their needs for protection going unnoticed and unmet.

The typical view of a victim can also impact policy and practice designed to protect people from harm; for example most of the refuge spaces in the UK are available to women only (and very few of those specifically meet the needs of women with learning disabilities). One of the functions of the FMU is to support victims and potential victims who are British nationals and offer guidance to frontline professionals involved in cases of forced marriage. The rise in reporting of cases (all cases) from approximately 400 in 2005 to 1,764 in 2018 highlights a rise in both awareness of forced marriage as an issue and also the need for the casework the FMU undertakes. Year on year the number of reported cases of men and women with a learning disability has also risen (see Table 5.2) with these cases now making up approximately 10% of all cases reported to the FMU (Clawson et al, under review).

Interestingly, the FMU statistics also show some differences between cases of people with learning disabilities and those without in terms of the gender of victims. Understanding these differences is crucial for safeguarding policy and practice – particularly given that much of the literature (and government policy) on forced marriage references it being an issue affecting predominantly young females. The statistics demonstrate that people with learning disabilities are more likely to be forced to marry at an older age and that males are just as likely to be victims as females as Table 5.2 shows.

The table shows that in 2010 almost 63% of recorded cases of people with learning disabilities related to females and 35% to males; this figure also reflects discoveries in Clawson's (2011) research, which found of the cases reported by practitioners, 38% were female and 45% male (remainder unknown). However, by 2015 the trend had changed, and almost 62% of recorded cases related to males and 38% to females. For people without learning disabilities the picture is very different, with a fairly consistent 80:20 split in female to male ratio. The findings suggest that in the wider population females are reportedly most at risk of forced marriage (although of course there are many reasons why males do not report forced marriage which will impact upon the figures – see Idriss' introductory chapter), but males with

Table 5.2 Comparison of FMU statistics for gender for ALL cases (2010–2015) and for Learning Disability (LD) cases only (2009–15)

Year	*Female (All recorded cases)*	*Female (LD cases only)*	*Male (All recorded cases)*	*Male (LD cases only)*
2009	No figs available	46.70%	No figs available	53.30%
2010	86%	62.70%	14%	35.30%
2011	78%	53.40%	22%	46.60%
2012	82%	55.60%	18%	42.60%
2013	82%	50.00%	18%	49.00%
2014	79%	45.20%	21%	54.80%
2015	80%	38.30%	20%	61.70%

Source: Patterson et al., 2018.

a learning disability may be more at risk or equally at risk of forced marriage as females. Some of the reasons for this are highlighted in the box below.

> Men with learning disabilities are at risk of forced marriage for a range of reasons including:
>
> - Increased likelihood of social isolation from community
> - Reliance on parents/family members for some/all aspects of daily living
> - Needs of aging parents to have alternative care plans in place
> - Impaired capacity to resist or avoid forced marriage
> - Lack of understanding what marriage is about
> - Speech, language and communication needs – not given choices or listened to
> - Unaware of right to and route to complain
> - Lack of access to a trusted person if wanting to disclose forced marriage
> - More easily tricked/duped/coerced or eager to please parents and family members, belief that 'parents know best'
> - Human rights not recognised or respected
> - Family members do not understand notion of 'capacity to consent' and believe they can make decisions on behalf of their son or daughter
> - Family members wanting spouse to provide care
> - In some communities the belief is that it is the woman's role to marry and care for husband

If widely held perceptions relating to gender and forced marriage are applied to people with learning disabilities, many cases involving male victims could go unrecognised. Practitioners and policy makers involved in safeguarding people with learning disabilities need to be aware of these potential differences so that risk can be effectively recognised and appropriately responded to (Clawson, 2016).

Why does forced marriage happen to men with learning disabilities, and what are the potential consequences?

In order to understand the unique features of forced marriage of men with learning disabilities it is necessary to have an awareness of the role that concepts of disability and care play in their everyday lives in a range of cultures. Motivators are strongly linked to culturally influenced ideas of disability and notions of care (Clawson & Fyson, 2017; Patterson et al., 2018) and can include both exploitative and abusive factors – for example, obtaining a Spousal Visa and financial or sexual exploitation, but these more commonly reflect perceived 'protective' factors. By far the most common motivator for forcing the marriage of a man with a learning disability is that of obtaining a wife to become his carer (Clawson, 2011;

Patterson et al., 2018). Perceptions of learning disability are culturally defined; for example, some South Asian parents draw upon biomedical explanations for a child's disability and others on theological explanations (Croot et al., 2008). Theological explanations include the belief that a disabled child is a gift or a blessing from God or a test, punishment or curse. For some there is a stigma or shame attached to having a disabled child (Lindsay, 2014) and in some communities there are perceived links to former wrongdoing or witchcraft (Stobart, 2006). As such, disability is viewed as negative or shameful (Edwardraj et al., 2010). People with learning disabilities have low social status and are viewed as having few rights, thus increasing their likelihood of social isolation and dependency on family members to provide care and make decisions on their behalf. Parents feel they are judged by others, including wider family and community members (Croot et al., 2008). Marriage is often seen as a way of eradicating stigma for the person with the learning disability and their siblings, particularly if the person with the learning disability is the eldest child of the family (Clawson, 2011; Patterson et al., 2018).

The list below shows the most frequently cited reasons for these marriages taking place:

Motivators for Forcing a Person with a Learning Disability to Marry

- Obtaining a carer for the person with learning disability
- Pressure from extended family/community: Marriage is a cultural norm
- Obtaining a visa for someone outside UK
- Marriage is a rite of passage and it might 'normalise' person with learning disability
- Reducing stigma
- Obtain financial security for the person with a learning disability
- Belief that it will cure the person of their learning disability
- Wanting son/daughter to 'be happy'
- Obtaining physical assistance for ageing parents

(Clawson, 2011; Patterson et al., 2018)

These motivators may go some way to explain why men with learning disabilities are as at risk of forced marriage as women – both men and women experience stigma and require care as their parents get older. This may influence their family's decision that marriage is the best option to meet everyone's needs. Some families are extremely unlikely to choose support from outside agencies (and so more likely to choose marriage as a care option), whatever the circumstances. For many families, seeking or receiving support from outside agencies, including social care, carries a stigma (Gilligan & Akhtar, 2006) which may prevent them from engaging with services; Singh and Orimalade state 'Cultural and religious attitudes are important in how care is sought, delivered and accepted' (2009: 405), they cite a study by Fatimilehin and Nardishaw (1994) which found that many South Asian families want care to be provided by a relative rather than outside agencies when parents are no longer able to provide it themselves. For families who do seek support from health and social care agencies, a range of common challenges to the provision of culturally sensitive and appropriate care emerges including language barriers, differences in cultural views (including gender and generational views) and differing values (IRISS, 2010; Lindsay et al., 2014) which may lead to further reluctance to seek support. Some families are unaware of support available from health and social care services or may not access it either because they do not know how or because they do not believe it will meet their relatives' needs. Additionally, the government policy of austerity in recent years has led to many services being reduced or cut and eligibility to such services restricted to those with the only highest level assessed need. One might argue that a reduction in government-funded support could, in itself, play its own role in leading families to choose marriage as a means of support when other resources are lacking.

When coupled with a strong tradition towards marriage, attitudes relating to marriage of sons with learning disabilities may be deeply held. Marriage can be seen as a way of 'normalising' or even 'curing' the person with a learning disability and is viewed as a rite of passage, which, if undertaken, enables the family to be freed from stigma (Groce et al., 2014). Indeed many families would not view the marrying of their son or daughter with a learning disability (with or without the capacity to consent to marriage) as a forced marriage (Clawson, 2011, 2013; Clawson & Fyson, 2017; Patterson et al., 2018). Some families believe they have the right to make decisions on behalf of their son, as 'capacity' in itself is not recognised as being required and they believe they are acting in his best interest. This is turn can create difficulties for practitioners who may also not recognise the risk factors or view the marriage as forced, particularly when working with families whose cultures differ from their own.

Challenges to safeguarding practice

Research and evidence from practice tells us that children and adults with learning disabilities are both subjected to more abuse and are less likely to be protected by safeguarding systems than their non-disabled peers (Cooke & Standen, 2002; Stevens, 2013; Stalker & McArthur, 2012; Sullivan & Knutson, 2000). In terms of forced marriage, safeguarding policy and practice tends to respond to the more obvious abusive motivators, but less well-understood are the 'compassionate' motives relating to men with learning disabilities hence, cases of forced marriage go unrecognised. Whatever the motivation, the consequences of forced marriage of men with learning disabilities cannot be underestimated, including sexual and physical assault, abandonment, financial and emotional abuse and psychological trauma as the case studies described earlier highlight. These factors need to be better understood – it cannot be assumed that if organised for the 'right' reasons to the 'right' person the marriage will not be abusive or traumatic. Additionally, there are risks for the spouse of the learning disabled man who may also be in need of protection from abuse. Many women do not know they are marrying a man to effectively act as his carer, many do not meet the man until the day of the marriage. Whether or not they are truly giving their own informed consent should be questioned. They are frequently young women who come from other countries to live in the UK and who may not speak English or understand their own rights. Some experience domestic servitude and are abused by the extended family of their spouse as the following case study shows:

> Neeta is 22 years old and from a village in rural Bangladesh. Her family are economically poor, she lives with her parents and five siblings in a small dwelling. Her parents were contacted by a relative from the extended family in England asking for their permission for Neeta to marry their son. The family and Neeta agreed, as it meant she would move to England and experience what they perceived to be a better life. Neeta did not meet her husband until their wedding ceremony, at which point she realised he had significant learning disabilities and would need caring for. He did not understand he was getting married. She did not feel she could back out of the agreed marriage. When she moved to England to live with her husband and his family, Neeta was forced to sleep on the floor and to do all the cooking and cleaning for the family. She was not given enough food to eat and was physically abused by her mother-in-law for not doing chores properly. Neeta was not allowed out of the house on her own and feared telling anyone what was happening to her; she did not speak English so needed a family member to translate conversations.

Many cases of forced marriage involving a man with a learning disability are not recognised as such by professionals supporting him, and the man himself may not have means to report or understand he has been forced to marry (Clawson, 2011, 2013). Frontline adult care practitioners, managers and policy makers are not always clear about what constitutes a forced marriage. Safeguarding professionals are sometimes unable to recognise that someone is potentially a victim of forced marriage as they may over-identify with parent/carer need for care support or be accepting of what they perceive to be cultural norms, particularly when working with someone from a culture different from their own. It is therefore perhaps unsurprising that when faced with both disability and cultural differences, some practitioners feel ill-equipped to recognise forced marriage and to challenge practices they might not understand. Some fear being perceived as racist or culturally insensitive or may simply fear 'getting it wrong' (Clawson, 2011: Patterson et al., 2018). In addition, a lack of clear guidance in safeguarding policies and procedures makes recognition of the problem and then dealing with it more difficult. As noted previously, forced marriage is against the law and is known to be associated with a range of physical, sexual, financial and emotional abuses, as such falling within the definitions of adult abuse. The safeguarding role of adult social care is recognised explicitly in statutory guidelines published by the UK Government Forced Marriage Unit (2014), yet is not always fully understood by those tasked with implementing the guidelines. Although there are some pockets of excellent safeguarding practice in the UK, many safeguarding adult boards do not adequately deal with the issue, and men with learning disabilities at risk of forced marriage may not always be appropriately safeguarded (Clawson, 2011, 2013, 2016).

Conclusion

Forced marriage of men with learning disabilities often presents differently to forced marriage per se, and this can make it difficult for families, practitioners and others to recognise it as such. This can result in cases going unnoticed and men remaining at risk of harm. Although the government definition of forced marriage states duress is a factor, this may not be the case for men with learning disabilities who could be more easily tricked or coerced into marriage; indeed they may even present as being happy about the prospect of marriage. Parents often seek marriage for their son or daughter with a learning disability to provide him or her with long-term care and very often, families believe they are making the right (or only possible) choice. There is a lack of understanding around the law on forced marriage and issues relating to capacity to consent and how this is assessed. Some men with learning disabilities are given no choice and/or will not ever have the capacity to give informed consent to marriage and all it entails. This may include engaging in a sexual relationship, having children and deciding where to live. Many practitioners are struggling to recognise forced marriage as such, and families are potentially leaving themselves open to prosecution, as they do not understand they may be forcing the marriage of their son or daughter. People with learning disabilities, and indeed their spouses, may be subjected to a range of abuses.

We have come a long way in terms of our understanding of forced marriage of men with learning disabilities over the past ten or so years, and changes to policy and legislation have gone some way in recognising the specific needs of this group. However, misunderstandings about the law and capacity to consent to marriage continue to exist in all stakeholder groups and so men remain at risk. Men (and women) with learning disabilities need to be empowered to make decisions and choices for themselves wherever possible; they also need to know where to go for support. There is a difficult balance to be had between ensuring the human right to marry (enshrined in the UN Convention on the Rights of Persons with Disabilities Article 23: The right of all persons with disabilities who are of marriageable age to marry and to found a family on the basis of free and full consent of the intending spouses) is upheld and that the right to be protected from harm is both recognised and acted upon.

There is need for better awareness-raising within all stakeholder groups. For men with learning disabilities to be better protected, families need to understand the legal implications of arranging a marriage for someone who lacks capacity to consent, but they also need to be provided with improved information about alternative support in caring for their relative. Indeed the very term *forced marriage* may hinder recognition, particularly where family members believe they are making the right decision in obtaining care. Work needs to be done to ensure that faith and community leaders and marriage registrars are better equipped and supported to understand what constitutes 'capacity to consent' and how this can be established. Practitioners in all agencies working with men with learning disabilities should be provided with training and improved resources to support them in both recognising forced marriage and assessing capacity to consent.

Policy and legislation can help in raising the profile of the issue but the very specific vulnerabilities of this group and the reasons why forced marriages take place need to be better understood in order for men with learning disabilities to be better supported and protected.

Acknowledgements

Thank you to all the people with learning disabilities, family members, faith leaders, marriage registrars and practitioners working in social work and social care, health services and the police who have given their time to help us better understand this issue and improve safeguarding policy and practice. Please visit www.nottingham.ac.uk/research/groups/mymarriagemychoice/ for more information on our research and access to our free resources including:

- 30-minute awareness raising film (available in four languages)
- Workbooks to accompany the film (one aimed at people with learning disabilities and one for family members)
- Case study document detailing composite cases outlining stories told to us as part of our research
- Guidelines and toolkit for assessing capacity to consent.

Note

1 The term *learning disability* is used throughout this document, as this is the term most frequently used by practitioners in the UK. *Learning disability* is defined as: (a) a significantly reduced ability to understand new or complex information, to learn new skills (impaired intelligence) with; (b) a reduced ability to cope independently (impaired social functioning); and (c) which started before adulthood, with a lasting effect on development ('Valuing People', White Paper 2001- Department of Health).

References

Care Act (2014) available at http://www.legislation.gov.uk/ukpga/2014/23/contents/enacted

Chantler, K. (2012) Recognition of, and Intervention in, Forced Marriage in *Journal of Trauma Violence and Abuse* 13(3), 176–183.

Chantler, K., Gangoli, G. & Hester, M. (2009) Forced Marriage in the UK: Religious, Cultural, Economic or State Violence? in *Critical Social Policy* 29(4), 587–612.

Clawson, R. (2011) *Forced Marriage of People with Learning Disabilities: Final Report.* Nottingham: Ann Craft Trust.

Clawson, R. (2013) Safeguarding People with Learning Disabilities at Risk of Forced Marriage: Issues for Inter-Aagency Practice in *Social Work & Social Sciences Review: An International Journal of Applied Research.*

Clawson, R. (2016) Safeguarding People with Learning Disabilities from Forced Marriage: The Role of Safeguarding Adult Boards in *Journal of Adult Protection* 18(5), 277–287.

Clawson, R. & Fyson, R. (2017) Forced Marriage of People with Learning Disabilities: A Human Rights Issue in *Disabiity & Society* 32(6), 810–830.

Cooke, P. & Standen, P.J. (2002) Abuse and Disabled Children: Hidden Needs? in *Child Abuse Review* 11(1), 1–18.

Croot, E., Grant, G., Cooper, C.L. & Mathers, N. (2008) Perceptions of the Causes of Childhood Disability among Pakistani Families Living in the UK in *Health and Social Care in the Community* 6(6), 606–613.

Edwardraj, S., Mumtaj, K., Prasad, J.H., Kuruvilla, A. & Jacob, K.S. (2010) Perceptions about Intellectual Disability: A Qualitative Study from Vellore in South India in *Journal of Learning Disability Research* 54(Part 8), 736–748.

Fatimilehin, I & Nardishaw, Z (1994) A Cross-cultural Study of Parental Attitudes and Beliefs about Learning Disability (Mental Handicap). *Journal of Applied Research in Intellectual Disabilities* 7(3), 177–201

Gangoli, G., Razak, A. & McCarry, M. (2006) *Forced Marriage and Domestic Violence among South Asian Communities in North East England.* Univ. of Bristol.

Gill, A. & Mitra-Khan, T. (2010) Moving toward a 'Multiculturalism without Culture': Constructing a Victim-Friendly Human Rights Approach to Forced Marriage in the UK In *Violence against Women in South Asian Communities: Issues for Policy and Practice*, edited by R.K. Thiara and A. Gill, 128–155. London: Kingsley.

Gilligan, P. & Akhtar, S. (2006) Cultural Barriers to the Disclosure of Child Sexual Abuse in Asian Communities: Listening to What Women Say in *British Journal of Social Work* 36, 1361–1377.

Groce, N., London, J. & Stein, M. (2014) Inheritance, Poverty, and Disability in *Disability & Society* 29(10), 1554–1568.

HM Government. (2014) *The Right to Choose: Multi-Agency Statutory Guidance for Dealing with Forced Marriage.* London: Crown Copyright.

HO/FCU (2010) Forced Marriage Unit Statistics Jan – Dec 2010 https://assets.publishing.service.gov.uk/government/uploads/system/uploads/attachment_data/file/804044/Forced_Marriage_Unit_Statistics_2018_FINAL.pdf

HO/FCU. (2012) Forced Marriage Unit: Statistics Jan – Dec 2012. www.gov.uk/government/uploads/system/uploads/attachment_data/file/141823/Stats_2012.pdf

HO/FCU. (2013) Forced Marriage Unit: Statistics Jan – Dec 2012. www.gov.uk/government/uploads/system/uploads/attachment_data/file/291855/FMU_2013_statistics.pdf

HO/FCU. (2014) Forced Marriage Unit: Statistics Jan – Dec 2013. www.gov.uk/government/uploads/system/uploads/attachment_data/file/412667/FMU_Stats_2014.pdf

HO/FCU. (2015) Forced Marriage Unit: Statistics Jan – Dec 2014. www.gov.uk/government/uploads/system/uploads/attachment_data/file/505827/Forced_Marriage_Unit_statistics_2015.pdf

HO/FCU. (2016) Forced Marriage Unit: Statistics Jan – Dec 2015. www.gov.uk/government/uploads/system/uploads/attachment_data/file/597869/Forced_Marriage_Unit_statistics-_2016.pdf

HO/FCU (2017) Forced Marriage Unit Statistics Jan – Dec https://assets.publishing.service.gov.uk/government/uploads/system/uploads/attachment_data/file/730155/2017_FMU_statistics_FINAL.pdf

HO/FCU (2018) Forced Marriage Unit Statistics Jan - Dec https://assets.publishing.service.gov.uk/government/uploads/system/uploads/attachment_data/file/35474/0031-12attachment1of2.pdf

Human Rights Act (1998) available at http://www.legislation.gov.uk/ukpga/1998/42/content

Institute for Research and Innovation in Social Sciences (IRISS). (2010) *Improving Support for Black and Minority Ethnic (BME) Carers.* Glasgow: IRSS.

Lindsay, S., Tetrault, S., Desmaris, C., King, G. & Pierart, G. (2014) Social Workers as 'Cultural Brokers' in Proving Culturally Sensitive Care to Immigrant Families Raising a Child with a Physical Disability in *Health & Social Work* 39(2).

NSPCC. (2003) *It Doesn't Happen to Disabled Children: Report of the National Working Group on Child Protection and Disability.* London: NSPCC Publications.

Patterson, A., Clawson, R., Fyson, R., McCarthy, M. & Kitson, D. (2018) My Marriage, My Choice: Summary of Findings. *University of Nottingham* www.nottingham.ac.uk/research/groups/mymarriagemychoice/documents/summary-full.pdf

Phillips, A. & Dustin, M. (2004) UK Initiatives on Forced Marriage: Regulation, Dialogue and Exit in *Political Studies* 52(3), 531–551.

Sandwell Metropolitan Borough Council v RG, GG, SK and SKG [2013] EWHC 2373 (COP)); XCC v AA & Anor (Rev 3) [2012] EWHC 2183 (COP) (26 July 2012)]). Available at https://www.familylaw.co.uk/news_and_comment/capacity-sandwell-metropolitan-borough-council-v-rg-gg-sk-and-skg-2013-ewhc-2373-cop

Singh, I. & Orimalade, A. (2009) Ethnic Minority Groups, Learning Disability and Mental Health in *Psychiatry* 8(10), 405–407.

Sobsey. D. (1994) *Violence and Abuse in the Lives of people with Disabilities: The End of Silent Acceptance?* Baltimore: P.H. Brookes.

Srinivasan, B. & Karlan, G. (1997) Culturally Responsive Early Intervention Programs: Issues in India in *International Journal of Disability, Development and Education* 44(4), 367–385.

Stalker, K. & McArthur, K. (2012) Child Abuse, Child Protection and Disabled Children: A Review of Recent Research in *Child Abuse Review* 21(1), 24–40.

Stevens, E. (2013) Safeguarding Vulnerable Adults: Exploring the Challenges to Best Practice Across Multi-agency Settings. *Journal of Adult Protection* 15(2), 85–95.

Stobart, E. (2006) *Child Abuse Linked to Accusations of Spirit Possession And Witchcraft.* Research report RR750. Department for Education and Skills.

Sullivan, P.M. & Knutson, J.F. (2000) Maltreatment and Disabilities: A Population-Based Epidemiological Study in *Child Abuse & Neglect* 24(10), 1257–1273.

UK Government (2007) *Mental Capacity Act Code of Practice.* https://assets.publishing.service.gov.uk/government/uploads/system/uploads/attachment_data/file/497253/Mental-capacity-act-code-of-practice.pdf

United Nations. (1948) UN Declaration of Universal Human Rights. www.un.org/en/universaldeclaration-human-rights/

United Nations. (2006) UN Convention on the Rights of Persons with Disabilities. www.un.org/development/desa/disabilities/convention-on-the-rights-of-persons-with-disabilities/article23-respect-for-home-and-the-family.html

Wind-Cowie, M., Cheetham, P. & Gregory, T. (2012) *Ending Forced Marriage.* London: Demos.

Chapter 6

Homophobic 'honour' abuse experienced by South Asian gay men in England

Roxanne Khan and Michelle Lowe

Introduction

> After protracted detention and torture, the detainees were released to families, and at least some were subjected to further humiliation by being forced to 'confess and repent' in front of their elder male relatives. . . . Officials then shamed the relatives for having gay family members and made the relatives shame the victims, thereby fuelling a climate in which family abuse, including honor killings, might occur.
>
> (Andreevskikh, 2017)

Since April 2017, media groups across Europe have reported on what has been called a 'gay genocide' and 'antigay purge' in Chechnya; it is alleged that men who are suspected of being gay have been victimised by the authorities and been threatened with so-called 'honour' killings by their families (Beard, 2018; Castro, 2019; Human Rights Watch, 2017). Further disconcerting is that homophobic honour-based violence is reported in other countries where homosexuality is condemned or considered a sin – this includes South Asian nations where same-sex sexual activity is not only taboo but a criminal offence with a maximum penalty of life imprisonment (Carroll & Mendos, 2017).

With a focus on female victims, studies with South Asian and Middle Eastern populations have identified a range of sociodemographic factors that explain why some people endorse honour abuse and killings (e.g. Eisner & Ghuneim, 2013; Gengler, Alkazemi, & Alsharekh, 2018; Khan, 2018; Lowe, Khan, Thanzami, Barzy, & Karmaliani, 2018). As the victimisation of girls and women is far more frequent, this has attracted a greater share of scholarly and public interest. Investigations into homonegative honour-based victimisation are still sparse (Khan, Hall, & Lowe, 2017; Lowe, Khan, Thanzami, Barzy, & Karmaliani, 2019). Thus, very little is known about the psychological, social and cultural factors associated with different types of honour abuse specific to gay men of South Asian origin in England.

To gain insight into lived realities and perceptions of homophobic honour abuse, this chapter draws together the fragmented literature in this area to provide a context for qualitative data collected from ten South Asian gay men living in England. Using an online questionnaire, three themes were explored, including: (1) respondents' demographic, social and familial background; (2) the homophobic victimisation experienced and witnessed and how this affected respondents' psychosocial wellbeing; (3) perceptions of the efficacy of emergency services and welfare agencies to respond to homonegative honour abuse. These findings indicate that extensive work needs to be undertaken to improve awareness of the difficulties faced by gay South Asian males at risk of 'honour' abuse and violence in the UK.

Background

> Ahmet Yıldız was just 26 years old when he was shot dead on 15 July 2008, in what has been widely regarded by Lesbian Gay Bisexual Transgender and Intersex (LGBTI) rights activists as a gay "honour" killing.
>
> Seven years on, his killer or killers are still at large and the lack of progress in bringing about justice is viewed by LGBTI organizations in Turkey as an indictment of the lack of protection of LGBTI individuals and a symbol of impunity for homophobic violence.
>
> Amnesty International, Public Statement (2015)

'Honour' abuse is a broad category that includes psychological, physical and sexual maltreatment, the most extreme of which is 'honour' killing (Oberwittler & Kasselt, 2014). In the United Kingdom (UK), there is no statutory definition of honour-based violence, and the term is used broadly to define criminal acts committed in defence of, or to protect, the honour of an individual's family or community (Crown Prosecution Service, 2018). To understand the causes, characteristics and situational contexts in which this abuse occurs, we draw from the established psychological and criminological literature to explain the powerful role of honour and shame as fundamental values in collectivist-orientated cultures. This is important to understand as it explains the motives of people who inflict harm on others in the name of so-called honour, as well as those who approve of it; understanding how they think, act and behave towards victims is the key for unpicking this seemingly paradoxical form of abuse. This chapter focuses on gay male victims of honour abuse (including forced marriage) and violence, a poorly understood topic on which the empirical research base is only recently emerging. To evolve this line of investigation, we also draw from a larger body of research that has explored the aetiology of homophobic abuse more broadly to identify the nature, characteristics, and the circumstances in which this abuse is experienced specifically by South Asian gay men in England.

Social context: the importance of family honour in collectivist cultures

Although 'honour'-based abuse and violence is commonly linked with Muslim communities in Middle Eastern, North African, South Asian (MENASA) and Turkish populations worldwide (Chesler, 2010; Cooney, 2014; Grzyb, 2016), punishments of sexualised behaviours are also reported in other 'moral' collectivist orientated communities and territories. For example, 'honour' crimes are reported in Catholic orientated Italy as well as Gypsy Roma Traveller communities (Araji, 2000; Asquith, 2015; Caffaro, Ferraris, & Schmidt, 2014; Giuffrida, 2019).

To unravel the intricate processes underpinning 'honour'-based abuse, rather than a narrow focus on religiosity as a singular cause, it perhaps prudent to adopt a holistic, less myopic approach to understanding its origins. Religiosity is undoubtedly significant, yet this should not underplay the influence of another core tenet binding all collectivist 'honour' cultures – that is, the *maintenance of family bonds* and *attaining and upholding a respectable social image* (Khan, 2018). These twin principles help explain why the public maintenance of family honour is of paramount importance in collectivist cultures (Rodriguez Mosquera, 2016). The concept of honour is a pervasive and powerful social construct that underpins collectivist ideologies (Rodriguez Mosquera, 1999, 2013). These shared beliefs are associated with a broad spectrum of attitudes, norms, roles, emotions, behaviours and cultural practices that prioritise socially prescribed values – especially that of family honour – above that of personal beliefs and ideals. There is also an expectation that members within collectivist cultures ensure that 'honour' norms are being observed by their own family and wider community (Vandello & Cohen, 2003). As Cooney (2014: 407) suggests 'from a purely explanatory point of view, family honor is most profitably viewed as a type of social control'.

In MENASA and Turkish communities, honour functions as an important social currency. Having honour in these communities may lead to fruitful personal and social benefits, such as greater marital prospects and business opportunities, and likewise, there is a heavy personal and social cost for the loss of honour or failure to restore it, including loss of self-esteem, social ostracisation, and economic boycott (Bond, 2014; Brandon & Hafeez, 2010; Mosquera, Manstead, & Fischer 2002). Ultimately, the loss of honour brings personal and social shame to the individual, his or her family and wider community (Bond, 2014). Understood in this way, it becomes easier to understand why some individuals from collectivist 'honour' cultures have been reported to use force or to aggress against others in response to what is perceived to be threats to their family's honour (Brown, Osterman & Barnes, 2009; Cohen et al., 1996; Cohen & Nisbet, 1996; Mosquera et al., 2002; Vandello & Cohen, 2003).

With this is mind, it is dispiriting that over 5,000 women are reportedly murdered every year in the name of honour (United Nations Population Fund,

2000) and that these so-called 'honour' killings are recorded in over 30 countries (Chesler, 2010). Any estimates are most likely a vast underestimation of the true extent of honour killings, as they do not include cases 'camouflaged as suicides, accidents, disappearances or deaths from natural cause' (Cooney, 2014: 407), yet it is still notable that many are committed in South Asian territories. In collectivist-orientated Pakistan, for example – where one-quarter of all global honour killings are reported to occur – over 700 women were reportedly murdered in one year alone and nearly two thousand women were estimated to have been murdered between 2004 and 2007 (Fatima, Qadir, Hussain, & Menezes, 2017; Nasrullah, Haqqi, & Cummings, 2009). Internationally, honour killings in South Asian diaspora were recorded in communities across North America (Chesler, 2009; Hayes, Freilich, & Chermak, 2016) and Europe, including Germany (Grzyb, 2016), Finland (Keskinen, 2009), Sweden (Wikan, 2008) and England (Dyer, 2015). This information helps to gauge the scope of these murders, while recognising that, as they are sketchily based on unreliable data, they only reflect the extreme end of a much larger problem.

Antigay 'honour' abuse, violence and killings in collectivist cultures

> A catalogue of serious mistakes and negligence by the Turkish authorities include the failure to investigate threats Ahmet Yıldız had received from members of his family in the months leading up to his murder, despite these threats having been reported to the authorities.
>
> After Ahmet Yıldız' murder it emerged that his complaint had not been investigated. . . .
>
> There has not been an investigation into the failure of the authorities to act on Ahmet Yıldız' complaints since the murder. An arrest warrant was only issued . . . three months after the killing, by which time the only named suspect in the case, Ahmet Yıldız' father was believed to have left the country and could not be apprehended, and seven years on, still hasn't been despite an Interpol red alert issued for him to be arrested. A prosecution was initiated in April 2009, naming Ahmet Yıldız' father as sole suspect.
>
> Amnesty International, Public Statement (2015)

'Honour'-based abuse and violence is rooted in the rigid gender roles prescribed in patriarchal collectivist cultures that promote hegemonic masculinities (Connell, 2005). In this way, males are legitimised to use forceful means to maintain their dominant social position over female counterparts – this is reflected in girls and women's familial, cultural, fiscal, relational and legal subordination. Therefore, it is a social expectation of hegemonic masculinity for males to use macho force to defend or restore honour, including the use of aggression and violence against females. Robust support for the relation between masculine ideology and men's perpetration of aggression toward women is shown in a meta-analysis of 39 studies (Murnen, Wright, & Kaluzny, 2002).

Hostility and aggression are also used to control and deter other marginalised expressions of masculinity, including gender identities perceived to defy culturally idealised forms of manhood, including homosexuality as this is thought to be 'not masculine' in collectivist-orientated cultures (Connell, 2005). In linking expressions of misogyny and homophobia, Kupers (2010: 112–113) argued that they 'are two sides of the same coin' manifested as toxic masculinity, which he described as 'the constellation of socially regressive male traits that serve to foster domination, the devaluation of women, homophobia and wanton violence'. Thus stemming from illiberal cultural norms, males and females who do not adhere to rigid, stratified gendered codes may face collective aggression for deviating from socially acceptable conventions (Lowe et al., 2019; Steinke, 2013; Vandello & Cohen, 2003).

In both national and migrant South Asian collectivist-oriented communities, honour abuse and violence often occurs when it is perceived that sexually improper behaviour has brought *sharam* (shame) on an individual, his or her family or community. Samad (2010) explains that in the main, same-sex intimacy and relationships are considered in South Asian cultures to reflect a serious social and sexual indiscretion that can be rectified via coercive control, forced marriage, verbal threats or physical violence.

This is most starkly illustrated at the extreme end of the spectrum, in the analysis of data in Turkey that shows 22 honour killings, from 2007 to 2009, were attributed to the victims' sexual identity (Democratic Turkey Forum, 2011). With reference to cultural perceptions of homosexuality in Turkey, Hurtas (2017) highlighted parallels between the brutal 'gay honour killings' of two young gay males, Ahmet Yildiz (age 26) and Rosin Cicek (age 17) which 'reveal a similar pattern of deep-rooted prejudice and social codes that override even the closest family bonds'. In both cases, the victims' families were thought to have been involved in their murders. This feature demarcates honour violence and killings from other forms of interpersonal violence, that is, victims' families often endorse abuse, violence, and sometimes, even torturous murder to restore family honour. As Khan (2018: 217) stated, 'the victim's kin and community were often the instigators of the abuse, and in many instances, they organised or committed these murders themselves'. Indeed, the sole suspect in Mr Yildiz's brutal murder was his father and, to add insult to injury, Mr Yildiz's family did not claim his body (Bilefsky, 2009). This is particularly poignant as in Islamic teachings, the burial of the deceased is regarded as a collective obligation and 'the entire Muslim community will be guilty if a Muslim body is not buried, unless the burial was beyond their knowledge or capacity' (Al Dawoody, 2018).

These reports of antigay honour killings cast a dark shadow, not least because they represent a specific form of familial abuse that is imbedded within wider structural processes where expressions of prejudice, abuse and violence are used for the dual aim of marginalising 'difference' and espousing hypermasculinity.

In light of this, it is unsurprising that homosexual men in South Asian collectivist territories and diaspora are reported to be at risk of antigay honour abuse from their immediate and extended kin, tribal and community leaders and groups (Mahendru, 2017). This feeling is sensed in the words of Dasgupta (2018) when he writes about growing up in India:

> I grew up in Calcutta under the shadow of Section 377 which effectively criminalised homosexuality and has been used almost exclusively against LGBTQ individuals who continue facing harassment and blackmail. Growing up as a queer teenager in the early 2000s I often heard harrowing tales from friends who had been beaten up by gangs when they went out cruising, or in some instances even taken to prison where police officers demanded a bribe before letting them off with a warning that they would tell their parents about their 'immoral lifestyle'. Academics . . . have rightly used the term 'India's shame culture' whilst referring to this. If one's sexuality is made public it not only brings 'shame' to the individual but also to their family and larger society".

Homophobic 'honour' abuse in England

Piecing together these fragmented reports, concerns have been emerging about South Asian gay males at risk of 'honour'-based abuse (particularly, forced marriage) in England (Jaspal, 2014; Khan, Hall, & Lowe, 2017; Lowe et al., 2019; Razzall & Khan, 2017; Samad, 2010). Since the first official honour killing in England in 1999, the majority of recorded honour crimes have been committed against females of South Asian origin (Aplin, 2017). As so few studies have examined 'honour'-based male victimisation, little is known about the abuse gay men experience. However, charities in England have reported concerns that South Asian males might be facing abuse that is comparable to their female counterparts, including forced marriage, threats or actual violence, sexual assault, and imprisonment (Razzall & Khan, 2017; Tri, 2017).

Although the prevalence of 'honour'-based violence in England cannot be easily or reliably ascertained, it is widely accepted that any figures are likely to represent only the tip of the iceberg (Khan, Saleem, & Lowe, 2018). Despite this, official data indicates that like their counterparts in South Asia, diasporic populations who identify as LGBT in England are also at risk of 'honour'-based violence. An examination of police recordings from 39 forces across England showed that 11,000 cases were recorded from 2010 to 2014 (Iranian and Kurdish Woman's Right Organisation, 2015). Only four police forces provided information on victim gender that, when combined, showed 271 male victimisation cases were recorded between 2010 and 2017 (Razzall & Khan, 2017). In the annual review of crimes in the UK from 2015 to 2016, almost a quarter of 'honour'-based violence victims (where gender was recorded) were males (Crown Prosecution Service, 2016). Statistics from the British Home Office's Forced Marriage Unit

(FMU) for 2014 and 2015 show that of the approximate 1,220 forced marriages reported, around one-fifth of the victims were males (FMU, 2016). Similarly, the most recent statistics available show that for 2018, of the 1,764 forced marriage reports, 17% involved males (FMU, 2018). Official homicide statistics also show that annually, males represent one-third of honour-killing victims in the UK (Dyer, 2015). Almost entirely, these figures represent South Asian victims.

Although victim sexual orientation was not reported in these data, it is most likely that at least a proportion of the men in these cases were victimised because of their sexual orientation. Data from the FMU supports this proposition, with reports that 30 (2%) victims in both 2015 and 2016 were South Asian gay men. Sexual orientation or sexual identity are only recorded by the FMU if victims volunteer this information at first contact, and victims are not routinely asked to disclose this personal information. Therefore, it is reasonable to estimate that 'honour'-based violence is most likely occurring at a higher rate than currently reported by gay South Asian males.

A number of small-scale studies conducted in the UK indicate that while gay British Asian males live in a country that is broadly tolerant of their sexual identity, they tend to live in families and communities that frown upon their sexual orientation. For example, in a poll of 500 British Muslims, not one person believed that homosexuality was "morally acceptable" (Gallup Coexist Index, 2009). Another study reported that of the 70 men interviewed about their experiences of 'honour'-based abuse and violence, a proportion were victimised due to their sexuality (Razzall & Khan, 2017). One interviewee stated that, 'I feared for my life. I felt I could be killed. . . . I would be disowned, kicked out of the house and forced to marry a woman, definitely'. This interviewee disclosed that once the news of his homosexuality spread to his wider community, he was warned that he would be punished for dishonouring both his family and his culture; he was threatened with the humiliation of being sexually violated by an electric hand drill. A recent police study of South Asian LGBT populations in northern England (Khan, Hall, & Lowe, 2017) found that a majority of participants reported both family and community 'honour'-based abuse and violence due to their sexual identity. Although the number of participants in these studies is small, it indicates that gay males are likely to be at risk for this abuse.

Methodology

This quantitative study used online questionnaires to explore the following areas:

1 *Demographic background*: For example, individual, family, social and cultural background including age, gender-identity, sexual orientation, relationship status, ethnicity, education, occupation, religion, family/community affiliation with honour culture, and adherence to honour codes.
2 *Type, extent and psychosocial impact of homonegative 'honour' abuse*: For example, any form of aggression (e.g. verbal threats and physical violence)

committed against, or witnessed by, respondents as a direct result of their sexual identity including their refusal to enter a forced marriage.

3 *Perceptions of available support*: For example, respondents' perceptions of emergency services and welfare agencies in England, in terms of their ability and efficacy to meet their needs as a vulnerable group at risk for 'honour'-based violence.

Precautionary measures were taken to ensure the privacy, confidentiality, and safety respondents participating in this study. Potential participants viewed a briefing page, prior to opening the questionnaire. This detailed the study's full aims, explained the procedures involved, and emphasised the anonymous nature of the study, as well as there being no obligation to participate. Participants were advised that they could withdraw from the study by closing the browser (and deleting their browser history) at any point. The last page debriefed participants by summarising the study aims and listing professional support agencies that offer professional and confidential support and advice to those affected by honour abuse and violence and other related issues raised in the questionnaire.

Findings

To gain insight into lived realities and perceptions of homophobic honour abuse, this study provides detailed qualitative analysis collected from ten South Asian gay men living in England. The online questionnaire explored three themes including: (1) participants' demographic, social and familial background; (2) the homophobic victimisation experienced and witnessed and how this affected respondents' psychosocial wellbeing; (3) perceptions of the efficacy of emergency services and welfare agencies to respond to homonegative honour abuse.

Theme 1 – demographic, social and familial background

Gender and sexual orientation

Participants were asked whether or not they identified as LGBT and whether or not they engaged with the wider LGBT community. Of the ten gay males who took part in the study, none self-identified as transgender. Seven participants stated that they identified as LGBT and three did not, while six stated they engaged with the LGBT community, but four did not.

Age and relationship status

Participants varied in age from 21 to 45 years (mean age = 31 years). Two participants were single, three dating, two co-habiting and three separated or divorced. No participants were married.

Educational status

Participants were mainly highly educated, with seven achieving Higher Education qualifications and three achieving Further Education.

Location

Participants were asked to reveal whether or not they were born in the UK, how many years they had resided in the UK if born outside, and their ethnic/national origin. Five participants were born in the UK, and five elsewhere. Of those not born in the UK, three were born in Pakistan, one in Bangladesh and one in the United States. Participants born elsewhere had resided in the UK between 7 and 37 years (Mean = 17 years). Regarding ethnic/national identity, five participants were Pakistani, two Indian, and one Bangladeshi. One participant stated "other" and one did not answer this question.

Religion and family ties

A total of four participants stated that they were religious; six participants were not. Religious denomination varied, with four stating their religion as Islam and two as Christian. Six participants did not, and four participants did not answer this question. Two participants actively rejected their faith.

Participants were asked to respond to three questions relating to the strength of their religious conviction, and that of their family, and how strongly/committed their family identified with the South Asian community (on a scale of 0 to 4, with 4 being very much). Participants overall revealed that their religious conviction was relatively low (mean = 1.7), but that of their family was high (mean = 3.7). Participants felt their family's commitment to the South Asian community was high (3.2). Participants were also asked (on a scale of 0 to 4, with 4 being very much), how important maintain *izzat* was to their family, and to what extent participants felt their family was shamed by their LGBT identity. Mean scores on both questions was high: 3.5 and 3.9 respectively.

Theme 2 – homophobic victimisation experienced and witnessed and how this affected respondents' psychosocial wellbeing

Participants were asked to respond to a series of six questions regarding their experiences of 'honour'-based abuse and violence that was committed due to their identifying as LGBT. Three questions covered abuse, violence and threats from their community, their family and strangers. Additionally, two questions addressed forced marriage: whether they themselves had been married (or expected to marry) without their consent and knowing of anyone in their community who identifies as LGBT being forced to marry. The final question asked

Figure 6.1 Respondents' experiences of 'honour' abuse

participants whether they had reported 'honour'-based abuse or violence to the police. Participants were asked to respond 'yes' or 'no' to each question. The number of participants reporting 'yes' and 'no' to each question are displayed in Figure 6.1.

Mental health

Participants were asked to state whether they had been affected by each of nine different mental health issues. Figure 6.2 shows the number of participants affected across each domain. Most participants stated that they had more than one mental health issue. The number of issues raised by each participant ranged from one to six mental health domains.

Theme 3 – perceptions of the efficacy of emergency services and welfare agencies to respond to homonegative 'honour' abuse

Participants were asked to respond in their own words to three questions, broadly addressing how they perceived the support efforts of emergency services and welfare agencies in England, in terms of ability and efficiency to meet the needs of

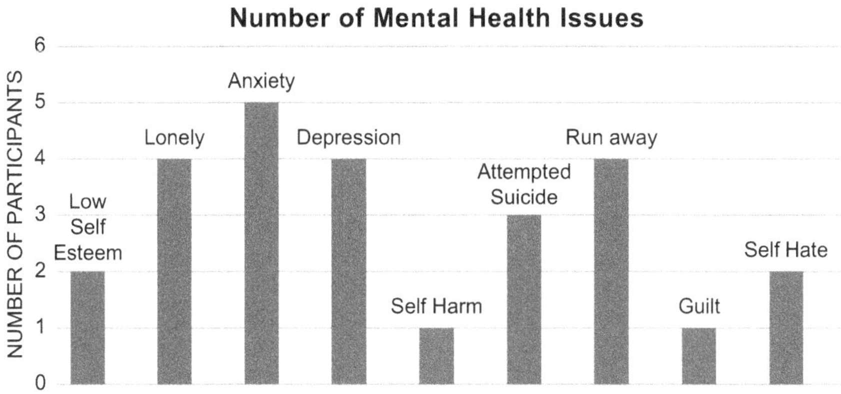

Figure 6.2 Number of mental health issues reported by participants

LGBT people within the South Asian community at risk of 'honour'-based abuse and violence.

1 The first question in this section asked participants to say why they felt so few reports of 'honour'-based abuse were made to the police from LGBT individuals. Eight participants gave their opinions, which, for some participants, focused around fear of damaging family reputations and/or being 'outed' within their community. One participant commented, for example: 'South Asian people dont [sic] accept LGBT people . . . I think that's why there is more police reports from south Asian LGBT people', 'Because they feel by telling the police it would out them', and 'Fear of family (being disowned etc.)'.

Other participants commented on lack of police resources to make reporters safe and the perceived lack of support, trust or racism from the police. For example: 'Lack of resources to make it safe after reporting; Lack of help to move away from prejudiced family; Lack of re-accommodation options; Lack of prosecutions; Lack of action against zealots; Lack of real action against community promoting harmful honour traditions', 'What can they do to help? . . . no one really trusts the police and they do not understand what it is like. I know there are asian [sic] police now but can we trust them, and what can they do anyway?', and, 'Because the police are intututionally [sic] racist and brown people hate/fear them'.

2 Next, participants were asked their opinion on what local support agencies (e.g. community, crime and safety, education, and faith groups) could do to encourage and support more open and transparent LGBT South Asian communities. Seven participants responded. Most comments related to

more awareness of LGBTQ issues in places of worship. For example, 'Ensure LGBT posters are placed in mosques', and, 'Have more open discussions in temples/mosques/churches about LGBTQ issues and that they exist in every community and it is nothing to be ashamed about; Try to separate sin from homosexuality'. One participant commented on wider issues, such lack of integration of Asians and fear of being blamed: 'encourage asians [sic] to come out and integrate more. so much bad stuff has happened with terrorism and so asians [sic] are scared of being blamed for this so it is a good time to get them out more. asains [sic] are so traditional and family obsessed but they are judgmental and need to integrate more.'

3 Finally, participants were asked their opinion on what is important for South Asians who identify as LGBT. Four participants responded to this question. Comments related to more support being needed within South Asian communities to support coming out and for mental health concerns to enable LGBT individuals to have a voice within their community, and better laws to protect LGBT people. For example, 'well, I see teenage boys who might be gay and they are religious and look so depressed. It is so sad. They will probably be married to women against their will and pretend to be straight just to get by', and, 'there certainly needs to be a voice for LGBTQ South Asian people. Someone to normalise being gay not only to themselves, but to their families. . . . I think mental health in the South Asian community is vastly understated and more research and support should be given in general as well as for the South Asian LGBTQ community. If we have more support groups, more openly gay south Asian people that people can identify and relate to that would be wonderful.'

Lessons learned: where do we go from here?

These findings indicate that extensive work needs to be undertaken to improve awareness of the difficulties faced by gay South Asian males at risk of honour abuse and violence in England and across the UK. The literature review and study findings overviewed in this chapter highlight a number of salient areas that research, policy and practice should focus on. One critical area for development includes improved education as part of the national schooling curriculum. It is encouraging that LGBT-inclusive teaching is now taking place to tackle anti-LGBT bullying in the UK. Indeed, from 2020 on, all secondary schools are obliged to teach pupils about sexual orientation and gender identity, while all primary schools are obliged to teach about family diversity – this may include LGBT families (Twocock, 2019).

Yet recent efforts to improve LGBT awareness and inclusivity in schools have been partially thwarted by large scale and high profile protests, led by parents and other, mostly religious, objectors across a number of schools in England's second largest city – Birmingham. One leading protester claimed that homosexuality was not a 'valid sexual relationship' (BBC News, 2019a). Another argued that the

British government's inclusivity policy was a 'totalitarian endeavour to indoctrinate our children in sexual ideologies', an 'assault on the family' and a 'war on morality'. The number of names on a petition set up by this demonstrator, signed over 11,400 times, illustrates the scale of these protests (Parveen, 2019). It is notable that a large proportion of the parents involved in this protest are British Asian Muslims (BBC News, 2019a, 2019b; Parveen, 2019), born and raised in England. The tenet of these parents' protests reflect the complex and multifaceted issues that underpin hostile attitudes towards homosexuality in many collectivist cultures, as reported by participants in this and other studies (see Lowe et al., 2019). For these reasons, efforts to improve awareness about LGBT inclusivity in schools would do well to consider the specific challenges faced by British gay people from South Asian backgrounds raised in religious families. Above all, the design and delivery of school educational programmes need to be culturally sensitive to protect the well-being of young people vulnerable to antigay honour abuse who may feel the way participants in this study described – anxious, guilty, afraid, depressed, ashamed, self-hating and suicidal.

Another significant lesson gleaned from this work is the importance of raising general awareness as well as professional awareness, with specific regard to the ways in which South Asian gay males might experience honour abuse. For example, both the literature review and study participants indicated that one of the most common ways in which gay South Asian males experience homophobic honour abuse is the use of coercive control and verbal abuse to force them into marriage (FMU, 2016, 2018; Jaspal, 2014; Khan, Hall, & Lowe, 2017; Razzall & Khan, 2017; Samad, 2010). With this in mind, It is important to note the Forced Marriage Unit (2018: 7) reported that:

> the majority of referrals (around 60%) come from professionals as well as other third parties e.g. non-governmental organisations. The other 20% of calls come largely from colleagues, friends or family members of the victim. The fact that victims self-reporting represents only a fifth of cases may reflect the hidden nature of forced marriage and the fact that victims may fear reprisals from their family if they come forward.

These findings indicate that there may be particular value in encompassing information on homophobic honour abuse against South Asian males in future public awareness campaigns. Indeed, increased awareness of forced marriages in the UK, for both males and females, most likely explains the two-fold increase in cases reported to the FMU in 2018 (N=1,764), representing a 47% increase compared with 2017 (N=1,196). This increase was partly credited to increased media attention and high-profile governmental campaigns.

Another important factor in raising awareness lies with religious and community leaders in collectivist communities in the UK. The extent to which 'honour'-based abuse and religiosity are associated is often debated (Lowe et al., 2019). Some have found support for this link (e.g. Chesler & Bloom, 2012; Gengler,

Alkazemi, & Alsharekh, 2018) and while others argue any links are tentative and misleadingly conflated with Islam in particular (e.g. Bhanbhro, Cronin De Chavez, & Lusambili, 2016). What is undisputable, however, is that 'honour'-based abuse, violence and killings are often justified by perpetrators, on religious grounds. Thus, there is a clear need for religious and community leaders to be involved in openly condemning these abusive acts and to play a visible part in changing patriarchal norms of hypermasculinity and rigid gender roles. A good example and role model is a leading imam from Manchester in the north of England, Irfan Chishti, who, in a leading newspaper (McVeigh, 2009), stated:

> It is not an Islamic issue, it's more of a tribal tradition that cuts across several faiths, but I can say categorically that it is not acceptable. It's difficult to ascertain the extent of this problem but I like to think that faith leaders are speaking out against it. Honour is a way of measuring dignity and respect and it is a very individualistic thing. Dishonour to one person is not the same as to another but we have to be very clear that there is never any justification for such horrific crimes.

Conclusions

In this chapter, the literature reviewed and study findings presented indicate that antigay honour abuse is a real and lived problem for gay males of South Asian origin living in England. The homonegative honour abuse they experience appears to stem from the complex interplay of multiple factors, including the power of honour and shame in culturally collectivist communities, institutionalised patriarchy, and other societal influences such as traditional families, cultural norms and institutional systems.

It is no surprise that respondents in this study reported myriad negative psychological effects resulting specifically from aligning their sexual identity and cultural orientation, including shame and low psychological well-being. The impact of this conflicting identity has been explored by Jaspal (2014), whose study of British Asian gay men found that they experienced a host of negative emotional experiences including 'invisibility', loss of control, sadness, humiliation, embarrassment and self-loathing. Also troubling are findings that a person's adherence to honour-related cultural values – such as *izzat* and *sharam* – and fears that they have dishonoured their family may predispose a person to suicide (Roberts, Miller, & Azrael, 2019). Indeed, research studies have found an association between honour cultures that emphasise strict gender-roles and hypersensitivity to reputational threats with higher rates of suicide (Crowder & Kemmelmeier, 2014). The volatility of this is further demonstrated when added to the mix are findings from other studies that highlight the vulnerability of British Asian gay men in the UK at risk for abuse from family members, with a third being victim to domestic abuse by a family member since the age of 16 years (Varney, 2013).

At time of writing, the protests at schools in Birmingham show no sign of abating. This suggests that despite progress in the domains of academia and social policy, there are clear pockets of homophobic familial and community resistance that impede efforts to achieve equal rights for LGBT people in the UK. It is in this milieu that the findings of a survey of school and collage-aged young people ought to be of great concern, as three in four gay and bisexual boys from ethnic minorities reported thoughts of taking their own life (Gusap & Taylor, nd). In light of these findings, we think a fitting end this chapter are the words of Matt Mahmood-Ogston (nd), who set up the Naz and Matt Foundation, after his Birmingham-born fiancé took his own life:

> On 30th July, 2014, my fiancé, my partner in everything, and eternal soulmate Naz (Dr Nazim Mahmood) sadly passed away, two days after his religious family confronted him about his sexuality. It was the first time they had heard about our 13-year relationship and our plans to marry. They told Naz to go to a psychiatrist to be 'cured'. They treated him like a disease that needed to be got rid of. The day after Naz passed away I was told by his family that he was living in 'sin' because of their religious beliefs. In the same breath I was also told that I was living in 'sin' because of 'my religion'. They told me not to tell anyone that Naz 'liked men' as it would bring 'shame' on their family. Out of respect I followed their wishes, until it reached a point and I decided I could not sit back and let this happen to anyone else ever again.

References

Al Dawoody, A. (2018). Respect for the dead under Islamic law: Considerations for humanitarian forensics. *Humanitarian Law and Policy*, retrieved from: https://blogs.icrc.org/law-and-policy/2018/11/01/respect-for-the-dead-under-islamic-law-considerations-for-humanitarian-forensics/

Amnesty International, Public Statement (2015). Turkey: Seven years on, still no justice for Ahmet Yıldız, retrieved from: www.amnesty.org/en/documents/eur44/2108/2015/en/

Andreevskikh, O. (2017, May). Report reveals the full brutality of anti-gay purges in Chechnya. *The Conversation*, retrieved from: https://theconversation.com/report-reveals-the-full-brutality-of-anti-gay-purges-in-chechnya-78373

Aplin, R. (2017). Exploring the role of mothers in 'honour' based abuse perpetration and the impact on the policing response. *Women's Studies International Forum*, *60*, 1–10.

Araji, S. K. (2000). Crimes of honor and shame: Violence against women in non-Western and Western societies. *Journal of Postmodern Criminology*, *8*, 1–15.

Asquith, N. L. (2015). Honour, violence and heteronormativity. *International Journal for Crime, Justice and Social Democracy*, *4*(3), 73–84.

BBC News (2019a, 22 May). Birmingham LGBT teaching row: How did it unfold?, retrieved from: www.bbc.co.uk/news/uk-england-48351401

BBC News (2019b, 21 March). Birmingham LGBT row: Parkfield School protests resume, retrieved from: www.bbc.co.uk/news/uk-england-birmingham-47652563

Beard, M. (2018, April). We must get justice for gay and bisexual men murdered in Chechnya. *The Guardian*, retrieved from: www.theguardian.com/world/2018/apr/06/we-must-get-justice-for-gay-and-bisexual-men-murdered-in-chechnya

Bhanbhro, S., Cronin De Chavez, C., & Lusambili, A. (2016). Honour based violence as a global public health problem: A critical review of literature. *International Journal of Human Rights in Healthcare*, *9*(3), 198–215.

Bilefsky, D. (2009). Soul-searching in Turkey after a gay man is killed. *The New York Times*, retrieved from: www.nytimes.com/2009/11/26/world/europe/26turkey.html

Bond, J. (2014). Honour as familial value. In A. K. Gill, C. Strange & K. Roberts (Eds.), *'Honour' Killing & Violence Theory, Policy & Practice* (pp. 89–107). Basingstoke: Palgrave Macmillan.

Brandon, J. & Hafez, S. (2010). *Crimes of the Community: Honour-based Violence in the UK*. Centre for Social Cohesion London, England.

Brown, R.P., Osterman, L.L., & Barnes, C.D. (2009). School violence and culture of honor. *Psychological Science*, *20*(11), 1400-1405. doi: 10.1111/j.14679280.2009.02456.x

Caffaro, F., Ferraris, F., & Schmidt, S. (2014). Gender differences in the perception of honour killing in individualist versus collectivistic cultures: Comparison between Italy and Turkey. *Sex Roles*, *71*, 296–318.

Carroll, A., & Mendos, L. R. (2017). *State-Sponsored Homophobia Report*. A world survey of sexual orientation laws. International Lesbian, Gay, Bisexual, Trans and Intersex Association (ILGA), retrieved on 26 February, 2019 from: https://ilga.org/sites/default/files/ILGA_State_Sponsored_Homophobia_2017_WEB.pdf

Castro, C. I. (2019, February). Forgotten, not gone: Chechnya revisited. *The McGill International Review*, retrieved from: www.mironline.ca/forgotten-not-gone-chechnya-revisited/

Chesler, P. (2009). Are honour killings simply domestic violence? *The Middle East Quarterly*, *16*(2), 61–69.

Chesler, P. (2010). Worldwide trends in honor killings, *The Middle East Quarterly*, *17*, 1–11.

Chesler, P., & Bloom, N. (2012). Hindu vs. Muslim honor killings. *Middle East Quarterly*, *19*(3), 43–52.

Cohen, D., & Nisbett, R. E. (1994). Self-protection and the culture of honour: Explaining southern violence. *Personality and Social Psychology Bulletin*, *20*(5), 551–567.

Cohen, D., Nisbett, R.E., Bowdle, B.F., & Schwarz, N. (1996). Insult, aggression, and the southern culture of honor: An "experimental ethnography." *Journal of Personality and Social Psychology*, *70*(5), 945–960.

Connell, R. W. (2005). *Masculinities* (second edition). Berkeley: University of California Press.

Cooney, M. (2014). Death by family: Honour violence as punishment. *Punishment & Society*, *16*(4), 406–427.

Crowder, M. K., & Kemmelmeier, M. (2014). Untreated depression predicts higher suicide rates in U.S. honor cultures. *Journal of Cross-Cultural Psychology*, *45*(7), 1145–1161. doi:10.1177/ 0022022114534915

Crown Prosecution Service (2016). Violence against women and girls (inclusive of data on men and boys) crime report 2015–2016, retrieved from: www.cps.gov.uk/publications/docs/cps_vawg_report_2016.pdf

Crown Prosecution Service (2018). Honour based violence, retrieved 2019 from: www.cps.gov.uk/legal/h_to_k/honour_based_violence_and_forced_marriage/

Dasgupta, R. (2018, July). This is what it was like growing up queer in India when homosexuality was illegal. *The Independent*, retrieved from: www.independent.co.uk/voices/india-gay-childhood-lgbt-illegal-homosexual-laws-section-377-a8469781.html

Democratic Turkey Forum (2011). The killing of Ahmet Yildiz (2008). Retrieved from: http://www.tuerkeiforum.net/enw/index.php?title=The_killing_of_Ahmet_Y%C4%B1ld%C4%B1z_(2008) 30 March, 2011.

Dyer, E. (2015). *Honour Killings in the UK*. London: Henry Jackson Society.

Eisner, M. and Ghuneim, L. (2013). Honor killing attitudes amongst adolescents in Amman, Jordan, *Aggressive Behavior*, 39: 405–417. DOI: 10.1002/ab.21485

Fatima, H., Qadir, T. F., Hussain, S. A. and Menezes, R. G. (2017). Pakistan steps up to remove "honor" from honor killing, *The Lancet Global Health*, 5: e145.

Forced Marriage Unit (2016). Forced marriage statistics for 2014 and 2015, retrieved from: www.gov.uk/forced-marriage

Forced Marriage Unit (2018). Forced marriage statistics 2018, retrieved from: www.gov.uk/government/statistics/forced-marriage-unit-statistics-2018

Gallup Coexist Index (2009). A global study of interfaith relations with an in-depth analysis of Muslim integration in France, Germany, and the United Kingdom, retrieved from: www.olir.it/areetematiche/pagine/documents/News_2150_Gallup2009.pdf

Gengler, J. J., Alkazemi, M. F., & Alsharekh, A. (2018). Who supports honor-based violence in the Middle East? Findings from a National Survey of Kuwait. *Journal of Interpersonal Violence*, 1–27. doi:10.1177/0886260518812067

Giuffrida, A. (2019, March). Italy accused of restoring honour killing defence after lenient femicide rulings. *The Guardian*, retrieved from: www.theguardian.com/world/2019/mar/18/italy-jail-terms-reduced-men-killed-wives-femicide?CMP=share_btn_tw

Grzyb, M. A. (2016). An explanation of honour-related killings of women in Europe through Bourdieu's concept of symbolic violence and masculine domination. *Current Sociology*, *64*(7), 1036–1053.

Guasp, A & Taylor J. Ethnicity (n.d.). Stonewall health briefing, retrieved from: www.stonewall.org.uk/get-involved/stonewall-research

Hayes, B. E., Freilich, J. D., & Chermak, S. M. (2016). An exploratory study of honor crimes in the United States. *Journal of Family Violence*, *31*(3), 303–314. https://doi.org/10.1007/s10896-016-9801-7

Hurtas, S. (2017). Honour killings haunt Turkey's gay community. *Turkey Pulse*, retrieved 2019 from https://www.europe-solidaire.org/spip.php?article42368

Human Rights Watch (2017, May) 'They have long arms and they can find me': Anti-gay purge by local authorities in Russia's Chechen republic, retrieved from: www.hrw.org/report/2017/05/26/they-have-long-arms-and-they-can-find-me/anti-gay-purge-local-authorities-russias

Iranian and Kurdish Woman's Right Organisation (2015). *Postcode Lottery: Police Recording of Reported 'Honour' Based Violence*. London, UK.

Jaspal, R. (2014). Arranged marriage, identity, and well-being among British Asian gay Men. *Journal of GLBT family studies*, *10*(5), 425–448.

Keskinen, S. (2009). 'Honour-related violence' and Nordic nation-building. In S. Keskinen, S. Tuori, S. Irni & D. Mulinari (Eds.), *Complying with Colonialism: Gender, Race and Ethnicity in the Nordic Region* (pp. 257–272). Farnham: Ashgate.

Khan, R. (2018). Attitudes towards 'honor' violence and killings in collectivist cultures: Gender differences in Middle Eastern, North African, South Asian (MENASA) and Turkish populations. In J. L. Ireland, P, Birch, & C. A. Ireland (Eds.), *International Handbook in Aggression: Current Issues and Perspectives*, Chapter 6, (pp. 216–226). London: Routledge.

Khan, R., Hall, B., & Lowe, M. (2017, December). *'Honour' abuse: The experience of South Asians who identify as LGBT in North West England.* Summary policy research report prepared for Lancashire Constabulary. HARM: Honour Abuse Research Matrix, United Kingdom.

Khan, R., Saleem, S., & Lowe, M. (2018). 'Honour'-based violence in a British South Asian community. *Safer Communities, 17*(1), 11–21.

Kupers, T. A. (2010). Role of misogyny and homophobia in prison sexual abuse. *UCLA Women's Law Journal, 18*(1), 107–130.

Lowe, M., Khan, R., Thanzami, V., Barzy, M., & Karmaliani, R. (2018). Attitudes toward intimate partner "honor"-based violence in India, Iran, Malaysia and Pakistan. *Journal of Aggression, Conflict and Peace Research, 10*(4), 283–292. DOI 10.1108/JACPR-09-2017-0324

Lowe, M., Khan, R., Thanzami, V., Barzy, M., & Karmaliani, R. (2019). Anti-gay 'honour' abuse: A multinational attitudinal study of collectivist vs individualist orientated populations in Asia and England. *Journal of Interpersonal Violence.* doi:10.1177/0886260519838493

Mahendru, R. (2017). 'I am not safe': On the run as a gay man in Afghanistan. *Open Democracy*, retrieved from: www.opendemocracy.net/5050/ritu-mahendru/i-am-not-safe-on-run-as-gay-man-in-afghanistan

Mahmood-Ogston, M. (n.d.). Naz and matt foundation: Be the person you were born to be, retrieved from: www.nazandmattfoundation.org/

McVeigh, T. (2009, October). Ending the silence on 'honour killing'. *The Guardian*, retrieved from: www.theguardian.com/society/2009/oct/25/honour-killings-victims-domestic-violence

Mosquera, P. M. R., Manstead, A. S. R., & Fischer, A. H. (2002). Honor in the mediterranean and Northern Europe. *Journal of Cross-Cultural Psychology, 33*(1), 16–36.

Murnen, S. K., Wright, C., & Kaluzny, G. (2002). If 'boys will be boys,' then girls will be victims? A meta-analytic review of the research that relates masculine ideology to sexual aggression. *Sex Roles, 46*(11–12), 359–375.

Nasrullah, M., Haqqi, S., & Cummings, K. J. (2009). The epidemiological patterns of honour killing of women in Pakistan. *The European Journal of Public Health*, 193–197.

Oberwittler, D., & Kasselt, J. (2014). Honour killings. In R. Gartner & B. McCarthy (Eds.), *The Oxford Handbook on Gender, Sex, and Crime*. Oxford: Oxford University Press.

Parveen, N. (2019, March). Activist warning of 'war on morality' wades into LGBT lessons row. *The Guardian*, retrieved from: www.theguardian.com/world/2019/mar/23/lgbt-lessons-row-campaigner-dr-kate-godfrey-faussett-role-sparks-concern

Razzall, K., & Khan, Y. (2017). Charities sound the alarm on male 'honour abuse'. *BBC News*, retrieved 2017 from: www.bbc.co.uk/news/uk-39485348

Roberts, K., Miller, M., & Azrael, D. (2019). Honor-related suicide in the United States: A study of national violent death reporting system data. *Archives of Suicide Research*, *23*(1), 34–46. doi:10.1080/13811118.2017.1411299

Rodriguez Mosquera, P. M. (1999). *Honor and Emotion. The Cultural Shaping of Pride, Shame and Anger*. Kurt Lewin Institute, the Netherlands.

Rodriguez Mosquera, P.M. (2013). In the name of honor: On virtue, reputation and violence. *Group Processes and Intergroup Relations*, 16 (3), 271–278.

Rodriguez Mosquera, P. M. (2016). On the importance of family, morality, masculine, and feminine honor for theory and research. *Social and Personality Psychology Compass*, 10, 431–442. doi: 10.1111/spc3.12262

Samad, Y. (2010). Forced marriage among men: An unrecognized problem. *Critical Social Policy*, *30*(2), 189–207. https://doi.org/10.1177/0261018309358289

Steinke, C. (2013). Male asylum applicants who fear becoming the victims of honour killings: The case for gender equality. *City University of New York Law Review, 17*: 233–262.

Tri.x. (2017). Male honour abuse, briefing 207, retrieved from: www.trixonline.co.uk/website/news/pdf/policy_briefing_No-207.pdf

Twocock, P. (2019). Historic announcement on LGBT inclusion in England's schools. *Stonewall*, retrieved from: www.stonewall.org.uk/about-us/news/historic-announcement-lgbt-inclusion-england%E2%80%99s-schools

UN Population Fund. (2000). *The State of the World's Population 2000: Lives Together, Worlds Apart: Men and Women in a Time of Change*. New York: Retrieved from http://www.unfpa.org/swp/2000/english

Vandello, J. A., & Cohen, D. (2003). Male honour and female fidelity: Implicit cultural scripts that perpetuate domestic violence. *Journal of Personality and Social Psychology*, *84*(5), 997.

Varney, J. (2013). Minorities within minorities: The evidence base relating to minority groups within the LGB&T community. *Manchester: LGBT Foundation*, retrieved from: www.refworld.org/docid/48abd5660.html

Wikan, U. (2008). *In Honour of Fadime: Murder and Shame*. Chicago: University of Chicago Press.

Chapter 7

Honour beliefs and identity among British South Asian gay men

Rusi Jaspal

Introduction

Lesbian, gay, bisexual and transgender (LGBT) communities in the United Kingdom have made significant strides in gaining equality over the last fifty years. Homophobia appears to be decreasing in British society. Many now feel able to disclose their identities to others. LGBT people are now able, and many choose, to get married and to become parents. Yet, the experience of ethnic and religious minority individuals who identify as LGBT does not fit comfortably within this narrative of equality. Many experience difficulties in reconciling their ethnicity, religion and sexuality, in obtaining parental acceptance of their sexual identity, and in coming out to significant others. They may face significant social and psychological stressors, such as rejection and discrimination, that adversely impact their identity, well-being and relationships (Jaspal, Lopes & Rehman, 2019).

In some collectivist cultures, there are coercive beliefs regarding 'honour', its role in the family's continuity and well-being, and the way in which it should be assessed, regulated and safeguarded (Soni, 2013). In these cultures, homosexuality may be regarded as a threat to honour and, thus, rejected as a cultural anomaly. LGBT people from collectivist cultural groups with strong honour beliefs may experience threats to their identity and negative emotional experiences and, consequently, feel unable to disclose their sexual identity to others. Some are clearly at risk of honour-based violence and forced marriage. As a case study, this chapter focuses on honour beliefs in the British South Asian community and the impact for identity and well-being among British South Asian gay men. Through the lenses of social representations theory and identity process theory from social psychology, this chapter focuses on the social psychological underpinnings of parental reactions to coming out, which may culminate in honour abuse and forced marriage, and identity and experience among British South Asians who come out as gay.

Family honour: social representation and identity

Honour is a difficult construct to define. It means different things to different groups and individuals. It is not easily delineable from other constructs, such as tradition and culture. However, there do appear to be some characteristics of honour that are shared across cultures. Vandello and Cohen (2003: 997) aptly define *honour* as 'virtuous behavior, good moral character, integrity, and altruism' and note that 'this ideal holds for males as well as females'. Their definition suggests that honour concerns cognition, affect and behaviour, and that it is more likely to be valued in collectivist, than in individualist, societies.

In South Asian communities, the Urdu term *izzat* is used to capture the concept of honour. Gill and Brah (2014: 73–74) define *izzat* as having 'multiple connotations and overlapping meanings related to respect, esteem, dignity, reputation and virtue' which is dependent on 'a wide spectrum of sociocultural relationships and ties that bind family and community groups together.' The antonym of izzat is *sharam*, which is the Urdu term for 'shame' – this amounts to a social or behavioural transgression which, in one way or another, undermines family honour. Although in South Asian communities, women are viewed as being central to family honour and their behaviour is particularly scrutinised (Gill, 2011), the conduct of men can also enhance or undermine family honour. As highlighted later in this chapter, religion, ethnicity and caste are of varying importance to South Asian communities and the norms, values and expectations associated with some or all of these identities can be integral to maintaining *izzat*. For instance, it is possible that, by marrying someone of another caste group or by leaving the Islamic faith, one would be accused of bringing *sharam* on the family (e.g. Jaspal, 2011a).

Honour beliefs clearly possess a psychological dimension in addition to cultural underpinnings. Why do people hold such beliefs? What social and psychological functions do they perform? What can happen if 'honour' is perceived to be violated? Both social representations theory (Moscovici, 1988) and identity process theory (Jaspal & Breakwell, 2014) can shed light on the social psychological underpinnings of honour and its significance for British South Asians.

Social representations theory

Social representations theory (Moscovici, 1988) provides a useful framework for exploring how members of any given group or community develop an understanding of, and are able to communicate about, their cultures and identities. Moreover, the theory provides insight into the broader social, political and ideological contexts in which people construct their identities, develop individual attitudes and relate to others. The theory can enable us to understand the development and maintenance of honour beliefs and how they relate to the issue of homosexuality, for instance. Social representations theory was originally designed to examine how esoteric topics become 'common sense' knowledge over time, that is, how they enter public consciousness and become topics that can be discussed.

At a basic level, a social representation can be defined as a collective 'elaboration' of a given phenomenon (such as honour), which in turn enables individuals to think and talk about it. This elaboration consists of emerging beliefs, values, ideas, images and metaphors in relation to a phenomenon. Social representations provide a cultural group with a shared social reality or 'common consciousness'. Family honour can be considered a social representation – it facilitates particular ways of thinking, talking and behaving and inhibits others. For instance, the social representation of family honour dictates compulsory heterosexuality in male family members and constructs homosexuality as a violation of family honour and, in some cultures, as a religious sin (Yip & Khalid, 2010).

Two principal social psychological processes converge in the creation of social representations:

- *anchoring* refers to the process whereby a novel, unfamiliar phenomenon is integrated into existing ways of thinking. For instance, in South Asian cultures, family honour is often linked to the 'essence' of the family, that is, the long-standing norms, values and traditions of the family. This means that a violation of family honour essentially amounts to a 'stain' on the family's reputation and implies that the norms, values and traditions of the family are inferior to those of other families in the cultural ingroup. Individuals may, thus, come to believe that moral and social transgressions are typical in that family and, thus, generalise the actions of one family member to the entire family unit. In view of this example of anchoring, it is easy to see why families may fear, and thus attempt to curb or conceal, the moral and social transgressions of a family member.
- *objectification* refers to the process whereby an abstract phenomenon is rendered concrete and tangible, often through the use of metaphors and personification. For instance, although the conduct of both males and females in the family can impact family honour, family honour is often personified in terms of female family members (and especially daughters) (Gill, 2011). Thus, females are often viewed a 'symbol' of family honour. Even in penalising homosexuality among male family members, British South Asian parents may point to the adverse effect that knowledge of their homosexuality could have for the marital prospects of daughters – the symbol of family honour (Jaspal, 2019).

Anchoring and objectification occur in a wide range of contexts, including the media, film and literature, political discourse and in everyday conversation. Interactions in these contexts all contribute to the genesis and development of social representations. Although introduced in one context (e.g. the print media), the representation may subsequently be taken up, elaborated or challenged in other contexts (e.g. a conversation in the local pub). In short, they emerge and develop as a result of social interactions *between people* (Jaspal, Nerlich & Cinnirella, 2014).

Identity process theory

Identity process theory is an integrative social psychological theory of identity construction, threat and coping. Identity process theory can enable us to understand both the psychological significance of family honour and the challenges individuals face in constructing, protecting and reconciling a gay identity. According to the theory, identity is constructed through two universal processes: assimilation-accommodation and evaluation.

- The *assimilation-accommodation* process refers to the absorption of new information in the identity structure (e.g. 'my son is gay') and of the adjustment which takes place in order for it to become part of the structure (e.g. 'my son is gay so my family's relationship with our cultural community may need to change').
- The *evaluation* process confers meaning and value upon the contents of identity (e.g. 'being gay is negative and sinful'). Family honour may be utilised as a 'lens' for evaluating homosexuality. In short, homosexuality may be constructed in negative terms because it is perceived as a threat to family honour.

These processes are guided by identity principles, which 'specify the end states that are desirable for identity' (Breakwell, 1986: 24). There are at least five identity principles.

- *Self-esteem* refers to personal and social worth.
- *Self-efficacy* can be defined as the belief in one's competence and control.
- *Distinctiveness* refers to feelings of uniqueness and differentiation from others.
- *Continuity* is essentially the psychological thread between past, present and future.
- *Coherence* refers to the perception that relevant aspects of identity are coherent and compatible.

When the identity principles are abrogated as a result of changes in one's social context (e.g. coming out as gay), identity is threatened, which is aversive for psychological well-being. For instance, the perception that one's sexual orientation is inconsistent with one's religious identity could plausibly challenge the coherence principle of identity, while the representation of homosexuality as a religious sin might challenge the self-esteem principle. Conversely, maintaining family honour potentially enables the individual to derive a sense of continuity since it facilitates a positive sense of lineage between past and present generations.

In response to identity threat, the individual will attempt to deploy strategies for coping with, or for reducing the negative impact of, the threat. A *coping strategy* is defined as 'any activity, in thought or deed, which has as its goal the removal or modification of a threat to identity' (Breakwell, 1986: 78). Coping strategies can function at intrapsychic, interpersonal and/or intergroup levels. For instance, it may be possible to deny the source or implications of a threat, such as one's sexual orientation (intrapsychic); to isolate oneself from individuals who denigrate one's sexual orientation (interpersonal); or to engage with like-minded others to form a group membership on the basis of a stigmatised identity element, such as one's sexual orientation (intergroup).

Although coping strategies are designed to reduce, assuage or eliminate the threat to identity, they vary in their level of effectiveness – some have only short-term benefits while others may be difficult to implement in the short term but are successful over time. In the remainder of this chapter, tenets of both social representations theory and identity process theory are invoked to illustrate the significance of honour beliefs in the lives of British South Asian gay men.

British South Asian communities

The category *British South Asian* is used to refer to UK residents of South Asian ancestry, including those of Indian, Pakistani, Bangladeshi, Sri Lankan and Maldivian descent. South Asians constitute a significant ethnic and religious minority umbrella group in the United Kingdom – the 2011 census revealed an estimated population of 4.2 million South Asians in the UK (Office for National Statistics, 2011). There are over 1.4 million British Indians, 1.1 million British Pakistanis and just under half a million British Bangladeshis resident in the United Kingdom.

South Asians are a collectivist society, in which family and community are of cultural importance – for many, these are the important facets of identity and sources of belongingness (Masood, Okazaki & Takeuchi, 2009). British South Asian identities are complex and multi-layered, and people within this umbrella community identify in a multitude of ways. Some define themselves as 'British Asian' or 'Asian', while others favour more specific ethno-national identities, such as 'Indian' or 'Pakistani'; ethno-regional identities, such as 'Panjabi' or 'Gujarati'; religious identities, such as 'Muslim', 'Hindu' or 'Sikh'; and even caste identities, such as 'Jat' or 'Khatri' (Jaspal, 2011b). Social context often determines the choice of identity and some are intersecting. In short, the category 'British South Asian' is diverse and best described in terms of an umbrella category or as a category of *communities*, encompassing many significant subgroup identities, albeit with some overlapping cultural characteristics.

One such characteristic shared by British South Asians of all ethnic and religious traditions concerns the importance that they collectively append to the cultural construct of izzat and their shared trepidation about permitting, or engaging in, behaviours that could result in sharam (Ghuman, 2003; Werbner, 2005). An essential tenet of maintaining izzat is the fulfillment of the cultural expectation of marriage, which is often arranged, to varying degrees, by the individual's family (Uddin, 2006). Any contravention of cultural norms concerning sexuality, such as coming out as gay, refusing to get married, or marrying someone against one's family's wishes, may be regarded as a threat to izzat and, thus, conducive to sharam (Jaspal & Siraj, 2011; Samad & Eade, 2003).

Parental reactions to homosexuality

Gay men tend to report social psychological difficulties in relation to coming out to their parents – they may experience changes in valued relationships, exposure to discrimination, and negative emotions, such as guilt, shame, and internalised homophobia. In one study (D'Augelli, Grossman & Starks, 2008), 71% of the young people perceived their parents' reaction to their coming out to be negative. This may be attributed partly to parents' lack of preparedness for their sons' coming out. Parents may hastily make comments or take actions which are construed by their gay sons' as disparaging and denigrating.

Some parents believe that coming out as gay is the result of bad parenting and attribute their child's sexual orientation to an adverse childhood event, which can lead to self-blame. Some elect a strategy of 'loving denial' (see Livingston & Fourie, 2016), which refers to knowledge, but lack of acknowledgement, of their child's sexual identity. This essentially silences the topic without resolving the issues that surround it. This strategy can superficially safeguard the parent-child relationship by downplaying a controversial topic but implicitly signals parental dismay at the child's sexual orientation and the preference to avoid acknowledging it. Such attributional styles and coping strategies can further stigmatise the child's sexual orientation, thereby causing tension in parent-child relations.

Parental acceptance of a child's sexual identity is associated with several positive psychological and interpersonal outcomes in gay men, such as higher self-compassion and lower internalised homophobia (Gertler, 2014). It is important to identify the factors that might facilitate parental acceptance. In their study of 72 gay men, Willoughby, Malik and Lindahl (2006) found that gay men who described their families as cohesive, adaptive and authoritative perceived their parents' reaction to their coming out as less negative than those whose families were disconnected, rigid and authoritarian. These data suggest that a positive family structure is associated with a better coming out experience and, thus, better interpersonal relations in adulthood.

Yet, in collectivist societies, families tend to be hierarchical and, in South Asian communities, patriarchal – they are more likely to be rigid and authoritarian. Not all parents are necessarily aware of, or understand, homosexuality. As Jaspal (2010) has argued, British South Asian parents may hold negative views of homosexuality and have little first-hand contact with gay people. This can make it difficult for them to understand and accept their own child's sexual orientation. They may focus on negative social representations of homosexuality that are associated with their cultural and religious identities (Yip, 2007).

Most British Indians are, at least nominally, of Hindu or Sikh faith (Ghuman, 2003). Neither Hinduism nor Sikhism officially prohibits homosexuality and, thus, homophobia within these communities can more accurately be attributed to cultural rather than theological factors (Jaspal, 2012). Conversely, Islam, which is the religion of most British Pakistanis, generally takes a negative stance on homosexuality and is opposed to Western conceptualisations of homosexuality in the sense of coming out as exclusively gay (Duran, 1993). Yet, in all British South Asian communities, religion is often drawn upon by individuals in order to substantiate their beliefs about homosexuality. Tenets of religion, such as the Story of Lot in the Koran, may be invoked in order to denigrate homosexuality, although there is by no means consensus concerning the interpretation of religious scripture in this regard (e.g. Jamal, 2001).

In his study of twelve parents of British South Asian gay men, Jaspal (2019) found that parents faced psychological distress due to their sons' coming out and experienced threats to the self-esteem and continuity principles of identity. Self-esteem was challenged due to widespread parental beliefs that their sons were committing a religious sin and that the esteem of their families would be reduced as a result of their sons' coming out. Continuity was jeopardised by parents' belief that they would lose valued relationships with friends, extended family members and ethnic and religious ingroup members as a result of their sons' coming out.

Due to limited social psychological resources for coping with these significant threats to identity, Jaspal's (2019) participants tended to favour denial as a coping strategy. Some apparently denied the reality of their sons' coming out despite having been given this information clearly and unequivocally, while others denied the true implications of this reality. For instance, although the parents participated in the study with the express knowledge that the research objective was to understand their reactions to their sons' coming out, they did not consistently acknowledge their sons' sexual identities during the course of the research project. Some of them continued to construe their sons' sexual orientation as a phase in their sexual identity development and believed that an arranged marriage might rectify this. This led some of them to continue to plan their sons' marriages and to discuss their plans candidly both with extended family members and with their gay sons.

Those parents who did resign themselves to the reality of their sons' sexual orientation tended to engage in the strategy of isolating themselves (and indeed their close family members) and, thus, avoided interpersonal contact with others. This strategy signalled an element of acceptance, on the one hand, and deflection on the other – parents chose to avoid contact with others to avoid having to acknowledge their sons' sexual orientation and its true implications. Although this strategy enabled them to save face in their respective communities, it could have negative consequences for identity – as members of a collectivist culture, British South Asians lament the loss of relationships with close ethnic and religious community members.

Given that South Asian communities are often concentrated in residential clusters, social and sexual transgressions can become the focus of gossip in close-knit communities and lead to sharam (Werbner, 2005). In some cases, marriage may be regarded and utilised by the family as a means of avoiding potential, or rectifying actual, transgressions of this kind. Marriage may be regarded as a panacea to homosexuality, for instance. Parents and other family members may cynically believe that sexual orientation is socially determined, mutable and, thus, rectifiable through a heterosexual marriage. Understandably, many young British South Asian gay men who are encouraged to get married refuse to do so – they may be unable, or simply unwilling, to enter into a heterosexual marriage. Yet, behaviours that are perceived to jeopardise family honour can trigger processes and outcomes that lead to a forced marriage when the individual in question refuses to comply.

According to the UK Home Office:

> [a] forced marriage is a marriage in which one or both spouses do not (or, in the case of some vulnerable adults, cannot) give free and full consent to the marriage and duress is a factor. Duress can include physical, psychological, financial, and emotional pressure, and sexual abuse. This form of marriage **is unacceptable** within the UK.
>
> (2012: 3, bold in original)

Some British South Asian parents do regard homosexuality as a serious social transgression which can be 'cured' by an arranged heterosexual marriage (Samad, 2010). The distinction between arranged and forced marriage (Home Office, 2012; Uddin, 2006) can become blurred due to the ambiguous boundaries between persuasion, coercion and force as well as an observed lack of understanding of what 'coercion' actually entails (Renteln, 2004). In British South Asian communities, there may be less acknowledgement of the fact that psychological and emotional pressure also constitutes a form of forced marriage (see further Chantler's chapter in this collection). Some parents deny, or are unaware of, the psychological and emotional pressure that their children experience in discussions about arranged heterosexual marriage. They may have a firm conviction that their actions will actually benefit their children. Samad and Eade (2003) have argued that arranged marriage and forced marriage ought to be viewed as points along a continuum rather than as dichotomous categories.

In essence, British South Asian parents are attempting to protect their identities from threat when they react adversely to their sons' coming out. Many believe that their izzat is at stake and that community members' knowledge of their sons' sexual orientation could bring about sharam. Their actions, though designed to protect identity, may actually result in psychological distress among British South Asian gay men.

British South Asian gay men: identity and experience

There is growing research into the identities and experiences of British South Asian gay men, much of which highlights the psychological distress that many face as a result of rejection from significant others due to their stigmatised sexual orientation (Jaspal & Cinnirella, 2010, 2012; Jaspal, Lopes & Rehman, 2019; Jaspal & Siraj, 2011; Yip, 2004).

Previous research into British South Asian gay men has focused on their perceptions of coming out (Jaspal & Siraj, 2011), interpersonal relations on the gay scene (Bassi, 2008) and their response to the cultural expectation of heterosexual marriage (Jaspal, 2014). Much of this work highlights the high risk of identity threat among British South Asians. In one of the first studies of this population, Bhugra (1997) noted feelings of regret, self-deprecation and self-hatred among many of his participants, given the 'traumatic discrepancy' between being Asian and gay. He attributed this traumatic discrepancy to attempts to construct 'a coherent sense of self from the two identities he seeks to attain: Asian and gay', alluding to threats to identity coherence (Jaspal & Cinnirella, 2010: 556). Homophobia from one's valued ethnic and religious communities can severely undermine the self-esteem principle of identity – individuals may fail to derive a positive self-conception on the basis of their gay identity (Yip, 2007).

British South Asian gay men may perceive their social, cultural and familial environment to be stigmatising towards homosexuality and, thus, unaccommodating of the sexual identity that they construct. They may refrain from coming out as gay. In their interview study of ten British Asian gay men (of Muslim faith), Jaspal and Siraj (2011) found that interviewees experienced shame when contemplating coming out to their parents, siblings and community members because of the stigma surrounding homosexuality. Many believed that, if they did come out to their parents, they would be stereotyped as being 'like white people'.

Some interviewees in their study actually feared physical violence from their family members due to pervasive honour beliefs. Crucially, izzat was a key issue – individuals believed that, by coming out as gay, they would be imperilling their family honour, which in turn could engender adverse consequences for themselves and their family members. Physical violence was just one potential consequence – others included denigration, ostracisation of the family, and adverse effects for the marital prospects of other siblings in the family. These honour beliefs can lead British South Asian gay men to reject the prospect of coming out, which in turn can undermine the self-esteem and coherence principles of identity. They may be unable to derive social support from others, due to their refusal to come out, and resort to denial, self-isolation and other maladaptive deflection strategies for coping with identity threat.

Some differences have been observed in the responses of British Indian and British Pakistani gay men to their sexual orientation (Jaspal, 2012). British Indians, most of whom are of Hindu or Sikh faith, generally report difficulties in disclosing their sexual orientation to other community members due to fear of stigma, rejection and threats to izzat. British Pakistani gay men, most of whom are of the Islamic faith, appear to experience both social *and* psychological difficulties in that they themselves may believe that their sexual orientation is a sin and that they are, therefore, 'bad Muslims'. For both British Indian and British Pakistani gay men, the family is an important aspect of identity and, given their collectivist cultural orientation, threats to izzat can be challenging at an individual level.

Individuals from British South Asian cultures generally wish to retain a connection with the family and with their respective communities, but many believe that coming as out as gay could jeopardise these community connections. Given the importance of the family, British South Asian gay men generally express trepidation about harming the family's izzat and bringing about sharam – they are concerned about the adverse impact on the lives of their parents, siblings and other family members. They generally acknowledge the different social structures that underpin the lives of their parents, which tend to be more collectivist and community-oriented than their own. For instance, while British South Asian gay men may have access to various social groups and contexts, such as the gay scene, their parents may continue to live within close-knit ethnic and religious communities, which are their primary sources of belongingness. Family honour constitutes a priority for many first-generation British South Asians and second-generation British South Asians are cognisant of the social value appended to izzat.

In their survey study of an ethnically diverse sample of 289 gay, lesbian and bisexual individuals, including those of British South Asian origin, Jaspal, Lopes and Rehman (2019) found that ethnicity was associated with depressive symptomatology, namely depression, psychological distress and suicidality. Moreover, the study showed that this relationship was mediated by situational stressors (i.e. rejection, discrimination, victimisation), psychological self-schemata (i.e. outness, internalised homophobia) and coping variables (i.e. drug use, help-seeking). In short, they found that those individuals who reported higher exposure to situational stressors, a negative psychological self-schema (i.e. internalised homophobia) and maladaptive coping (i.e. drug use) were more likely to manifest psychological distress, depression and suicidality. These data suggest that situational stressors and resultant negative psychological self-schemata predispose gay men (and indeed other sexual minorities) to depressive symptomatology. British South Asian gay men do appear to face situational stressors and to develop negative self-schemata due to coercive honour beliefs, which, in the absence of social support, can result in maladaptive coping strategies. These strategies can include denial, fantasy, isolation and, as Jaspal, Lopes and Rehman's (2019) study suggests, drug use.

As indicated earlier in this chapter, an arranged heterosexual marriage may be regarded as a means of changing one's sexual orientation. Understandably, this perception can have a significant impact on identity processes among British South Asian gay men whose parents and family members pressure them into a heterosexual marriage. In another study, Jaspal (2014) asked twelve British South Asian gay men to keep a personal diary to document their relationship with their parents amid parental pressure to get married. Study participants consensually described various forms of psychological and emotional coercion from their parents, such as repeatedly having to consider marital proposals, being asked to provide a reason for rejecting proposals, and enduring the guilt of letting their parents down. Despite having disclosed their sexual orientation to their parents, some individuals reported parental dismissal of this information and denial of its implications – their parents clearly believed that a heterosexual marriage would succeed in changing their sons' sexual orientation.

Parental pressure to get married appeared to cause identity threat – especially in relation to the self-esteem and continuity principles of identity – and significant psychological distress. In their diaries, individuals described feelings of anxiety, shame, and guilt in relation to their sexual orientation and believed that they were bringing shame on their families. In response to such identity threat, British South Asian gay men may attempt to cope by engaging in various deflection strategies. Some study participants engaged in the strategy of fantasy and denied their current reality by 'escaping' psychologically to their childhood so that they did not have to contemplate marriage. Others disengaged from family members, avoiding first-hand contact with them, in order to evade the topic of marriage and the threats to identity that consideration of this topic entailed.

Yet, a sizeable number of British South Asian gay men did come to view marriage in terms of a dilemma – on the one hand, they accepted their sexual orientation and, thus, did not wish to enter into a heterosexual marriage but, on the other hand, they themselves believed that a heterosexual marriage is more consistent with the norms, values and expectations associated with their ethno-religious identities. In such cases, individuals believe that a heterosexual marriage could simplify their lives, from an ethno-religious perspective at least. They too may come to view marriage as a panacea and as a means of safeguarding izzat. In conjunction with deflection strategies, such as fantasy and denial, contemplating an arranged marriage can easily become a reality – often with unfavourable consequences for identity among all involved.

Conclusions

Honour beliefs are pervasive in British South Asian communities. These beliefs are grounded in long-standing social representations that are associated with ethno-religious identities. They can therefore be coercive and inescapable for both British South Asian gay men and for their parents if they wish to forge a sense of belonging in their ethno-religious communities. Yet, these beliefs can cause considerable psychological distress to British South Asian gay men struggling to assimilate and accommodate their sexual orientation in their identity and lead them to evaluate their emerging sexual identities negatively. This itself is associated with the onset of internalised homophobia, which can have insidious social psychological consequences, such as poor mental health and sexual health outcomes.

It is noteworthy that honour beliefs can also cause identity threat among the parents of British South Asian gay men struggling to understand and accept their sons' sexual identity, which may be perceived as being at odds with family honour. Parents may come to engage in irrational behaviours designed to protect family honour and, by extension, their identities. This can include honour abuse against their gay children. When viewed through the lens of identity process theory, behaviours that are described as 'honour abuse' may actually constitute maladaptive coping strategies. British South Asian gay men's uncritical acceptance of these behaviours, such as acquiescing to an arranged heterosexual marriage, may also be a maladaptive coping strategy. These strategies may have short-term benefits for honour and identity but are unlikely to be successful in the long term, causing secondary threats to identity, further patterns of maladaptive coping and psychological distress.

On the basis of this chapter, at least three practical recommendations can be made to support those at risk of identity threat due to honour beliefs:

- First, there is a need for greater awareness and understanding of sexual orientation in British South Asian communities. The widespread social representation of homosexuality as a 'chosen' and, thus, mutable state must be challenged. Social representations of honour (izzat) and shame (sharam) must also be challenged within British South Asian communities. Clearly, community leaders will need to take a proactive stance on challenging long-standing honour beliefs, understandings and practices. Similarly, young British South Asians ought to be informed about diversity in a positive and proactive way – ideally within the context of sexuality education programmes in schools – so that future generations are more accepting and accommodating of both their own and others' (sexual) identities.
- Second, British South Asian parents appear to have few sources of social and psychological support in relation to their children's coming out. In view of pervasive honour beliefs, this can be a psychologically aversive experience and coping is difficult. The availability of culturally competent support networks and psychological support services would facilitate effective coping and potentially reduce the risk of engagement in maladaptive strategies, such as honour abuse. An evidence-based self-help guide for British South Asian parents would be a very useful resource.
- Third, although the Home Office (2012) does acknowledge non-violent forms of coercion, in practice there must be greater social, legal and institutional acknowledgement of subtler forms of forced marriage, which involve psychological and emotional coercion in the ways described by British South Asian gay men themselves (e.g. Jaspal, 2014). The boundaries between arranged marriage and forced marriage can easily become blurred – with distressing consequences for British South Asian gay men. Honour beliefs are clearly a causal factor.

Using social representations theory and identity process theory, it has been shown that honour beliefs can shape, protect and challenge identity processes among both British South Asian gay men and their parents. These theories will undoubtedly help to inform interventions to challenge honour beliefs that curtail identity development and psychological well-being among British South Asian gay men. These interventions must focus on re-configuring negative social representations of homosexuality, facilitating a positive sexual identity among British South Asian gay men, and supporting the parents of British South Asian gay men struggling to reconcile homosexuality and honour.

References

Bassi, C. (2008). The precarious and contradictory moments of existence for an emergent British Asian gay culture. In C. Dwyer & C. Bressey (eds.), *New geographies of race and racism* (pp. 209–222). Farnham, UK: Ashgate.

Bhugra, D. (1997). Coming out by South Asian gay men in the United Kingdom. *Archives of Sexual Behaviour*, 26, 547–557.

Breakwell, G.M. (1986). *Coping with threatened identities.* London: Methuen.

D'Augelli, A.R., Grossman, A.H., & Starks, M.T. (2008). Families of gay, lesbian, and bisexual youth: What do parents and siblings know and how do they react? *Journal of GLBT Family Studies*, 4(1), 95–115.

Duran, K. (1993). Homosexuality in Islam. In A. Swidler (ed.), *Homosexuality and world religions* (pp. 181–198). Harrisburg, PA: Trinity Press.

Gertler, L.M. (2014). *The coming out experience, internalized homophobia and self-compassion in LGBQ young adults.* Unpublished PsycD thesis, The Wright Institute, Berkeley, USA.

Ghuman, P.A.S. (2003). *Double loyalties: South Asian adolescents in the West.* Cardiff: University of Wales Press.

Gill, A. (2011). Reconfiguring 'honour'-based violence as a form of gendered violence. In M.M. Idriss & T. Abbas (eds.), *Honour, violence, women and Islam* (pp. 218–231). Oxford: Routledge.

Gill, A. & Brah, A. (2014). Interrogating cultural narratives about 'honour'-based violence'. *European Journal of Women's Studies*, 21(1), 72–86.

Home Office (2012). The right to choose: Guidance and instruction on forced marriage. Available at www.basw.co.uk/system/files/resources/basw_93347-2_0.pdf Accessed on 3 August 2019.

Jamal, A. (2001). The story of Lot and the Qu'ran's perception of the morality of same-sex sexuality. *Journal of Homosexuality*, 41(1), 1–88.

Jaspal, R. (2010). Identity threat among British Muslim gay men. *The Psychologist*, 23(8), 640–641.

Jaspal, R. (2011a). Caste, social stigma and identity processes. *Psychology and Developing Societies*, 23(2), 27–62.

Jaspal, R. (2011b). Delineating ethnic and religious identities in research with British South Asians. *Psychological Studies*, 56(2), 214–244.

Jaspal, R. (2012). 'I never faced up to being gay': Sexual, religious and ethnic identities among British South Asian gay men. *Culture, Health and Sexuality: An International Journal for Research, Intervention and Care*, 14(7), 767–780.

Jaspal, R. (2014). Arranged marriage, identity and psychological wellbeing among British Asian gay men. *Journal of GLBT Family Studies*, 10(5), 425–448.

Jaspal, R. (2019). Parental reactions to British South Asian young men who come out as gay. *Journal of GLBT Family Studies* https://dx.doi.org/10.1080/1550428X.2019.1684412.

Jaspal, R. & Breakwell, G.M. (eds.) (2014). *Identity process theory: Identity, social action and social change.* Cambridge: Cambridge University Press.

Jaspal, R. & Cinnirella, M. (2010). Coping with potentially incompatible identities: Accounts of religious, ethnic and sexual identities from British Pakistani men who identify as Muslim and gay. *British Journal of Social Psychology*, 49(4), 849–870.

Jaspal, R. & Cinnirella, M. (2012). Identity processes, threat and interpersonal relations: Accounts from British Muslim gay men. *Journal of Homosexuality*, 59(2), 215–240.

Jaspal, R., Lopes, B., & Rehman, Z. (2019). Depressive psychopathology in Black & Minority Ethnic lesbian, gay and bisexual people in the UK. Paper presented at the 33rd Annual Conference of the European Health Society, Dubrovnik, Croatia, 4–7 September.

Jaspal, R., Nerlich, B., & Cinnirella, M. (2014). Human responses to climate change: Social representation, identity and socio-psychological action. *Environmental Communication: A Journal of Nature and Culture*, 8(1), 110–130.

Jaspal, R. & Siraj, A. (2011). Perceptions of 'coming out' among British Muslim gay men. *Psychology and Sexuality*, 2(3), 183–197.

Livingston, J. & Fourie, E. (2016). The experiences and meanings that shape heterosexual fathers' relationships with their gay sons in South Africa. *Journal of Homosexuality*, 63(12), 1630–1659.

Masood, N., Okazaki, S., & Takeuchi, D. T. (2009). Gender, family, and community correlates of mental health in South Asian Americans. *Cultural Diversity and Ethnic Minority Psychology*, 15(3), 265–274.

Moscovici, S. (1988). Notes towards a description of social representations. *European Journal of Social Psychology*, 18, 211–250.

Office for National Statistics (2011). 2011 Census. Available at www.ons.gov.uk/census/2011census Accessed on 2 August 2019.

Renteln, A.D. (2004). *The cultural defense*. Oxford: Oxford University Press.

Samad, Y. (2010). Forced marriage among men: An unrecognized problem. *Critical Social Policy*, 30, 189–207.

Samad, Y. & Eade, J. (2003). *Community perceptions of forced marriage*. London: Foreign and Commonwealth Office.

Soni, S. (2013). *'Izzat' and the shaping of the lives of young Asians in Britain in the 21st century*. Unpublished PhD dissertation, University of Birmingham, UK.

Uddin, M.S. (2006). Arranged marriage: A dilemma for young British Asians. *Diversity in Health and Social Care*, 3, 211–219.

Vandello, J.A. & Cohen, D. (2003). Male honor and female fidelity: Implicit cultural scripts that perpetuate domestic violence. *Journal of Personality and Social Psychology*, 84(5), 997–1010.

Werbner, P. (2005). Honor, shame and the politics of sexual embodiment among South Asian Muslims in Britain and beyond: An analysis of debates in the public sphere. *HAGAR International Social Science Review*, 265(1), 25–47.

Willoughby, B.L.B., Malik, N.M., & Lindahl, K.M. (2006). Parental reactions to their sons' sexual orientation disclosures: The roles of family cohesion, adaptability, and parenting style. *Psychology of Men & Masculinity*, 7(1), 14–26.

Yip, A.K.T. (2004). Negotiating space with family and kin in identity construction: The narratives of British non-heterosexual Muslims. *Sociological Review*, 52, 336–350.

Yip, A.K.T. (2007). Sexual orientation discrimination in religious communities. In M.V.L. Badgett & J. Frank (eds.), *Sexual orientation discrimination: An international perspective* (pp. 209–244). London: Routledge.

Yip, A. K. T. & Khalid, A. (2010). Looking for Allah: Spiritual Quests of Queer Muslims. In K. Browne, S. Munt & A.K.T. Yip (eds.) *Queer Spiritual Spaces* (pp. 81–110). London, UK: Ashgate.

Chapter 8

'You must keep your 'honour', a man without 'honour' is no man at all'

'Honour, masculinity and violence in Afghanistan

Sayed Mahdi Mosawi

Introduction

'Honour' can be described as the backbone of Afghan culture. It is the foundation upon which social status is built and conformity praised. The folklore, local languages and everyday life in Afghanistan give much emphasis on reputation, good name and respect. Dupree considers the main function of etiquette and social manners as preserving *izzat* or so-called honour (Dupree, 1998), and the code in Afghanistan contains a wide range of common values, such as hospitality, generosity, chivalry and protecting the family's reputation. In the Afghan context, 'honour' is essentially gendered and requires men and women to maintain honour in distinct ways. On the one hand, to protect their honour, women are expected to conform to notions of femininity that emphasise sexual chastity, modesty, virginity and *Purdah* – the latter which is also defined as seclusion (Abirafeh, 2009). Here, Afghan women are considered as the symbols and embodiments of honour (Emadi, 2002). On the other hand, safeguarding honour is dominantly intertwined with the concept of *Mardānagi* – masculinity (Mojab, 2005) and how to be an Afghan 'man'. In this regard, 'honour' mandates that the men of the household assume the responsibility of intervention when the reputation of the family is at stake in order to maintain the status quo (Dupree, 2004). So-called honour killings and 'honour'-based abuse against women are the main instances that are most often highlighted in the existing literature. A report summary on violence against women by the Afghanistan Independent Human Rights Commission recorded 277 cases of femicides between March 2017 and March 2018, of which 136 cases were described as so-called honour killings (AIHRC, 2018). Also from January 2016 to December 2017, the United Nations Assistance Mission in Afghanistan recorded '280 cases of murder and honour killings of women' (UNAMA & OHCHR, 2018: 22). While many cases of violence against women go unreported or ignored, the aforementioned statistics provide a glimpse of the issue of so-called honour killings that target women throughout the country.

However, there is a key aspect that is often neglected within the existing literature and that is HBA involving Afghan men. The dominant debate on HBA and violence in Afghanistan focuses on males as perpetrators of abuse. For instance, in defining so-called honour killings, the emphasis focuses upon 'a man's right to kill a woman' because of her immoral actions that damage the family's honour (UNAMA & OHCHR, 2010: 33). Another instance is where HBA is explained as a 'means of punishing women' who are out of control or who engage in extramarital affairs outside of marriage (AIHRC, 2013: 87). Such a view is limited because it fails to take into account abuse and violence that men experience in the name of so-called honour. Inflicting abuse and violence can be considered to be an important source of injury among men (Connell, 2001) and within a cultural climate such as Afghanistan (where honour is very prominent) it is expected that the consequences of HBA and so-called honour killings contribute to the lives of both women and men, although admittedly in different forms and degrees. A brief literature review online reveals many extreme incidents in Afghanistan where men have also been killed based on a supposed justification of dishonouring the family and community. Male victims have been accused of *Zinā* – adultery – fornication and elopement and are subsequently lynched and shot dead by informal group members like the Taliban,[1] the victims' family, kin and people within the community at large. For example, the Taliban publicly executed a young man and woman in central Afghanistan in May 2019. The victims had eloped to pursue their love but were arrested by militants and killed at the order of the Taliban court (Karimi, 2019). In 2017, an armed mob including hundreds of local people and the relatives of a woman (Fateha, who ran away with her lover, Hedayatullah) stormed a police station in eastern Afghanistan. The mob dragged the lovers outside the station and seriously assaulted them. The police said that this was then followed by the execution of Fateha, shot dead by her brother, while Fateha's (arranged) husband shot and killed the young man (Nader and Nordland, 2017; Bezhan and Bashir, 2017). A similar incident recently occurred in 2019, where a group of brothers and the father of a young woman who had eloped with a man, attacked the male lover's house. As a result of the violent confrontation, three men were killed (Zarifi, 2019). These cases of male homicides are only but a few examples of violence against male victims in Afghanistan. There are other instances of HBA and so-called honour killings that Afghan men are forced to confront but which are not recognized or reported within mainstream society. This chapter intends to develop an understanding of men's lived experiences of HBA in the post-conflict era in Afghanistan. It aims to explore and comprehend HBA in the everyday life of men living in Kabul city. Dealing with such an issue is important because it fills a crucial gap in the existing literature by revealing the experiences of Afghan men and their stories of HBA. It also moves beyond current narratives that merely pay attention to men as perpetrators of HBA – men are also victims. Moreover, this chapter looks at the different types of HBA that men experience and does not solely focus on 'extreme' cases of so-called honour killings. Finally, this chapter seeks to highlight the significance of HBA as a harm that jeopardises the health, safety and well-being of both women and men.

'Honour', masculinity and violence: the conceptual background

'Honour' is a basic social code that plays a significant role in regulating gender – 'a living system of social interactions' (Connell and Lecture, 2002: 14) that establishes hierarchies in cultures that deeply value it. In honour cultures, the concept of honour is particularly entwined with the notion of masculinity (Cohen, 2007). Gilmore (1990: 43–44) gives the examples of the Mediterranean where 'male honour' is extensively pronounced as a domestic duty. He adds that honour is about 'being good at being a man', and to be a man it is required to accept the 'expandability' and 'sacrifice' in the service of family, kin group members and societal values. Begikhani et al. (2015) also note that in honour-based patriarchal societies, a man is the ultimate head of the family and is considered as the defender of his family and their honour. As a result, men are expected to be constantly on the guard against threats and challenges to the individual and collective honour and to maintain it by demonstrating their power and strength. In a culture of honour, it is usually men who feel obliged to protect the reputation and honour by taking much greater risks (Barnes et al., 2012), displaying physical aggression and also using force and violence (Cohen et al., 1996; Cohen, 2007; Brown and Osterman, 2012). Such violence can occur against women or other men. The issue of honour violence against women is well-discussed within debates on gender-based violence (Leverenz, 2007; Gill, 2011; Westmarland, 2015). This type of abuse, and in extreme cases, femicide, are justified by the alleged sexual misconduct of women who endanger the whole family's reputation and signify a source of shame and humiliation (Pitt-Rivers, 1966; Abou-Zeid, 1966). However, in order to understand and discuss HBA, it is not enough to uncover violence in women's lives only. One must also 'expose the way violence works in the men's lives . . . [both as] . . . perpetrators and victims' (Stanko, 1994: 44–45). As Connell explains, men should not be seen as a homogenous group. Rather, there are multiple masculinities within a given cultural setting. This means that different understanding and ways of 'doing masculinity' may exist in a specific context (Connell, 2006). Accordingly, men may be the victims of HBA too (Home Affairs Committee House of Commons, 2008; Roberts et al., 2014). For instance, in the conflict situations, sexual violence and rape against men are used to 'feminise' them and humiliate their status as a man in the eyes of their communities (Wright and Welsh, 2014). Also, in the everyday context, men can be the perpetrator or victim of confrontational homicides (Wilson and Daly, 1985), such as 'pub fights' or what may be termed as as 'honour contests' (Polk, 1994). These types of events occur amongst men and may be sparked by what might appear to be trivial arguments, such as 'a minor jostle, an insult, a comment to a woman companion, or in some cases simply challenging eye contact' (Polk, 2003: 135). But for the male participants, it is 'often provoked by what is seen as a challenge to their standing as males, in a word, to their honour' (Benson and Archer, 2002). The male victims of such assaults are impacted differently, ranging from short term shock, fear, anger, and disbelief at the time of the assault to long-term impacts and a sense of disruption to life routines after the abuse (Stanko and Hobdell, 1993). Men are also the victims of so-called honour killings, though much less in comparison with women. The main reason for murdering male victims involves the alleged engagement in pre- or extra-marital sex (Chesler, 2010). While there have been attempts to understand male victimisation within intimate relationships (Cook, 2009; Lien and Lorentzen, 2019), the experiences of male victims of HBA has been neglected within the contemporary sociological exploration of masculinity and violence. As Newburn and Stanko point out, 'much of this neglect is based upon a widely held but largely untested assumption that a central element of masculinity involves an unwillingness to talk about or admit "weakness"' (Newburn and Stanko, 2002: 267). In this sense, men avoid being viewed as vulnerable and weak by avoiding talking about their victimisation in HBA cases. This chapter considers the 'honour' code that paves the way for understanding violence against men and considers experiences and stories of Afghan men as perpetrators and victims.

Context of the study, Afghanistan: an overview

Afghanistan society contains a multitude of ethnic, linguistic, religious sects and kin-based groups in which *Qawm* (communal group) and *Qabila* (tribe) units constitute the base of the social structure. The social organisation of *Qawm* and *Qabila* is based on the agnatic ties and blood relations (Moghadam, 1992). It is socially united and shares a common language and place of origin. Eickelman (1981) explains that in Afghanistan, *Qawm* can also include relatives by marriage, some neighbours and others. Almost all the people of Afghanistan are Muslims with the majority being *Sunni* and minorities including *Shi'as*, *Esmāilis* and *Sufis* as well as small communities of non-Islamic religions, such as Hindus and Sikhs.

Existing literature

A search within the existing literature relating to the Afghanistan context reveals that there has been no study that explicitly concentrates specifically on HBA and male victims. There are, however, some studies that focus their attention on masculinities and the honour code (see e.g. Azarbaijani-Moghaddam, 2009; Baldry et al., 2013). Accordingly, the review of previous works is synthesised and outlined below, highlighting the concept of masculinities, masculine honour and men's violence. Afghanistan is described as a patriarchal society where notions of masculinities are defined in terms of men's responsibilities and social roles within the family and community. Men are perceived as the main breadwinners of the family, *Nafaqa*[2] (i.e. maintenance) providers, safeguarders and decision-makers. Non-conformity to the social expectations dishonours men and places them within the spectrum of shame (Echavez et al., 2016). However, attending to these traditional roles is perceived as highly challenging for men in Afghanistan, particularly considering the ongoing conflict and insecurity within the country (Myrttinen, 2018). Promundo's study (Gereš, 2018) shows that due to the financial insecurity, political instability and insurgency, young men are currently finding their sense of manhood under threat as they struggle to meet their social roles as the providers and protectors of the family. When referring to masculine honour, it is characterised by a man's ability 'to protect a woman's virtue, ensuring no other man (or his eyes) has access to "his" women' (Schmeidl, 2009: 79). Afghan women are considered as the symbols of honour for men, the family, clan and nation. They are central to the honour-shame complex (Kandiyoti, 2005; Moghadam, 2002). As a consequence, a woman's action that is perceived to be dishonourable can be symbolised as her male relatives' inability to practice their power and control over 'their' women.

In the context of honour and men's violence, the main focus is given on the *Pashtunwali* – the way of being a Pashtun – the Taliban and *Jihad*. As a part of *Pashtunwali*, studies introduce honour as a fundamental component that determines a code of conduct and prescription of a 'good' Pashtun (Casimir and Jung, 2009; Pstrusińska, 2017). Schmeidl (2009) also mentions that among Pashtuns, men are usually given a gun as a rite of passage into manhood. In this sense, weapons and their ownership are associated with a man's honour and masculinity. The honour theme is also significant in *Jihad* ideology and the Taliban. Poulton (2003) emphasises the issues of honour and manhood in understanding *Jihad* and committing suicide attacks. The example that he provides includes Afghan male refugees who attend mosques and *Madrasas* in Pakistan and who are educated by *Mullahs* with *Wahhabist* propaganda; they are indoctrinated to see the West as 'the devil' and include 'suicide as martyrdom and a source of honour' (Poulton, 2003: 408). This was also a similar factor with the Afghan *Mujahidins*' resistance as Muslim fighters whose 'life and death was the same in *Jihad* [against the Soviet Union] and the ultimate goal was to earn the honour of becoming *Shahid* [martyr]' (Olesen, 1995: 278).

The Afghanistan political conditions since the 1980s and 1990s have shaped the definition of Afghan masculinity as one that includes threat and use of violence (Gilani, 2008). This is especially because of the Taliban regime, under which the 'arbitrariness of death' endangered men's role to protect their families. It also reinforced masculine violence and its representation in both private and public spheres. After their fall in 2001, the Taliban continued to follow their gender discourse, which comprised extreme religious interpretations of Islamic scriptures and tribal codes and applied them to their propaganda and insurgent operations. Schmeidl (2009: 80) states that in Southern Afghanistan, the Taliban challenged Pashtun men by questionning their manhood and asking 'Are you men (Pashtun), or are you women? How long will you tolerate a foreign dominated government in Kabul?' This is an example of male violence politically being linked to male honour (Möller-Leimkühler, 2018).

This literature reveals the significance of Afghan masculine concepts in terms of traditional roles – provider, protector and procreator within the family and community. It shows that honour is mostly attached to and manifested through masculine attributions. The authors provide examples of how honour contributes to male violence against women. While a few works draw attention to the impact of honour on men's interpersonal violence in war, it merely focuses on the male's perpetration. In almost all the works, Afghan men are observed merely as perpetrators of violence and not the victims of HBA at the hands of other men.

Research method

To understand how honour contributes to men's different experiences of HBA in Afghanistan, this chapter profited from a qualitative research design. There are two main sources of data in this chapter: in-depth interviews and observations. The data and stories were first gathered through semi-structured interviews with 21 Afghan men. The participants were selected using purposive sampling. Cases were selected on the basis of their 'information-rich' qualities and those cases where the men had a great deal to discuss about their experiences of HBA (Patton, 2015). Since discussing honour issues can be culturally very sensitive, especially when it might be linked to victimisation, the search for participants began by establishing contact and opening a dialogue with those who were interested in exchanging their views and experiences of honour. Through building trust and establishing relationships with these participants, new subjects were found. The focus of the study was limited to three major ethnic groups – Pashtun, Tajik and Hazara. The participants were between the ages of 18 and 53. Concerning the educational background of the participants, there were two participants who had no formal education; two participants had some education in *Madrasa* schools; three had left their primary or high school before graduation; eight had graduated from the twelfth grade; and six had formal university education. Among the cases, seven males were single; thirteen were married; and one man was engaged. All of the participants attended interviews voluntarily. Besides the interviews, the 'observation in person' technique (Bottorff, 2004) was used as another strategy to observe and document HBA amongst men in their everyday context in public places. The study site was Kabul, the capital city located in Eastern Afghanistan. For the analysis, interviews were transcribed and thematised along with the observation data through the coding process using the Maxqda program.

Findings of the study

In this chapter, the term *honour*[3] contextually refers to a combination of *Izzat*, *Āberu* and *Haysiyat* (face) that was repeatedly quoted by the participants in order to describe their stories of HBA. The findings are categorised into three main themes. The first relates to the meaning and significance of honour from the point of view of the male participants. The second theme considers men's involvement in the use of violence against other men in the context of honour, and the third category relates to men as victims of HBA and forced marriages in their everyday lives.

Meanings and significance of 'honour'

(a) Masculine notions of 'honour'

The first category of findings describes the meanings of 'honour' for the participants. How did the men perceive honour? The first reaction in most of the cases was remarkably similar: there was a sense of surprise and unexpectedness, followed by a short silence and when reflecting upon their thoughts, the participants described their thoughts very strongly with an emphasis upon something highly valuable. There were two categories ascribed to the meaning of honour: one is about the 'face' and social value that men claim and obtain through social interactions. For example, when a man conforms to socially accepted norms (e.g. demonstrating his ability to be a good husband or father), this makes him an 'honourable' man. According to the second category, there are 'symbols' that explicitly represent a man's honour within the community, such as a virtuous wife, daughter or sister. The interviewees described the meaning of *A ¯beru* and *Haysiyat* as a source of credit and also the possibility of representing and maintaining a good image and face in public interactions with others. According to the participants, preserving and proving *A ¯beru* and *Haysiyat* is an integral part of their everyday life and is, in particular, awarded to men who conform to religious, moral and social values. The following quote includes common metaphors mentioned by a number of the participants while describing their sense of *A ¯beru* and *Haysiyat*:

> I do not know what to say about *Āberu* and *Haysiyat*. [Pause] you know the lives of our people are centered around these matters. [Laughter . . .] I have not been thinking about the meaning of *Āberu* yet, though I am using it all the time. That is how it is. When I say I am a *Bā -Āberu* man [a man with dignity and honour], it means that I can hold my head up before my relatives, friends, and people [*Sar Boland Hastam*]. It means they can count on me. But God forbid the poor man who loses his *Āberu* or is considered as a man with no *Haysiyat*, then he does not dare to look in the face of his people [*Ruy Nadārad Samt-e Digaran Bebinad*].
>
> (Pashtun man, 30 years old)

Here, several features are implied for the *Āberu* by men: the first is that it includes a self-image or a man's evaluation and consciousness about his own social standing and value amongst other group members and the public. That is to say 'his estimation of his own worth, his claim to pride' and face (Pitt-Rivers, 1966: 21). Second, there is a collective image that is recognised and shared by others about 'positive social value' of the person and acknowledges his claim and right to pride

(Goffman, 1967: 5). Third, *Āberu* and *Haysiyat* can be achieved or lost based on a man's actions and its evaluation by group members and actors associated with him.

The second category of meanings includes symbols that stand for and represent honour. Almost all the participants except for two men considered *Nāmus* to be equal and synonymous to honour. According to their point of view, *Nāmus* predominantly refers to a man's female family members:

> A man's *Nāmus* is his *Izzat* [honour] and *Āberu* [face]. Let me make this clear to you. For me as a man, my wife, mother, sister, daughter and nieces are considered as my *Nāmus*. And these are my *Izzat*. In general, those intimate female family members are considered as a man's *Nāmus* that is highly important in our country.
>
> (Tajik man, 45 years old)

(b) 'Honour' and masculinity: when 'honour' calls for men

In Afghanistan everybody, including women and children, can claim *Izzat* (honour) and *Āberu* (face) qualities. However, there is a close connection between honour and being a 'man' that requires further clarification. First, a man's good image and face depend on his actions and ability to fulfil masculine roles. The majority of the participants described a 'man' as being the head of the family who is in charge of all the associated members and their conduct. This means that the result of any social evaluation for a specific conduct is not only related to the individual family member who performed it, but also includes the male figurehead who assumes the role as head of the household. As a result, a man's *Āberu* and *Izzat* is associated with the deeds of his family members:

> I am a man. A man is responsible of his *Khāna* [home; it refers to the family in this context]. A man has to be the breadwinner of his family and should treat his family and community members well. He should try to help them for the betterment of the society. A man is responsible for earning money to maintain his children and his family's necessities such as food, education and security. He should help and persuade his children, boys and girls, to pursue an education. They should be well mannered. He should not let the children associate with naughty or bad boys. [Smiling] If your son will be a burglar or a drug addict in the future, the people would say, look at this man; he is X's son [*Bacheh-ye Felāni*; refers to the father name]. And of course you will be disgraced [*Be-Ezzat*] by that time.
>
> (Hazara man, 30 years old)

Such a perspective considers men to be responsible for the family's actions and behaviour, which in essence is not unique to the Afghan context. Bourdieu in his work on the Kabyle (1966) describes a man who is known as a shameless and brazen person within his community – people avoid him at all costs because they believe that he is a man without shame and who does not respect people. Once the man damaged the wall of his next-door neighbour. The victim, who was a weaker man, went to the brother of the offender and complained about the damage and sought compensation. When the brother asked why the victim did not use violence and aggression against his guilty brother, the victim stated:

> One must be an *amahbul* [shameless and brazen] to do what Si N [your brother] has done, and I'm not going to make myself ridiculous and be put to shame. . . . If you've an *amahbul* in the family, it's up to you to deal with him first, before others do.
>
> (Bourdieu, 1966: 194)

A second link between honour and masculinity is the strong emphasis on *Nāmus* – female family members as the key bearer of honour in the community and the role of men as the active guardians of *Nāmus*. In this sense, male participants thought that men's principal duty is to maintain the honour of the family:

> I work so hard. I have no education but do my best to find a manual work every day, earn some money and meet the needs of my family. What is all the fuss about? You tell me! It is to preserve my *Nāmus*'s *Āberu* and *Izzat*. I want to keep the face of my family before other people [*Āberu-dāri Kardan*].
>
> (Tajik man, 47 years old)

(c) Maintaining 'honour' at all costs

Participants of the study not only described their sense of honour, but also the significance of preserving honour for them as men. Most of the participants believed that there should be no excuse for a 'real man' to keep the face and honour that is a part of his social existence. They also tied their argument to religious ideology by stating that 'God created men to protect the family and honour' or 'Islam requires men' to protect the family name:

> Indeed the family needs a man and that is why they call him a 'man'. It is very difficult for a woman to defend herself, or the children to protect themselves. So, this is a man who is supposed to protect them. And you are not a man if you don't. A real man should not fear anything, not water nor fire [local metaphor, *Na az Āb Betarsa na az Ātash;* in this context it means that a man should be strong and well prepared at all times], because he is a man. God created man for working, defending his *Izzat* and *Āberu*, defending his *Nāmus* and country. Suppose there is a war – it is the man who should defend the family.
>
> (Hazara man, 51 years old)

Since protecting honour, face and family reputation is a must and is integral to defining manhood, the participants stated that they would be spurred on to take all possible risks and sacrifices to defend their honour. Applying violence was also justified and sometimes considered a 'natural' reaction and a deliberate strategy to avoid dishonour and *Bad Nāmi* (i.e. a bad name). Although the participants rejected violence in a general sense, in many parts of the transcribed interviews, they acknowledged that violence would be applicable when the issue concerned *Izzat* and *Āberu*:

> A man is a man; he is made for difficulties. I personally do not like violence. With violence, everything just gets worse. However, I have to admit that sometimes it is unavoidable. Like, I cannot be careless about my and my family's *Izzat* and *Āberu*. I fought tooth and nail to preserve it. We cannot let people talk behind our family or my daughters. I will react violently then. You know, you must keep your honour, a man without honour is no man at all.
>
> (Pashtun man, 41 years old)

My Nāmus, my Izzat is everything to me

Men's experiences of violence were clearly evident in the transcripts. Abuse and violence had occurred because of 'honour'-based issues, which varied and which took place within different contexts. Based on the men's stories, men occupied different positions – on some occasions, they were perpetrators and sometimes they were victims. On some occasions, they also appeared to be observers or mediators who wanted to end 'honour' disputes amongst other men. However, the findings most commonly focused on the men's experiences as both perpetrators and victims. As other studies have clarified (see e.g. Stanko, 1994; DeKeseredy and Schwartz, 2005), such a view is crucial towards understanding male violence.

Several participants shared their stories of confrontations with other men when they felt that their *Nāmus* or that the honour of female family members were under threat. This occurred when a *Nā-Mahram* – a non-*Mahram*/strange man – attempted to establish a sexual relationship with a female family member, or sexually harassed a woman associated with that participant. In such situations, verbal abuse and physical violence occurred as a response. For two of the participants, verbal fights occurred because a strange man had harassed a female relative, which later turned into a physical fight:

> If I told you that I did not use violence, I would be lying to you. In this society, it is unavoidable sometimes. Believe me. Especially if it concerns your *Nāmus*. My *Nāmus*, my *Izzat* is everything for me and I will do whatever I can to keep it safe. [Smiling] Let me share with you one of my experiences in this regard. One day, my wife, children and I went out shopping. When we reached the shopping mall, I noticed two men were staring at my wife and

> smiling. When they continued their gazing, I could not tolerate this. I ran to them and shouted at them with anger; grabbed one's collar and pushed him away with force. I said 'what is wrong with you, *Bi-nāmus*' [i.e. an insult that refers to a man who does not care about his female family members at all]? We then started punching each other until the surrounding people broke up the fight between us.
>
> (Tajik man, 47 year old)

Sexual insults were also exchanged between the men against one another, and the masculine identity of the man concerned was attacked. In particular, when applied to the settings of arguments and fights, it was intended to provoke and threaten the addressee's sense of male honour and manhood. This finding corresponds with Spierenburg's work that emphasises, in societies with pronounced notions of honour, how a man's reputation 'often depends on physical bravery and forceful response to insults' (Spierenburg, 1998: 2). Frevert (1998: 54–63) also provides further examples of German culture in the nineteenth century, where insults amongst men led to the immediate challenge to a duel and the killing of one of the men who engaged in battle – an example of how men have historically attempted to defend their honour in Europe. In the current study, a young Pashtun man explained the reason behind men's use of sexual insults against each other:

> When two men fight and one uses *Daw-e Nāmusi* [i.e. sexual swear words], he knows that this is the weak point of all men. If a man insults another by saying that 'You're a fool' or 'stupid', that does not affect him a lot. I mean using swear words for a man himself is not that much serious but if that person uses bad words against his intimate female members, then it will affect a man a lot. Why so? Because all men feel responsible for their closest people. *Nāmus* is every man's weak point, I believe. But they use such insults because they all know that it will affect the man who is insulted in a very bad way. This encourages the other side to get involved in a physical fight and does more harm. All men are ready to defend their *Nāmus*, *Izzat*, and *Āberu* and cannot allow anyone to cross the line concerning their *Nāmus*. Keeping and defending honour and *Nāmus* is a crucial duty for all men.
>
> (Pashtun man, 23 years old)

Ten of the participants also discussed that they heard about or witnessed incidents in extreme cases where a man had been killed because his honour was involved:

> I have heard many cases where men have been killed because of *Nang*, *Nāmus* and *Izzat*. I have even witnessed a case personally in Kabul. Once we wanted to go to another city and we were waiting for the inter-city buses. There was a young male bus attendant who was looking for passengers to fill his bus. I do not know why he did it, but he grabbed a young woman's

> hand who was standing close to the bus and invited her onto his bus. In the meantime, the woman's husband witnessed everything and was upset. He was calm to begin with and asked the bus attendant to apologise to his wife for grabbing her hand. When the bus attendant denied he had done anything wrong, the husband got angry. I also sought to mediate between the two along with other men, but to no avail. The argument then became physical. At this point, the husband pulled out a gun and shot the male bus attendant. It was really scary. And we couldn't do a thing.
>
> (Pashtun man, 41 years old)

This example illustrates the impact that 'honour'-based violence has on men, not only as perpetrators but also as victims. Based on this anecdote (and if true), the perpetrator saw a strange male touch his wife and immediately assumed this to be sexual and regarded this as an insult to his masculine 'honour'. He then wanted the bus attendant to express regret at his actions. He did not look for or consider an explanation or the reason behind the attendant's action (in this instance, supposedly to attract commuters onto his bus). The male participant who witnessed the incident did not know why the bus attendant did what he did or whether he wanted to sexually touch the woman concerned. Yet, the perpetrator chose to shoot the victim to avenge the perceived offence to his honour by committing a homicide in public. This is an example of how men can be killed in extreme cases in so-called honour killings in Kabul, if there is even a perception that they have dishonoured another man or that the male victim has dishonoured one of his female family members. In the present example, even a fleeting touch of the hand of a woman can be enough to justify killing a man in the name of honour.

Afghan men as victims of HBA and forced marriages

This part complements the previous discussion by unfolding an invisible feature of men's experiences where they suffer from the impacts of HBA. Within the stories of the participants, all the men faced at least one type of HBA – most frequently psychological abuse. However, while expressing their thoughts, none of the participants applied the term *victim* to their experiences. This is because in most cases, the participants recognised abuse and violence as part of their manly life and therefore thought of it as 'normal'. Moreover, it seemed to go against their sense of manhood to even admit to considering themselves 'victims' because the general perception among the participants was that a 'man is created for difficulties' – he should always be strong, tough and ready to fight. This development ties well with the Fontes's analysis that men are socialised to be self-sufficient, which means that 'they should not require help from others – that is if they are real men. Men are also socialized to be strong, physically and emotionally. This means they should not express physical and emotional pain, sadness, or fear – that is, if they are real men.

Men are also socialized to be the protectors in society, especially of women and children'. Thus, if men discuss their victimisation, society regards them as 'wimps' (Fontes, 2007: 306).

(a) Men, HBA and marriage – the cost I paid for my love

Among the participants, one man shared a story of his love marriage and the abuse that he faced thereafter, due to crossing the lines of accepted traditional norms. When he was a young man, he fell in love with a young girl from the same community. However, the family of girl rejected his offer of marriage because he was from a poor background and was perceived as lower in status. Elder persons in his community attempted to mediate, but this did not work. As a result, the young woman eloped with the young man and they got married. But there were verbal threats and attempts to murder both the man and his wife:

> If I tell you about my own story, then you would know that I paid much because of *Ăberu* – 'honour' – issues. [Laughter] my only fault was that I wanted to live with the one that I loved. I was very young at that time, about 18 years old. We really loved each other. From the outset, nobody knew about our relationship. We would have been in trouble if they had known about our secret love. My wife's family is very rich and well known on the political front. But we did not care about such things and we only wanted to live together. The first time that I asked my father to act as a suitor, he rejected this. It was not very common at that time for a man to tell his family that he has fallen in love with a woman he wants to marry. But I did it. My father told me that the families are not compatible and as he knew of the girl's father, saying that they would not accept the proposal. So, he told me not to do this otherwise we would fall flat on our faces. But I insisted, quite a lot. Anyway, I convinced my father at the end and they went to the girl's home. As was predicted, her father and family refused my proposal and did not listen to the elders who we had asked to intercede on our behalf. There was no way left then. One day, my wife eloped to our house. You know, my father was a great man! When this happened, he really supported us. He invited a Mullah to perform the marriage ceremony and we became *Mahram* (lawfully married/related). But believe me, from that same day my fears and anxiety started. My father, brother and uncle were guarding outside the home to prevent any attack from my wife's family. In the community, all the people were talking about our marriage. My wife stayed at home all the time, and I was also accompanied by my brother whenever I went outside. It was impossible to last like that. Since it was not safe, my father decided to move to another location which was far from the

> community. There has not been any social contact between my wife and her family since that time, but there have been two major physical attacks that we have been subjected to. One of them occurred several years after we had left; it was at the time that my wife's father had passed away. When we heard the news, my wife was very upset. She had not met her family at all since we married. So, I thought, as a long time had passed, it would be possible to attend the funeral ceremony. And in this way, my wife would feel better and our problems would be resolved. We attended, but we left in a hurry! Do you know why? Because the older brother wanted to attack me and my wife with a knife. There was also another time that the same brother found my house and since I was not home, he attacked my 5-year-old son and kicked his leg and left when the neighbours arrived. You know, for most of my family life, I have always been worried and stressed about my family's safety. For a long time, I could not let them stay at home alone or even pass through our old neighbourhood.
>
> (Hazara man, 48 years old)

This case is an example of how a man was not only a victim of HBA but also a potential victim of a so-called honour killing. Although his wife was also a target (as women are often the targets of such killings), in this case, it would seem that the brother was more intent on harming the man than his sister for marrying against the family's wishes. The long-lasting impact, stress, fear and anxiety on the male victim is clear to see. However, such a case is not unique to the Afghanistan context. As Cooney (2019) explains, traditional families strongly oppose love marriages and prefer to make marriage decisions collectively. As a result, couples who wish to be together elope at their own risk of being killed if their location and identities are ever discovered. Elopment for the sake of a love marriage may result in both the woman and the man being hunted down and killed, and sometimes it is just the man who is murdered. Nafisa Shah in her research on HBA in Southern Pakistan mentions a number of cases involving love-marriages where men have been murdered for marrying a girl whose family disapproved (Shah, 2016).

(b) Cousin marriages – it was arranged when I was a child

In Afghan culture 'cousin marriage' is a common method of forced marriage, where two people are forced against their will to enter into marriage for the sake of familial honour. According to this practice, families may arrange and in some cases force their sons and daughters to marry their cousins in order to keep with endogamy, cultural traditions and to keep property directly within the family (Berrenberg, 2003). Honour plays a significant role in cousin marriages and Bourdieu in his work on the 'sense of honour' explains that 'the need to safeguard blood purity and keep the family honour intact is the reason most frequently given to justify marriage with the parallel cousin' (1979: 127). One of the participants discussed his experiences related to (forced) cousin marriage, though he considered himself fortunate enough to be able to cancel the arrangement:

> I grew up with a sense of hate regarding my (female) cousin [his father's brother's daughter]. I think she disliked me too. The reason was simple. Everybody was saying that we are cousins and we belong to each other! [Sighing] In fact, it was my father who proposed this to his brother when she was born. He happily acknowledged it. So, we were supposed to get married. We call this *Lafz Dadan* [suiting a girl from her family and make it publicly known when they accept it]. The funny thing is that this all happened in our childhood when we did not even know what marriage meant. Anyway, the pressure on me got more and more intense when I reached 17 or 18 years old. Every day I felt it more, and I could not cope with it. I did not want her at all. You know, when you do not want someone, you should not be forced to marry her. So, I made my choice and at the beginning made excuses that we did not suit each other. But they were saying, 'What is wrong with you? You will be fine when you get together.' So, afraid of my future, I was so stressed that I really wanted to run away. Luckily, I found an opportunity when I went to university. I deliberately moved to another city. Then I created a rumor that I was going to get married there. My father threatened me a lot that he would not forgive me if I refused to marry his niece. However, I did not let them decide on my behalf. I still faced all the pressures and I heard all the blaming. My relatives talked behind my back and in such a way that it ruined my family and my (female) cousin's family because I was supposed to be her husband. I am telling you this, this is not fair. My uncle cut the relationship with me and my family because of this. Even after his daughter got married to someone else, they still don't talk to us.
>
> (Tajik man, 25 years old)

According to Emadi (2005: 172), it is common in Afghanistan (and in other traditional communities) that when two families agree for their children to marry, they are obligated to honour the agreement in all cases. In the case of the young man just mentioned, honour was strongly linked to the process of forcing him to accept the marriage. It was arranged during his childhood and the family and community were expecting him to comply with that promise made on his behalf. When he refused the marriage in his adulthood, he was stigmatised and placed under pressure to accept the marriage proposal. The case can be considered to be an example of early boy child marriage, as the marriage agreement was made when he was very young (Gastón et al., 2019: 6). His experience adds further light to the invisbility that exists amongst young boys all over the world who are potential victims of child marriage at an early age.

(c) Do not disgrace me!

Finally, two of the participants recalled their exposure to violence and physical abuse during their childhood and adolescence. They explained that they were required to be a 'good son' amongst their kin and community members. This was fulfilled when they showed politeness and respect towards their elders and obeyed their commands. A Pashtun man explained his childhood and how he had faced physical and psychological abuse by his father because he had crossed the lines of hospitality rules:

> I do not know if you consider this as violence or not, but this story is imprinted in my mind. I was about ten or eleven years old and I was the oldest son. We had many guests coming to our home. In our culture, as you know, it is very important to take care of your guests. Anyway, as the oldest son, I had to always be there to serve the guests. Once, I was playing outside with the other boys and forgot to come home early, clean and bring lunch for the guests. When I came home, the tablecloth had already been spread and the food had been already served by my father. I immediately understood that I had made a big mistake – I could see the anger on my father's face [Laughter]. When the guests left, my father called me. He just slapped me on the face hard and shouted at me, not to ever forget to respect our guests. 'You disgraced me in front of our relatives [*Bi- Āberu Kardi*]. Do not do that ever again!' I cried at that time and I was angry.
>
> (Pashtun man, 41 years old)

This quote demonstrates the normalisation of violence for the male interviewee as he was not sure whether such an incident could be considered violence, abuse or not. It also highlights the significance of the socialisation process through which he was exposed to aggression and physical violence to learn about the significance of honour and *Āberu* – making sure that one's face or appearance is respectable in front of others. As a young man in Afghan culture, he was a victim of 'honour'-based domestic abuse, all because he was playing outside and was perceived by his father to have disrespected his elders and guests by not serving them or conforming to socially-accepted rules of behaviour.

Conclusion

The issue of HBA and male victims has been sidelined within the existing academic literature and amongst the activism against gender-based violence in Afghanistan. This needs to be unfolded. Men's different positions regarding HBA are mainly overshadowed by discussions of men as predominantly perpetrators of so-called honour killings of women, while HBA can also profoundly affect men's lives as victims (Kimmel, 2001). Therefore, it is crucial from the author's perspective to examine Afghan men's stories and to explore their experiences of victimisation. This chapter has helped to reveal how the 'honour' code in Afghanistan can negatively impact men and not just women. As the current study has highlighted, men tend to remain silent when they are abused. This can be due to their misrecognition of HBA, which they may perceive as 'normal' and as part of their everyday life. Their silence may also be caused by their desire to conform to notions of what it is to be a 'real man' and not to be viewed as weak or vulnerable. HBA against men was justified by the necessity to maintain individual and collective face and honour, as well as protecting female family members (*Nāmus*). Love marriages that were met with disapproval, forced cousin marriages and early-boy child marriage were just some of the harmful practices that the male participants had experienced in the name of honour. These male victims carried the enduring consequences of their experiences, psychologically and socially, living in fear, stress, anxiety and in isolation. HBA against men needs to be comprehensively recognised and practically addressed in social policies and programs. Awareness-raising through formal and informal education in Afghanistan that focuses on HBA and its consequences for men (and not just women) need to be developed. The author's position is that unless we uncover the experiences of male victims of HBA, we cannot truly understand the nature of HBA and thereby develop strategies to address such practices. All victims of HBA need to be recognised and validated – laws, social policies and strategies need to be developed which support both female and male victims of HBA and forced marriages in Afghanistan and in other countries too.

Notes

1 Taliban or Taleban is an Islamic fundamentalist group comprised of *Madrasa* students, *Mullahs* Pashtun tribesmen and some of the ex-*Mujahidin* held the power over three quarters of Afghanistan from 1996 until 2001 when the U.S. invasion overthrew the regime. Since then, the military organization is waging insurgent war within the country. They also impose their extremist interpretation of Shari'a-Islamic law in the territories they control and reportedly execute, stone, or lash women and men because of alleged adultery.

2 Based on Islam, *nafaqah* is a man's responsibility to fulfill all the needs of the wife and the children including housing, food, medical care, clothing, and education. While Nafaqa is a woman's right, it is raised as a man's duty.

3 Pashto and Dari (Afghan Persian) are the official languages in Afghanistan and are very rich in providing multiple words that relate to the concept of 'honour', demonstrating the centrality of the code within Afghan culture. Terms like *Izzat* (honour), *Āberu*, *Haysiyat* (face), *Qadr va Ehterām* (respect), *E'tebār* (prestige), *Šaraf*, *Nang* (honour), *Nām* (name), *Šohrat* (fame and reputation), *Manzelat* (status) and *Qorur* (pride) are just some of the examples that are almost synonymous and mostly translated as *honour* in English. However, the connotations of the mentioned terms vary and need to be understood from the perspective of the social actors to whom they apply within a cultural-specific context (Casimir and Schnegg, 2002), as well as the way that they are constructed within social interactions.

Bibliography

Abirafeh, L. (2009) *Gender and International Aid in Afghanistan: The Politics and Effects of Intervention*. Jefferson, NC: McFarland & Co.

Abou-Zeid, A. (1966) 'Honour and Shame among the Bedouins of Egypt', in Peristiany, J. G. (ed.) *Honour and Shame: The Values of Mediterranean Society*. Chicago: The University of Chicago Press, pp. 243–259.

Afghanistan Independent Human Rights Commission (AIHRC) (2013) *National Inquiry Report on Factors and Causes of Rape and Honor Killing in Afghanistan*. Kabul. Available at: www.aihrc.org.af/media/files/PDF/Natioan%20Inquiry%20final%20-%20for%20meru.pdf (Accessed: 28 October 2018).

Afghanistan Independent Human Rights Commission (AIHRC) (2018) *Summary of the Report on Violence against Women: The Causes, Context, and Situation of Violence against Women in Afghanistan: Fiscal Year 1396 [21 March 2017–20 March 2018]*. Kabul. Available at: www.aihrc.org.af/media/files/Research%20Reports/Summerry%20report-VAW-2017.pdf (Accessed: 20 December 2018).

Azarbaijani-Moghaddam, S. (2009) 'Manly Honor and the Gendered Male in Afghanistan', in *Viewpoints Special Edition: Afghanistan 1979–2009: In the Grip of Conflict*. Washington, DC: The Middle East Institute, pp. 184–187.

Baldry, A. C., Pagliaro, S. and Porcaro, C. (2013) 'The Rule of Law at Time of Masculine Honor: Afghan Police Attitudes and Intimate Partner Violence', *Group Processes & Intergroup Relations*, 16(3), pp. 363–374.

Barnes, C. D., Brown, R. P. and Tamborski, M. (2012) 'Living Dangerously: Culture of Honor, Risk-Taking, and the Nonrandomness of "Accidental" Deaths', *Social Psychological and Personality Science*, 3(1), pp. 100–107.

Begikhani, N., Gill, A. K. and Hague, G. (2015) *Honour-Based Violence Experiences and Counter-Strategies in Iraqi Kurdistan and the UK Kurdish Diaspora*. London & New York: Routledge Taylor & Francis Group.

Benson, D. and Archer, J. (2002) 'An Ethnographic Study of Sources of Conflict between Young Men in the Context of the Night Out', *Psychology, Evolution & Gender*, 4(1), pp. 3–30.

Berrenberg, J. (2003) 'Beyond Kinship Algebra: Values and the Riddle of Pashtun Marriage Structure', *Zeitschrift für Ethnologie*, 128(2), pp. 269–292.

Bezhan, F. and Bashir, M. (2017) 'Young Afghan Lovers Lynched by Armed Mob in Latest Horrific "'Honor" Killing', *RadioFreeEurope, RadioLiberty*, 16 February. Available at: www.rferl.org/a/afhanistan-honor-killing-fateha-lynched/28314022.html (Accessed: 02 October 2018).

Bottorff, J. L. (2004) 'Observation, Types Of', in Lewis-Beck, M. S., Bryman, A. and Liao, T. F. (eds.) *The Sage Encyclopedia of Social Science Research Methods*. Thousand Oaks, CA: Sage Publications.

Bourdieu, P. (1966) 'The Sentiment of Honour in Kabyle Society', in Peristiany, J. G. (ed.) *Honour and Shame: The Values of Mediterranean Society*. Chicago: The University of Chicago Press, pp. 191–241.

Bourdieu, P. (1979) *Algeria 1960: The Disenchantment of the World, the Sense of Honour, the Kabyle House or the World Reversed: Studies in Modern Capitalism*. Translated by: Nice, R. Cambridge: Cambridge University Press.

Brown, R. P. and Osterman, L. L. (2012) 'Culture of Honor, Violence, and Homicide', in Shackelford, T. K. and Weekes-Shackelford, V. A. (eds.) *The Oxford*

Handbook of Evolutionary Perspectives on Violence, Homicide, and War Oxford Library of Psychology. Oxford: Oxford University Press, pp. 218–232.

Casimir, M. J. and Jung, S. (2009) '"Honor and Dishonor": Connotations of a Socio-Symbolic Category in Cross-Cultural Perspective', in Röttger-Rössler, B. and Markowitsch, H. J. (eds.) *Emotions as Bio-cultural Processes.* New York: Springer, pp. 229–280.

Casimir, M. J. and Schnegg, M. (2002) 'Shame across Cultures: The Evolution, Ontogeny and Function of a "Moral Emotion"', in Schölmerich, A., Keller, H. and Poortinga, Y. H. (eds.) *Between Culture and Biology: Perspectives on Ontogenetic Development Cambridge Studies in Cognitive and Perceptual Development.* Cambridge: Cambridge University Press, pp. 270–300.

Chesler, P. (2010) *Worldwide Trends in Honor Killings.* Middle East Quarterly. Available at: www.meforum.org/2646/worldwide-trends-in-honor-killings) (Accessed: 01 June 2019).

Cohen, D. (2007) 'Culture of Honor', in Baumeister, R. F. and Vohs, K. D. (eds.) *Encyclopedia of Social Psychology.* Thousand Oaks: Sage Publications.

Cohen, D., Nisbett, R. E., Bowdle, B. F. and Schwarz, N. (1996) 'Insult, Aggression, and the Southern Culture of Honor: An "Experimental Ethnography"', *Journal of Personality and Social Psychology*, 70(5), pp. 945–960.

Connell, R. W. (2000) 'Arms and the Man: Using the New Research on Masculinity to Understand Violence and Promote Peace in the Contemporary World', in Breines, I., Connell, R. and Eide, I. (eds.) *Male Roles, Masculinities and Violence: A Culture of Peace Perspective: Vol. Cultures of Peace Series.* Vendôme: UNESCO, pp. 21–33.

Connell, R. W. (2001) 'Masculinities and Men's Health', in Baron, B. and Kotthoff, H. (eds.) *Gender in Interaction: Perspectives on Femininity and Masculinity in Ethnography and Discourse.* Amsterdam & Philadelphia: John Benjamins Publishing Company, pp. 139–152.

Connell, R. W. (2006) 'Understanding Men: Gender Sociology and the New International Research on Masculinities', in Skelton, C., Francis, B. and Smulyan, L. (eds.) *The SAGE Handbook of Gender and Education.* London: Sage Publications, pp. 18–31.

Connell, R. W. and Lecture, C. (2002) 'Understanding Men: Gender Sociology and the New International Research on Masculinities', *Social Thought & Research*, 24(1&2), pp. 13–31.

Cook, P. W. (2009) *Abused Men: The Hidden Side of Domestic Violence.* Londres: Praeger.

Cooney, M. (2019) *Execution by Family: A Theory of Honor Violence: Routledge Studies in Crime and Society.* London & New York: Routledge & Taylor & Francis Group.

DeKeseredy, W. S. and Schwartz, M. D. (2005) 'Masculinities and Interpersonal Violence', in Kimmel, M. S., Hearn, J. and Connell, R. W. (eds.) *Handbook of Studies on Men & Masculinities.* Thousand Oaks, CA: Sage Publications, pp. 353–366.

Dupree, N. H. (1998) 'Etiquette in Afghanistan', in Yarshater, E. (ed.) *Encyclopedia Iranica.* New York: Bibliotheca Persica Press. Available at: www.afghandata.org:8080/xmlui/bitstream/handle/azu/3392/azu_acku_pamphlet_gt150_d87_1998_w.pdf?sequence=1&isAllowed=y (Accessed: 20 December 2017).

Dupree, N. H. (2004) 'The Family during Crisis in Afghanistan', *Journal of Comparative Family Studies*, 35(2), pp. 311–331.

Echavez, C. R., Mosawi, S. M. and Pilongo, L. W. R. (2016) *The Other Side of Gender Inequality: Men and Masculinities in Afghanistan*. Kabul: Afghanistan Research and Evaluation Unit.

Eickelman, D. F. (1981) *The Middle East an Anthropological Approach*. Englewood Cliffs: Prentice-Hall.

Emadi, H. (2002) *Repression, Resistance, and Women in Afghanistan*. Westport, CT: Praeger.

Emadi, H. (2005) *Culture and Customs of Afghanistan*. Westport & London: Greenwood Press.

Fontes, D. L. (2007) 'Male Victims of Domestic Violence', in Hamel, J. and Nicholls, T. L. (eds.) *Family Interventions in Domestic Violence: A Handbook of Gender-Inclusive Theory and Treatment*. New York: Springer Publishing Company, pp. 303–318.

Frevert, U. (1998) 'The Taming of the Noble Ruffian: Male Violence and Dueling in Early Modern and Modern Germany', in Spierenburg, P. (ed.) *Men and Violence Gender, Honor, and Rituals in Modern Europe and America*. Columbus: Ohio State University Press, pp. 37–63.

Gastón, C. M., Misunas, C. and Cappa, C. (2019) 'Child Marriage among Boys: A Global Overview of Available Data', *Vulnerable Children and Youth Studies*, 14(3), pp. 219–228.

Gereš, N., Heilman, B., Hashimi, S. I., Kakar, R., Kelberg, M., Hakobyan, L., El Feki, S. and Barker, G. (2018) *Reflections on Gender, Patriarchy, and Peace: Results from the International Men and Gender Equality Survey (IMAGES) in Afghanistan*. Washington, DC: Promundo-US, UN Women, and Global Affairs Canada. Available at: https://promundoglobal.org/wp-content/uploads/2019/01/IMAGES-Afghanistan-WEB.pdf (Accessed: 10 January 2019).

Gilani, S. (2008) 'Reconstituting Manhood: Examining Post-Conflict Remasculinisation and Its Effects on Women and Women's Rights in Afghanistan', *In-Spire: Journal of Law, Politics and Societies*, 3(2), pp. 53–71.

Gill, A. (2011) 'Reconfiguring "Honour"-Based Violence as a Form of Gendered Violence', in Idriss, M. M. and Abbas, T. (eds.) *Honour, Violence, Women and Islam*. New York: Routledge, pp. 218–231.

Gilmore, D. D. (1990) *Manhood in the Making: Cultural Concepts of Masculinity*. New Haven, CT: Yale University Press.

Goffman, E. (1967) *Interaction Ritual: Essays in Face to Face Behavior*. New York: Pantheon Books.

Hamel, J. (2005) *Gender Inclusive Treatment of Intimate Partner Abuse: A Comprehensive Approach: Springer Series on Family Violence*. New York, NY: Springer Publishing Company.

Holy, L. (1989) *Kinship, Honour and Solidarity: Cousin Marriage in the Middle East: Themes in Social Anthropology*. Manchester: Manchester University Press.

Home Affairs Committee House of Commons (2008) *Domestic Violence, Forced Marriage and "Honour"-Based Violence: Sixth Report of Session 2007–08*, HC 263-I. London. Available at: https://publications.parliament.uk/pa/cm200708/cmselect/cmhaff/263/263i.pdf.

Kandiyoti, D. (2005) *The Politics of Gender and Reconstruction in Afghanistan* [Occasional Paper], Switzerland: United Nations Research Institute for Social Development (UNRISD)OPGP 4). Available at: www.unrisd.org/80256B3C005BCCF9/

(httpPublications)/3050BE40DA5B871CC125704400534A7A?OpenDocument# (Accessed: 15 March 2014).

Karimi, J. (2019) 'Police: Taliban Shotgunned a [Young] Girl and Boy in Ghor Province', *Pajhwok Afghan News*, 26 May. Available at: https://bit.ly/2MCw6mW (Accessed: 26 May 2019).

Kaufman, M. (2007) 'The Construction of Masculinity and the Triad of Men's Violence', in O'Toole, L. L., Schiffman, J. R. and Edwards, M. L. K. (eds.) *Gender Violence: Interdisciplinary Perspectives*. 2nd ed. New York: New York University Press, pp. 33–55.

Kimmel, M. S. (2001) *Male Victims of Domestic Violence: A Substantive and Methodological Research Review*, A Report to the Equality Committee of the Department of Education and Science. Available at: https://vawnet.org/sites/default/files/assets/files/2016-10/GenderSymmetry.pdf (Accessed: 04 August 2018).

Leverenz, D. 2007. 'Honour', in Flood, M., Gardiner, J. K., Pease, B. and Pringle, K. (eds.) *International Encyclopedia of Men and Masculinities*. London & New York: Routledge.

Lien, M. I. and Lorentzen, J. (2019) *Men's Experiences of Violence in Intimate Relationships: Palgrave Studies in Victims and Victimology*. Cham: Palgrave Macmillan.

Moghadam, V. M. (1992) 'Development and Patriarchy: The Middle East and North Africa in Economic and Demographic Transition', in *UNU/WIDER Conference on Trajectories of Patriarchy and Development*. Helsinki: World Institute for Development Economics Research of the United Nations University. Available at: http://citeseerx.ist.psu.edu/viewdoc/download;jsessionid=532607A0558AD95E09A4113FF487E509?doi=10.1.1.636.3710&rep=rep1&type=pdf (Accessed: 10 October 2018).

Moghadam, V. M. (2002) 'Patriarchy, the Taleban, and Politics of Public Space in Afghanistan', *Women's Studies International Forum*, 25(1), pp. 19–31.

Mojab, S. (2005) 'Honor: Iran and Afghanistan', in Joseph, S. (ed.) *Encyclopedia of Women and Islamic Cultures*. Brill: Leiden-Boston.

Möller-Leimkühler, A. M. (2018) 'Why Is Terrorism a Man's Business?', *CNS Spectrums*, 23(2), pp. 119–128.

Myrttinen, H. (2018) *Navigating Norms and Insecurity: Men, Masculinities, Conflict and Peacebuilding in Afghanistan: International Alert & PTRO*. Available at: www.international-alert.org/sites/default/files/Afghanistan_MasculinitiesConflictPeacebuilding_EN_2018.pdf (Accessed: 11 January 2019).

Nader, Z. and Nordland, R. (2017) 'Mob Kills Eloped Lovers after Storming Afghan Police Station', *The New York Times*, 13 February. Available at: www.nytimes.com/2017/02/13/world/asia/nuristan-province-afghanistan-honor-killings.html (Accessed: 02 October 2019).

Newburn, T. and Stanko, E. A. (2002) 'When Men Are Victims: The Failure of Victimology', in Jewkes, Y. and Letherby, G. (eds.) *Criminology: A Reader*. London: Sage Publications, pp. 262–274.

Olesen, A. (1995) *Islam and Politics in Afghanistan*. Wiltshire: Curzon Press.

Patton, M. Q. (2015) *Qualitative Research & Evaluation Methods: Integrating Theory and Practice*. 4th ed. Los Angeles: Sage Publications.

Pitt-Rivers, J. (1966) 'Honour and Social Status', in Peristiany, J. G. (ed.) *Honour and Shame: The Values of Mediterranean Society*. Chicago: The University of Chicago Press, pp. 19–77.

Polk, K. (1994) 'Masculinity, Honour and Confrontational Homicide', in Newburn, T. and Stanko, E. A. (eds.) *Just Boys Doing Business? Men, Masculinities and Crime.* London & New York: Routledge, pp. 166–188.

Polk, K. (2003) 'Masculinities, Femininities and Homicide: Competing Explanations for Male Violence', in Schwartz, M. and Hatty, S. E. (eds.) *Controversies in Critical Criminology.* Oxon & New York: Routledge, pp. 133–145.

Poulton, R. E. (2003) 'Honour, Guns and Jihad: Improving Childhood and Communications in Afghanistan Would Promote Peace', *Conflict, Security & Development*, 3(3), pp. 407–416.

Pstrusińska, J. (2017) 'Content of Paštunwali: The Pashtun Code of Conduct', *Rocznik Orientalistyczny, T. LXX*, 1, pp. 5–19.

Roberts, K. A., Campbell, G. and Lloyd, G. (2014) *Honor-Based Violence: Policing and Prevention: Advances in Police Theory and Practice Series.* Boca Raton: CRC Press.

Schmeidl, S. (2009) 'The "Undoing of Gender Inequalities" in Traditional Societies: The Example of Post-Conflict Afghanistan', in Christine, E. and Seifer, R. (eds.) *Gender Dynamics and Post-Conflict Reconstruction.* Frankfurt am Main: Peter Lang GmbH, Internationaler Verlag der Wissenschaften, pp. 71–92.

Shah, N. (2016) *Honour and Violence: Gender, Power and Law in Southern Pakistan.* New directions in anthropology, 39. Oxford: Berghahn Books Ltd.

Spierenburg, P. (1998) 'Masculinity, Violence, and Honor: An Introduction', in *Men and Violence: Gender, Honor, and Rituals in Modern Europe and America the History of Crime and Criminal Justice Series.* Columbus: Ohio State University Press, pp. 1–29.

Stanko, E. A. (1994) 'Challenging the Problem of Men's Individual Violence', in Newburn, T. and Stanko, E. A. (eds.) *Just Boys Doing Business? Men, Masculinities and Crime.* London & New York: Routledge, pp. 32–45.

Stanko, E. A. and Hobdell, K. (1993) 'Assault on Men: Masculinity and Male Victimization', *The British Journal of Criminology*, 33(3), pp. 400–415.

UN Assistance Mission in Afghanistan (UNAMA) and Office of the United Nations High Commissioner for Human Rights (OHCHR) (2018) *Injustice and Impunity: Mediation of Criminal Offences of Violence against Women.* Kabul. Available at: https://unama.unmissions.org/sites/default/files/unama_ohchr_evaw_report_2018_injustice_and_impunity_29_may_2018.pdf (Accessed: 23 December 2018).

United Nations Assistance Mission in Afghanistan (UNAMA) and Office of the United Nations High Commissioner for Human Rights (OHCHR) (2010) *Harmful Traditional Practices and Implementation of the Law on Elimination of Violence against Women in Afghanistan.* Kabul. Available at: https://unama.unmissions.org/sites/default/files/harmful_traditional_practices_english.pdf (Accessed: 06 November 2018).

Westmarland, N. (2015) *Violence against Women: Criminological Perspectives on Men's Violences.* London & New York: Routledge.

Wilson, M. and Daly, M. (1985) 'Competitiveness, Risk Taking, and Violence: The Young Male Syndrome', *Ethology and Sociobiology*, 6(1), pp. 59–73.

Wright, H. and Welsh, P. (2014) *Masculinities, Conflict and Peacebuilding: Perspectives on Men through a Gender Lens.* London: Saferworld. Available at: https://bit.ly/2Ku4DSv (Accessed: 01 June 2019).

Zarifi, Y. (2019) 'Three Men Killed, Girl Injured for Eloping in Nuristan', *Pajhwok Afghan News*, 12 May. Available at: www.pajhwok.com/en/2019/05/12/3-men-killed-girl-injured-eloping-nuristan (Accessed: 13 May 2019).

Chapter 9

The so-called honour killings of men by men in Turkey

Bingül Durbaş

Introduction

In the past two decades, there has been an increasing amount of interest in the issue of Honour-Based Abuse[1] (HBA) in the international arena, from the media, Parliaments, women's rights organisations, international organisations and academics. In line with this international attention, various reports have offered cultural explanations for these crimes and perceive and define HBA as cultural, stemming from the cultural traditions and religion of internal minority groups, and in some cases, as a way of stigmatising these communities (Korteweg and Yurdakul, 2010). On the other hand, as 'honour' crimes are committed predominantly against women and girls, a wide range of feminist literature in academia has extensively examined and debated such violence as gender-based. Concepts of patriarchy, gender and sexuality are predominantly used to illustrate the gendered nature of the violence committed against women and girls in the name of 'honour'. However, far too little attention has been paid to HBA committed against men – men can also be the victims of honour crimes. This chapter dismisses the cultural-essentialist approach to honour crimes and instead, it locates HBA as a particular manifestation of universal heteronormative, heterosexual, patriarchal gender-based violence, which is rooted in hegemonic masculinity; this itself is based on the subordination of women and subordinated masculinities. This chapter also focuses on Turkey's legal responses to so-called honour killings. The purpose of this chapter is to explore the legal treatment of so-called honour killings that have been perpetrated by men in Turkey in relation to male victims. In particular, it examines the notion of provocation in Criminal High Court cases and the killing of men committed by other men, analysed from a feminist perspective to show the way in which the gendered approaches of the judges towards the their legal judgments of honour killings. My understanding of the term *gender* follows Connell's interpretation, which relates to 'a social practice' that 'responds to situations and is generated within definite structures to social relations' (Connell, 2005: 71–72). *Hegemonic masculinity* is 'the configuration of gender practice which embodies the currently accepted answer to the problem of the legitimacy of patriarchy which guarantees (or is taken to guarantee) the dominant position of men and the subordination of women' (Connell, 2005: 77) and the existence of subordinated masculinities (Connell, 1987: 183). These perceptions indicate that while power is gendered and women are subordinated by patriarchy, within patriarchy itself, hegemonic masculinity can exercise power over other men, demonstrating subordinated masculinities that are attributed to intersectional and structural inequalities of gender, sexual orientation, class, ethnicity and race.

Honour-based abuse/violence as gender-based violence

The high profile honour killings of women and girls committed by minority ethnic groups in the West (e.g. the murder of Hatun Sürücü in Germany; of Surjit Athwal, Rukhsana Naz, Heshu Yones, Banaz Mahmod, Tülay Gören and Shafilea Ahmed in Britain; of Fadime Şahindal in Sweden; of Aqsa Parvez and Amandeep Atwal in Canada; and of Kezban Vural in the Netherlands) drew enormous media attention and HBA has been discussed in policy debates by governments, particularly in the immigrant-receiving countries of Western Europe and North America. In line with this attention, numerous studies have considered HBA in terms of cultural/religious explanations as the root causes of these crimes (Hirsi Ali, 2007; Wikan, 2008; Chesler, 2010). Framing HBA in relation to cultural tradition ignores the main and most important point, the gender aspect, and disregards the fact that HBA is neither unique to certain minority, ethnic or immigrant communities, nor to the Muslim world, but also occurs in societies with other majority groups (Idriss and Abbas, 2010). This perspective also implies the increased stigmatisation of minority communities and the ethnicisation of such crimes by portraying the cultures of 'the other' as backward, barbaric and dysfunctional; it directs the focus of violence as contrasting with 'the superiority of a concatenation of cultural values associated with liberalism, autonomy, individualism and sexual freedom' (Abu-Lughod, 2011: 36). This approach has also resulted in exclusionary and anti-immigrant policies in Muslim-immigrant receiving countries (Korteweg and Yurdakul, 2010: 3), which can, in turn, increase gender-based violence in all communities. Dicle Koğacıoğlu (2004) drew attention to an important implication of these conceptualisations. She questioned such framings and their relationship to the role of state institutions in perpetuating HBA by reminding us that these crimes occur despite modern nation-state institutions responsible for preventing violence, providing protection and pursuing prosecutions. She argued that reducing these crimes to being an issue within certain cultures and traditions enables state institutions, which see themselves as 'modern and enlightened', to abandon their responsibilities by blaming the internal cultures and traditions of others as being 'native, timeless, unchanging' and being the cause of such crimes (Koğacıoğlu, 2004: 120).

However, a great deal of the existing feminist research into HBA and violence has approached the issue as gender-based violence (Sev'er and Yurdakul,

2001; Mojab and Abdo, 2004; Pervizat, 2005; Welchman and Hossain, 2005; Gill, 2006; Reddy 2008; Ertürk, 2009; Birdal, 2010; Yıldız Tahincioğlu, 2011; Begikhani et al., 2015). In general, this approach (partly or completely) dismisses cultural explanations (at least the essentialist cultural explanations) as a means of understanding these crimes by focusing only on the gender dimension, and instead locates them within the wider spectrum of violence against women and girls (VAWG). Some of this literature has framed such crimes explicitly as particular manifestations of universal patriarchal gender violence (Mojab and Abdo, 2004; Welchman and Hossain, 2005; Ertürk, 2009). From this perspective, the discrimination against and the subordination of women in different societies across cultures is established through oppressive gender relations, which are deeply patriarchal, one of the most common features in societies throughout the world. Patriarchy, the exercise of gender power, exists by manipulating a range of social formations such as culture, religion, the economy and language. Social values, state institutions and legislation also have a role in perpetuating patriarchal gender relations (Mojab and Abdo, 2004: 3). This system of male domination, which is seen as beneficial by some social groups, is maintained through the use and threat of violence. This system, where it is used to gain and maintain control over women, has different particularities and presentations in different contexts. HBA is one of the particularities in the context of heterosexual patriarchal gender regimes (Ertürk, 2009). In this chapter, HBA is approached as a particular manifestation of universal heteronormative, heterosexual, patriarchal gender violence built on hegemonic masculinities through the subordination of women and subordinated masculinities.

With regards to the concept of honour, it has been examined in a considerable amount of literature across different disciplines in the field of social science, in various geographical areas within anthropological, historical and sociological frameworks (Peristiany, 1966; Schneider, 1971; Ortner, 1978; Delaney, 1987; Gilmore, 1987). Overall, these studies identify various meanings within the concept of honour, while the term is commonly used across all cultures to denote virtue and integrity in an individual's character. The concept of honour associated with HBA, however, relates to an individual male and collected male dominated prestige, social status and reputation in society. The concept of honour, in this case, is generally conceptualised in relation to women's sexuality. It is often expressed in terms of men's ability to control female family members, their lives, bodies and sexual autonomies, associated with their purity and chastity, before, during, and after marriage. As specific comprehensions of masculinity are rooted in the perceptions of female virginity and chastity, it is assigned different meanings in different communities, but is manifested through patriarchal control over women and girls and communicated via the concepts of honour and shame (Shalhoub-Kevorkian, 2005: 1190). The concept of honour is used in combination with the term *shame* to apply to anything perceived as challenging the notion of purity in order to regulate gender relations, which are organised hierarchically, based on female dependency and male authority, through violence and the threat of violence. Any perceived improper acts or behaviour by women and girls may thus trigger violence. The term abuse is used to cover both 'verbal abuse and improper treatment' (Faqir, 2001: 65) and violence such as acts that can lead to actual murder, such as threats of or actual violence (Shalhoub-Kevorkian, 2003: 581), as well as permanent control, discipline and scrutiny of their actions, decisions and choices about their lifestyle, of their bodies and sexuality during their life cycle (Sen, 2005). In these cases, the victims of HBA are mainly women and girls.

So-called honour killings are committed predominantly by family members of the female victims, including blood relatives such as brothers, fathers, male cousins and nephews, but also by husbands and ex-husbands. Although these crimes are committed predominantly against females, in some cases, men can also become victims of these crimes. In some cases, more than one perpetrator commits the crime. Neither are men the only perpetrators of honour crimes – in some cases, women also collude, sometimes by acting as instigators, sometimes as co-perpetrators and sometimes as the sole perpetrator of HBA, including actual killings (Sen, 2005; Payton, 2010; Eldén, 2010; Durbaş, 2015; Aplin, 2017; Bates, 2018; Doğan, 2018) as a response to the patriarchal bargains in line with the conventional gender norms of the male dominated collectivities (Kandiyoti, 1988). Furthermore, local communities have a role in sanctioning/perpetuating such crimes by monitoring and reporting the sexual behaviour of members of the community, to make sure that they are in line with the accepted gender norms (Baker et al., 1999).

Male victims of HBA – issues of masculinity

As pointed previously, not all honour crimes are against women; men can be the victims of these crimes (see further discussion of this in Idriss, in this collection). The concept of honour refers to socially accepted and defined gender roles (Sen, 2005: 48) in conjunction with the concept of masculinity, which is enacted through gender domination. If a man is felt to transgress the honour boundaries of another man in some way, for instance by insulting one of his women folk – which reflects his ability to control her, and hence his honour – then he may be the victim of an honour crime, possibly together with the woman in question. A man's ability to comply with the responsibilities that society demands is mainly determined by society's expectations and preferences regarding women and girls' behaviour within their families in patriarchal societies. This is evaluated by the community in relation to a man's dedication to live and act in an exemplary fashion, in accordance with the requirements of an 'honourable' man, in society's terms. Failure could see the community framing him as 'inadequate' and incapable of guarding the honour of the family (Lindisfarne, 1994: 85–87). This triggers a hegemonic masculinity struggle between men over the patriarchal control of women's bodies, lives and sexuality. Men may suspect other men of attempting to seduce their female family members (Goksel, 2006: 56). This struggle occurs between two or more men claiming authority over female family members in order to ensure they live in the way that society demands. A man who challenges or is deemed to challenge another man's authority over female family members may be marked as an outsider or enemy, which can potentially frame a man and/or his family in a negative way, causing them to react to reclaim their honour (Lindisfarne, 1994: 87).

Furthermore, LGBTQ+ people can also be victims of HBA, including killings, because of their sexual orientation. For example, in Turkey, 26-year-old Ahmet Yıldız was killed in 2008 by his father for being gay.[2] His murder is regarded as the first LGBTQ+ 'honour' killing case in Turkey. His father's trial is still ongoing in 2019, although he has been absent from court (he has escaped) since he committed the crime. The Turkish state claims that they are still looking for him. The court has adjourned the trial for the last ten years for this particular reason. HBA and violence against heterosexual men in general and against LGBTQ+ in particular, indicates that such crimes are committed because the victim has failed to comply with the requirements of the heteronormative, 'heterosexual patriarchal gender order' (Ertürk, 2009: 65), which represents the norms and values of the accepted ways of being, behaving and living in family and community in certain societies. The state law practises and responses in relation to protecting the innocent, crime prevention and prosecuting the guilty are also reflected within this framework. The role of state institutions in helping to perpetuate these crimes is highlighted in some of the literature on HBA, particularly in relation to ineffective or non-state intervention in such crimes (Shalhoub-Kevorkian, 2002; Welchman and Hossain, 2005; Gill, 2009; HMIC, 2015, Idriss, 2018), in failing to record of cases of so-called honour killings, failure to conduct investigations and in relation to pursuing prosecutions (Faqir, 2001; Sev'er and Yurdakul, 2001). This also includes the discriminatory nature of the courts and legal discourse in dealing with so-called honour killings (Arın, 2001; Shalhoub-Kevorkian, 2002; Hoyek et al., 2005; Pervizat; 2005; Pimentel et al., 2005; Warraich, 2005; Khan, 2006; Durbaş, 2016). It is argued in this chapter that the state is an institution that is accountable for perpetuating these crimes and thus reproducing, regulating and maintaining oppressive gender relations and gender roles rooted in hegemonic masculinity. The state is a patriarchal entity with a hierarchical and gendered identity because state institutions, including the courts and the police, are dominated by men (Franzway et al., 1989). In addition, the state is both 'nominally' and 'substantially' patriarchal because high-level positions in state institutions are dominated by men (Savage and Witz, 1992: 37); men are also in positions of authority in legal, religious and political institutions, operating in line with the requirements of hegemonic masculinity. Accordingly, gender regulation is a key area for the state. It governs this through a heteronormative, heterosexual, hierarchical, patriarchal gender order by treating people in relation to various identities including husband, father, sister, mother, homosexual, all of which are based on patriarchal principles (Connell, 1987: 130). In the next section, I explore the way in which the Turkish courts have a role in legitimising certain types of honour killings against men and which are committed by men. Consequently, this reproduces, regulates and maintains the social construction of gender roles and the gender order rooted in hierarchical hegemonic masculinities based on the subordination of women.

Notions of provocation in cases of so-called honour killings against male victims

With the aim of exploring the way in which gendered norms and approaches, based on hegemonic masculinity, are reflected in Criminal High Court decisions for so-called honour killings committed against men by other men in Turkey, this section examines a selection of cases based on the notion of provocation, where the Turkish courts have reduced sentences mainly by blaming the male victims' alleged actions as a justification/excuse for the violence committed against them. The following situations are attributed as reasons and were considered as 'provocation' and were accepted by the Turkish courts as mitigating circumstances, where: (a) men were killed by the brothers of girls and women for harassing and/or raping them, or for having a relationship with the defendants' sisters, or separating from the defendant's sister after starting a family; (b) men were killed by sons for having a relationship with the defendant's mothers; (c) men were killed by male relatives (other than brothers, fathers or husbands) for having a relationship with female relatives; and (d) men were killed by other men in relation to adulterous relationships. The material presented in this section is based on 19 Criminal High Court Cases of the so-called honour killings of men by men that the author has been collecting in Turkey since 2007, before, during and after her PhD. These cases occurred between 2005 and 2008. So far, the author has collected a total of 200 Criminal High Court and Supreme Court Cases of so-called honour killings dating back from the late 1980s onwards across all regions of Turkey, obtained directly from the Criminal High Courts, lawyers and high-ranking judges dealing with such crimes. Nineteen of the 200 cases concerned male victims of murder or attempted murder by other men. The remaining 181 victims were women and girls. The 19 cases were collected in the First and Second Criminal High Courts in ten cities across six out of seven regions in Turkey. Two male victims survived their attempted murders in relation to the cases brought to court. However, the narratives of the surviving male victims are noticeably absent from court records. All of the court cases are now closed, and the ongoing court case of Ahmet Yıldız is excluded from this sample as the trial is ongoing. All translations from Turkish to English are the author's. Various limitations may have a potential impact on this study – given the nature of the research topic and the multi-layered and complex issues and challenges, it is important to protect the identity and ensure the safety of the participants. Taking into consideration that many cases of so-called honour killings are not reported and recorded appropriately, the 200 case files are not intended to reflect the prevalence of this crime in Turkey either. Employing qualitative research methods, the analysis process conducted by the author has inductive and analytical elements in order to provide an understanding of how these cases operate and the 'legal' reasoning (including the provocation defence) attributed to these crimes within Turkish courts to justify/excuse these so-called honour killings. With regards to Turkey's legal framework, Turkey's legal system has been modified by the incorporation of continental European systems. There is no jury system in the Turkish court system, and trials are heard by a panel of judges, including a presiding judge, member judges and a prosecutor. In relation to so-called honour killings in the Turkish Penal Code, some of the Articles of the old Turkish Penal Code of 1926 were amended, and a new Penal Code was accepted in June 2005. No Article within the old Penal Code covered so-called honour killings. The new Penal Code of 2005 does not address the issue directly, but did introduce a clause whereby *töre* (custom/tradition) is not a mitigating factor, but still made no mention of *nāmus* (honour).

Rape, harassment and having a relationship with the defendant's sister

The rape and harassment of the sisters of defendants by the male victims was one of the underlying reasons leading to their murder. In addition, having a consensual relationship with the sister of the defendant, or separating from the defendant's sister after starting a family, were other reasons attributed to killing the men, because the defendants considered these to be a major transgression which triggered violence against the male victims. These cases further illustrate that the judges reduced the sentences of defendants who were found guilty of murder by accepting the reasons given in court and by blaming the victims for provoking the defendants (two of the cases also referred to the socio-cultural structure of the society) (Case 2, 3, 8, 11,12, 13 and 14). In one of these cases, the reason given in court was that the married male victim was seeing (in terms of a relationship) the underage sister of the defendant, who stated the victim was harassing her, and so he was murdered by the defendant during an argument. The court reduced the sentence of the defendant as the judges agreed that 'the defendant was under provocation because of the behaviour of the victim towards the defendant's sister, [which] caused his anger, and, taking account of the nature of Turkish society, this was [a] gross [provocation]' (Case 2). Accordingly, his sentence was reduced from life imprisonment to 15 years imprisonment, and later to 12 years and 6 months imprisonment because of his good behaviour during the trial. In this case, there was another male defendant, the friend of the first defendant, but he did not benefit from a reduced sentence due to provocation. In another case, the defendant, who was working in another town, was informed by a male friend that his sister was pregnant by the male victim. He returned and killed the male victim, the presumed father of his sister's unborn child. The court agreed to grant the defendant a reduced sentence due to 'gross provocation' because when 'the defendant spoke to the victim, who he assumed had raped his sister, but which the victim denied, this angered the accused and as a result, he stabbed him to death' (Case 11a). His sentence was reduced by two-thirds due to provocation from life imprisonment to 8 years, and by one-sixth to 5 years, 6 months and 20 days for his good behaviour during the trial. Furthermore, the Supreme Court approved the court's judgement (Case 11b).

Cases 2 and 11 indicate that, when there were perceived crimes such as harassment and rape that the male victims had (been alleged[3] to have) committed against the sisters of the male defendants, these perceived crimes were given as mitigating reasons in court and were accepted without challenge as the triggers that resulted in their murders. Furthermore, the perceived acts of the male victims were considered 'gross provocation' only for the defendants who were the brothers of the women and girls that the male victims had been involved with, not for any other male or unrelated defendants. The judges limited the provocation defence to the male relatives of the girls and the women in question. However, the Criminal High Court cases of so-called honour killings committed by women against men for the same reasons (i.e. of rape and harassment) that I have examined (forthcoming) indicate that these claims have not been treated in the same way by the judges. These court cases which I have examined tended to dismiss women's claims of rape and harassment. For example, the high-profile case of Nevin Yıldırım clearly demonstrates this point.[4] Nevin Yıldırım, a 26-year-old Turkish woman, had been subjected to systematic rape from a man, and in the end, she killed him to stop this violence. At the time, she was also pregnant as a result of her rape and wanted to have an abortion. Not only she was denied an abortion by the state, but her claims of rape were also dismissed by the judges, so she was granted neither a sentence reduction due to provocation, nor did she have her sentence reduced for good behaviour during her trial, as is routinely given to male defendants. She was sentenced to life imprisonment. The Supreme Court also recently approved this decision in May 2019. This indicates the different treatment of so-called honour killing perpetrators by the courts, which systematically appears to favour male perpetrators.

Other cases demonstrate that if male victims enter a consensual relationship with the defendant's unmarried sister, at the disapproval of their families, this can also be regarded as provocation of the defendant and act as an excuse for the killing of the male victim. In one of these cases, the defendant's brother killed the male victim for having a relationship with his sister that he, the defendant, disapproved of. He also shot his sister, who miraculously, survived. She later stated in court that she was forced to be engaged to a distant relative at her father's wishes, but she never wanted to marry him and that she was speaking to her boyfriend/victim whom she really wanted to marry. More importantly, she felt the need to emphasise to the court that she had not had a sexual relationship with the victim and that she was still a virgin. She also added that she did not want to file a complaint against her defendant brother for shooting her. The court granted a sentence reduction for provocation to her brother for committing the crime:

> even though, it was understood that the relationship between the underage surviving sister and the victim was without the consent of her family, as was

> for them have a sexual relationship with the intention of marriage and that although the victim's attempt to elope with her boyfriend was consensual, taking into consideration the social cultural structure within which the crime took place, these actions are considered as provocation.
>
> (Case 13)

However, as the case concerned a consensual relationship, the court only granted a minimum reduction for provocation reduction, instead of that for gross provocation.

Men also kill other men when their sisters' partners send them back to their family home wishing to separate from them, or if men other than their husbands allegedly have a relationship with their married sisters. The courts, similarly, accepted these events as provocation and reduced the sentences of the defendants, blaming the male victims for the attack. In one particular case, it was claimed that the male victim and the sister of the defendant had started living together after they eloped with her consent and with the intention of marrying. After they had a child, the male victim changed his mind and sent the woman back to her parent's house. This angered the defendant (brother of the woman) and as a result, he shot the victim dead after an argument. In this case, the court record does not indicate any legal reasoning for granting him a gross provocation reduction for the murder (Case 8). This case demonstrates that the defendant's sister being sent back to her parent's house by her husband was considered the main transgression by the male victim, which disgraced her family 'honour' and ultimately led to his death, which was justified/excused by the court.

In relation to claims of adultery, in one case, it was claimed that three defendant brothers and their male friend killed a man because he was having an affair with the brothers' married sister and was constantly stalking and harassing her. When the gossip in the town where they lived spread to the rest of the community, one of the brothers ordered his other brother to 'to attend to her, to look after her, to protect her'. When after the defendants were informed by another male friend about the time and place where the male victim and their sister were going to meet, the male victim was murdered. The court accepted the reason given and acquitted two of the defendant brothers of committing the crime of murder, but sentenced them to two years and six months in prison for hiding evidence in relation to the crime. In this case, only one brother was sentenced for murdering the male victim, but even then the court reduced his sentence due to gross provocation:

> For the married sister to have a relationship with someone, whether with her consent or not, is an attack on the *irz* and honour of the defendants, which made the defendants uncomfortable and the defendant committed the crime as a result of the anger and grief caused by the victim that had lasted a long time. Therefore, a reduced sentence due to provocation is given, taking into consideration the nature of the unjust acts that had taken place.
>
> (Case 12)

These cases also illustrate the collective nature of many of these crimes. In Case 2, the defendant brother committed the crime with his male friend; in Case 11, the defendant's male friend informed him about his sister's pregnancy; in Case 12, three brothers and their male friend were also involved in the crime and the court's legal reasoning referred to the 'gossip' within the community about the alleged relationship as a major cause why the crime had been committed in the first place.

In another case, it was claimed that the defendant brother killed his friend for having a relationship with his married sister and for not taking this seriously when confronted about it by the defendant before the crime was committed. The court accepted the reason claimed by the defence, who attempted to prove there was a relationship between the victim and the defendant's sister. Although no evidence was found, the court granted a reduced sentence due to gross provocation, as:

> there were some telephone communications between the two married people [the male victim and the sister of the defendant] and this would not be tolerated by society . . . it has been understood that the victim underestimated the impact of the affair with the defendant's sister. He did not show any remorse or regret, and when the defendant spoke to the victim about this, he did not take the situation seriously, all of which caused the defendant great anger and grief. Thus, there is a link between the victim's unjust acts and the defendant's act of murder. If such an unjust act had not been perpetrated by the victim, this crime would not have taken place.
>
> (Case 3)

As a result of this reasoning, the defendant's sentence was reduced from life imprisonment to 16 years imprisonment due to gross provocation, and then to 13 years and 4 months due to his good behaviour during the trial. This case demonstrates that the so-called unjust act of the male victim, communication between two adults and the claim that the victim did not show any regret about the alleged adultery were all regarded as gross provocation for the defendant brother and that this and the alleged adulterous relationship of his sister with the victim had damaged his honour. Overall, this collection of cases demonstrates that the alleged rape/harassment of sisters of the defendants, or having a relationship with the sister of the defendant without her family's consent, or separating from the defendant's sister after starting a family, or having a relationship with the sisters of the defendants and not heeding the defendant's warning when confronted were all given as mitigating reasons which were accepted by the Turkish courts. In addition, the acts of the male victims were seen as the main transgressions, as personal attacks on the honour of the defendant brothers through their womenfolk. These Turkish judges then accepted these mitigating arguments to apply sentence reductions based on the provocation defence which, in some cases, was automatically applied without any explanation, other than by mainly blaming the male victims for the crimes committed against them. By doing this, the judges legitimised the violence committed against male victims by the brothers of the girls and women that the male victims were involved with and were alleged to have harmed.

Having a relationship with the defendant's mother

Some of the cases concerned men being killed by the sons of women they were involved with, for having a relationship with the defendant's mother (Case 1 and Case 19). The courts reduced the sentences of the defendants in these cases who were found guilty of murder. Although it is not a crime in Turkish law for adults to enter into relationships, such relationships are framed as acts of provocation for the sons of the women concerned. In addition, in some of the cases, judges also had to investigate whether the male victims and the mothers of the defendants actually had sexual intercourse and whether or not it was consensual. In one particular case, two defendant brothers were on trial for killing the man who had a relationship with their widowed mother. In this case, the court records show that the court tried to find evidence of the alleged relationship, and in particular, whether sexual intercourse had occurred between the male victim and the mother of the defendants. After a thorough investigation and evaluation of the behaviour of the male victim and the defendants' mother, it was concluded that their relationship had indeed been consensual. Despite this, the court found that the consensual relationship between the male victim and the defendants' mother to be gross provocation: 'it has been understood that the defendants committed the crime thinking and accepting that the victim had an illicit sexual relationship with their mother' (Case 19). Thus, the court imposed a reduced custodial sentence based on gross provocation for both defendants. The youngest defendant also benefited from age reduction as he was under 18 years of age at the time of the criminal offence. In another case where a man was killed by the son of a woman because of his alleged relationship with her, the court also granted him a reduced sentence as the court found this relationship also provocative for the defendant:

> it has been understood that the defendant committed the crime under provocation due to the relationship between his mother and the victim. [As] no evidence has been found that the victim was harassing his mother, it is accepted that the relationship was consensual, thus provocation was not gross.
>
> (Case 1)

These cases demonstrate that the lawful acts of victims, of having a relationship with defendants' adult mothers, were (and are still) considered as provocation of the defendant sons, leading them to kill the men that their mothers were involved with and thereby acquire reduced sentences. Thus, the Turkish judges have legitimised violence of the sons against the men their mothers they were involved with.

Having a relationship with the defendant's female relatives

Men may also kill, or attempt to kill, other men for allegedly having a relationship with distant female family members, and not just immediate sisters or mothers, and for damaging their 'family honour' (Case 17 and Case 4). The Turkish courts, as in prior cases, also granted these defendants reduced custodial sentences by blaming the male victims for provoking the defendants through their 'illegitimate' relationships. In one case, a man was killed by the defendants for having a relationship with the defendants' stepbrother's wife. In this case, one of the defendants claimed that when the defendant's stepbrother's wife was kidnapped by the male victim, this was regarded by him as a matter of 'honour' and thus decided to kill him with the aid of his brothers (although the husband changed his mind and made peace with his wife). The Turkish court in this case, while stating that adultery is a concern for any husband, cannot be considered serious for other people, but nevertheless allowed the provocation defence to reduce the defendants' sentence: 'It has been accepted that the wife of their stepbrother being kidnapped by the victim and for them to live together for a while constitutes the unjust provocation of the defendants' (Case 17).

Adultery as provocation

Finally, the cases presented in this section illustrate that male victims were murdered (or attempted to be murdered in one of the cases) predominantly by the husbands of the women with whom the male victims had committed adultery, This was the alleged reason behind the murders (Cases 5, 6, 7, 9, 10, 15 and 18). The Turkish courts similarly reduced the sentences of the defendants who were found guilty of murder by blaming the male victims, and sometimes, the women in question, for provoking the defendants by having an affair or for making the defendants think that they were involved in an adulterous relationship. For example, in one case the defendant husband claimed that he killed a man for his alleged adultery with his wife. The court records show that the judges went into great detail to explain how unacceptable the actions of the male victim had been, and to some extent, those of the woman. The court stated: 'the victim had an adulterous relationship with the defendant's wife and although it was consensual, as a married woman with two children, she had a duty of loyalty to her husband. Despite this, the male victim had a sexual relationship with her and entered the defendant's house without his knowledge, (Case 7). Although, the court acknowledged that adultery is not defined as a crime in the Turkish Penal Code, the judges used it to justify/excuse the death by blaming the male victim as the judges agreed that: 'According to the Turkish Civil Code, the husband and wife have a duty to be loyal to each other, thus the victim attacked the defendant husband's right. So, taking this into consideration, the court accepts the killing was the result of his [i.e. the male victim's] unjust acts, and pressurised the defendant into reacting' (Case 7). Accordingly, the Turkish court granted a sentence reduction due to gross provocation, from life imprisonment to 15 years, and then to 12 years and 6 months for good behaviour during the trial.

In a similar case, the defendant killed a man for his alleged adultery with his wife (although it was a religious marriage, which is considered illegal according to the Turkish Civil Code). Again, the Turkish court conducted an investigation into the alleged adultery and, despite no evidence being found, the Turkish court accepted that the adultery claim was based on deep suspicion and gossip and ruled that the crime was a matter of 'honour', and thus accepted the gross provocation defence which reduced the defendant's sentence: 'The conclusion is that the crime was committed as a result of the intense suspicion arising from gossip in the village and so the sentence is reduced due to gross provocation' (Case 15). This case shows that even a suspicion about the possibility of adultery, as a result of gossip, is enough for Turkish courts to consider reasonable and allows the courts to reduce the sentences of perpetrators. Only in one of the cases sampled did the court reject the defence of provocation. In this case, a man was killed by his wife's lover after gossip spread in the village about the alleged adultery between the defendant, and the victim's wife and the defendant had been warned about his behaviour by the victim's brothers. Later, during an argument, the victim/husband was killed by the defendant/lover. In this case, the court rejected the defence of provocation without any explanation (Case 16).

Conclusion

Although the current study is based on a limited number of cases, the cases presented in this chapter illustrate how men can also be the victims of so-called honour killings. Furthermore, these findings show how some women and girls are strictly controlled by their families. The attributed reasons in the previous cases were regarded, whether real or perceived, as transgressions committed by the male victims upon the male defendants and the relatives of the women and girls that the victims were involved with. The male victims' actions were seen as a threat and attack upon the 'honour' of the male defendants, perhaps because they were interpreted as an attack and challenge to their hegemonic masculinity, which is rooted in the control of female family members through oppressive gender relations. Failure to control female family members' lives, sexuality and/or chastity meant that they were perceived to have failed to meet the requirements of hegemonic masculinity. Through killing the male victims, the defendants were able to reclaim their hegemonic masculinity and maintain the gender order within their family and society. The Turkish judges also accepted the reasoning of the defendants and blamed the male victims for their 'unjust acts' and for upsetting and provoking the defendants into committing the crimes by framing the facts of the cases accordingly, thus constructing their legal discourse in line with the accepted gender norms based on the oppression of women by men. This shows that the provocation defence was granted when male victims breached socially accepted norms concerning the women's male family members – brothers, sons, brothers-in-law and husbands. Women were only addressed in relation to their familial roles, and not as independent citizens. Judges, through accepting the attributed reasons given by the defendants, allocated some responsibility to the male victims for prompting the 'unjust acts' against them, hence legitimising the violence committed against the male victims. In doing this, the Turkish judges have signified a message of approval, encouragement and even legitimacy for violence against male victims, as well as the oppression of women, by pushing the blame onto the male victims for their own deaths for failing to live according to the accepted gender norms and values required by family and society. This is extremely worrying for gender rights and for Turkish law in general. All sovereign states are required by international law to prevent violence and protect citizens from violence and to prosecute and punish those who carry out acts of violence. Turkey has signed relevant EU and international treaties, in particular, the Convention on the Elimination of All Forms of Discrimination Against Women (CEDAW), the Declaration on the Elimination of Violence Against Women and the Istanbul Convention which specifically addresses honour crimes and, more importantly, as a signatory to these documents, the Turkish state is obliged to take steps to combat such crimes through 'due diligence to prevent, investigate and punish acts of violence against women' (Ertürk, 2004: 169). Turkey has also amended various Articles of the Turkish Penal and Civil Codes as part of legal reform, especially between 2002 and 2004, which aim to eliminate violence against women and achieve gender equality in both private and public spheres. However, Turkey has failed to live up to its responsibilities – the cases examined in this chapter show that it has disregarded many of the related mandatory Articles in international law, failed to fulfil its commitments to securing gender equality and justice through selective and/or non-application of the law and consequently violated the rights of individual citizens. This, in particular, has grave implications for women and girls; the current situation is that the state ignores women's rights and treats them as second-class citizens. This is also evidenced by Turkey's human rights violations before the European Court of Human Rights (ECrtHR). These cases show the Turkish state's failure to properly deal with domestic violence, which the ECrtHR continues to criticise Turkey (see e.g. Opuz (2009); Durmaz (2014); Civek (2016); Kılıç (2016); and M.G. (2016).[5] Despite these rulings, Turkey continues to fail in its obligations to eliminate gender-based violence. It also continues to fail to properly prevent, investigate, prosecute and sentence HBA/violence perpetrators before the courts. This was already known in relation to female victims of such crimes, but the cases examined within this chapter reveal that male victims can be added to this too.

Notes

1 The terms *honour-based abuse/violence*, *honour crimes* and *honour killings* are used interchangeably in this chapter.
2 Sources: https://m.bianet.org/bianet/lgbti/198745-onur-haftasi-nda-ahmet-yildiz-davasinin-10-yili-konusuldu and https://kaosgl.org/sayfa.php?id=27408

3 While acknowledging and emphasising that the courts regularly dismiss the claims of female victims of rape and sexual violence and blame them for the violence they were subjected to rather than the male perpetrators, I refer to the 'alleged' harassment and rape of the woman and girls in this paper in a way that does not seek to absolve the male victim if a crime was, indeed, committed, nor seek to blame the male victim either.

4 Sources: https://bianet.org/english/women/208765-supreme-court-of-appeals-upholds-life-sentence-of-nevin-yildirim and https://catlakzemin.com/nevin-yildirim-davasi-dunden-bugune/

5 Source: www.coe.int/en/web/istanbul-convention/echr-case-law

References

Abu-Lughod, L. (2011) 'Seductions of the Honor Crime', *Differences*, 22(1), pp. 17–63.

Aplin, R. (2017) 'Exploring the Role of Mothers in 'Honour' based Abuse Perpetration and the Impact on the Policing Response', *Women's Studies International Forum*, 60, pp. 1–10.

Arın, C. (2001) 'Femicide in the Name of Honor in Turkey', *Violence against Women*, 7(7), pp. 821–825.

Baker, N. V., Gregware, P. R. and Cassidy, M. A. (1999) 'Family Killing Fields: Honor Rationales in the Murder of Women', *Violence against Women*, 5(2), pp. 164–184.

Bates, L. (2018) 'Females Perpetrating Honour-Based Abuse: Controllers, Collaborators or Coerced?', *Journal of Aggression, Conflict and Peace Research*, 10(4), pp. 293–303.

Begikhani, N., Gill, A. K. and Hague, G. (2015), *Honour-Based Violence: Experiences and Counter-Strategies in Iraqi Kurdistan and the UK Kurdish Diaspora*. Ashgate.

Birdal, N. B. K. (2010) *The Interplay between the State and Civil Society: A Case Study of Honor Killings in Turkey*. Unpublished PhD Thesis. University of Southern California.

Chesler, P. (2010) 'Worldwide Trends in Honor Killings', *Middle East Quarterly*, 7(2), pp. 3–11.

Civek v. Turkey, Case of (2016) Application no.55354/11). [online] Available at:https://hudoc.echr.coe.int/eng#{%22itemid%22:[%22001-161058%22]} [Accessed 8 Nov. 2019].

Connell, R. W. (1987) *Gender and Power: Society, the Person and Sexual Politics*. Stanford: Stanford University Press/Oxford: Polity Press.

Connell, R. W. (2005) *Masculinities*. Los Angles: University of California Press, 2nd Ed.

Delaney, C. (1987) 'Seeds of Honour, Fields of Shame', in Gilmore, D. D. (ed.) *Honour and Shame and the Unity of the Mediterranean*. Washington, DC: American Anthropological Association, pp. 35–48.

Doğan, R. (2018) 'Do Women Kill for Honor? Conceptualizing Women's Involvement in Honor Killings', *Deviant Behavior*, 39(10), pp. 1247–1266.

Durbaş, B. (2015) Perpetrators of Domestic Violence: Interpretation of the Role of Women in Honour-based Violence. 2 July 2015 Paper presented at British Society of Criminology Annual Conference. Plymouth University Law School, Plymouth. 30 June–3 July.

Durbaş, B. (2016) *Gender, Culture, Family and State: A Case Study of Honour Killings in Turkey*. Unpublished PhD Thesis. University of Sussex.

Durmaz v. Turkey, Case of (2014) (Application no. 3621/07). [online] Available at:https://rm.coe.int/CoERMPublicCommonSearchServices/DisplayDCTMContent?documentId=09000016805a32ba [Accessed 8 Nov. 2019].

Eldén, A. (2010) 'Men's Violence and Women's Responsibility: Mother's Stories about Honour Violence', in Idriss, M. M. and Abbas, T. (eds.) *Honour, Violence, Women and Islam*. London: Routledge, pp. 128–141.

Ertürk, Y. (2004) 'Violence in the Name of Honour within the Context of International Regimes', in Mojab, S. and Abdo, N. (eds.) *Violence in the Name of Honour: Theoretical and Political Challenges*. Istanbul: Bilgi University Press, pp. 165–176.

Ertürk, Y. (2009) 'Towards a Post-Patriarchal Gender Order: Confronting the Universality and the Particularity of Violence against Women', *Sociologisk Forskning*, 46(4), pp. 61–70.

Faqir, F. (2001) 'Intrafamily Femicide in Defence of Honour: The Case of Jordan', *Third World Quarterly*, 22(1), pp. 65–82.

Franzway, S., Court, D. and Connell, R. W. (1989) *Staking a Claim: Feminism, Bureaucracy and the State*. Sydney: Allen and Unwin.

Gill, A. (2006) 'Patriarchal Violence in the Name of Honour', *International Journal of Criminal Justice Sciences*, 1(1), pp. 1–12.

Gill, A. (2009) 'Honor Killings and the Quest for Justice in Black and Minority Ethnic Communities in the United Kingdom', *Criminal Justice Policy Review*, 20(4), pp. 475–494.

Gilmore, D. D. (1987) *Honour and Shame and the Unity of the Mediterranean*. Washington, DC: American Anthropological Association.

Goksel, I. (2006) 'Virginity and Masculinity', in Jones, A. (ed.) *Men of the Global South: A Reader*. London: Zed Books, pp. 55–58.

Her Majesty's Inspectorate of Constabulary (HMIC) (2015) *The Depths of Dishonour: Hidden Voices and Shameful Crimes*. Report, 8 December.

Hirsi Ali, A. (2007) *The Caged Virgin: A Muslim Woman's Cry for Reason*. London: Pocket Books.

Hoyek, D., Sidawi, R. R. and Mrad, A. A. (2005) 'Murders of Women in Lebanon: "Crimes of Honour" between Reality and the Law', in Welchman, L. and Hossain, S. (eds.) *'Honour': Crimes, Paradigms and Violence against Women*. London: Zed Book, pp. 111–136.

Idriss, M. M. (2018) 'Key Agent and Survivor Recommendations for Intervention in Honour-Based Violence in the UK', *International Journal of Comparative and Applied Criminal Justice*, 42(4), pp. 321–339.

Idriss, M. M. and Abbas, T. (2010) *Honour, Violence, Women and Islam*. Abingdon: Routledge.

Kandiyoti, D. (1988) 'Bargaining with Patriarchy', *Gender and Society*, 2(3), pp. 274–290.

Khan, T. S. (2006) *Beyond Honour: A Historical Materialist Explanation of Honour Related Violence*. Karachi: Oxford University Press.

Kılıç v. Turkey, Case of (2016) (Application no.63034/11). [online] Available at: https://hudoc.echr.coe.int/eng-press#{%22itemid%22:[%22001-164689%22]} [Accessed 8 Nov. 2019].

Koğacıoğlu, D. (2004) 'The Tradition Effect: Framing Honor Crimes in Turkey', *Differences: A Journal of Feminist Cultural Studies*, 15(2), pp. 119–151.

Korteweg, A. and Yurdakul, G. (2010) *Religion, Culture and the Politicization of Honour Related Violence: A Critical Analysis of Media and Policy Debate in Western Europe and North America*. Paper Number 12. Geneva: UNRISD.

Lindisfarne, N. (1994) 'Variant Masculinities, Variant Virginities: Rethinking "Honour and Shame"', in Cornwall, A. and Lindisfarne, N. (eds.) *Dislocating Masculinity: Comparative Ethnographies*. London: Routledge, pp. 82–96.

Mojab, S. and Abdo, N. (2004) *Violence in the Name of Honour: Theoretical and Political Challenges*. Istanbul: İstanbul Bilgi Üniversitesi Yayınları.
M.G. v. Turkey, Case of (2016) (Application no.646/10). [online] Available at: https://rm.coe.int/CoERMPublicCommonSearchServices/DisplayDCTMContent?documentId=090000168062cf75[Accessed 8 Nov. 2019].
Opuz v. Turkey, Case of (2009). (Application no. 33401/02). [online] Available at: https://rm.coe.int/CoERMPublicCommonSearchServices/DisplayDCTMContent?documentId=09000016805a320d [Accessed 8 Nov. 2019].
Ortner, S. B. (1978) 'The Virgin and the State', *Feminist Studies*, 4(3), pp. 19–35.
Payton, J. (2010) 'Collective Crimes, Collective Victims: A Case Study of the Murder of Banaz Mahmod', in Idriss, M. M. and Abbas, T. (eds.) *Honour, Violence, Women and Islam*. New York, NY: Routledge, pp. 67–79.
Peristiany, J. G. (ed.) (1966) *Honour and Shame: The Values of Mediterranean Society*. University of Chicago Press.
Pervizat, L. (2005) *Uluslararası İnsan Hakları Bağlamında Namus Cinayetleri: Kavramsal ve Hukuksal Boyutu ve Türkiye Özelinin Değerlendirilmesi*. Unpublished PhD Thesis. Marmara Üniversitesi Sosyal Bilimler Enstitüsü Siyaset Bilimi Ve Uluslararası İlişkiler Bilim Dalı, İstanbul.
Pimentel, S., Pandjiarjian, V. and Belloque, J. (2005) 'The "Legitimate Defence of Honour", or Murder with Impunity? A Critical Study of Legislation and Case Law in Latin America', in Welchman, L. and Hossain, S. (eds.) *'Honour': Crimes, Paradigms and Violence against Women*. London: Zed Books, pp. 245–262.
Reddy, R. (2008) 'Gender, Culture and the Law: Approaches to Honour Crimes in the UK', *Feminist Legal Studies*, 16(3), pp. 305–321.
Savage, M. and Witz, A. (eds.) (1992) *Gender and Bureaucracy*. Oxford: Blackwell.
Schneider, J. (1971) 'Of Vigilance and Virgins: Honor, Shame and Access to Resources in Mediterranean Societies', *Ethnology*, 10(1), pp. 1–24.
Sen, P. (2005) '"Crimes of Honour": Value and Meaning', in Welchman, L. and Hossain, S. (eds.) *'Honour': Crimes, Paradigms and Violence against Women*. London: Zed Books, pp. 47–63.
Sev'er, A. and Yurdakul, G. (2001) 'Culture of Honor, Culture of Change: A Feminist Analysis of Honor Killings in Rural Turkey', *Violence against Women*, 7(9), pp. 964–998.
Shalhoub-Kevorkian, N. (2002) 'Femicide and the Palestinian Criminal Justice System: Seeds of Change in the Context of State Building?', *Law and Society Review*, 36(3), pp. 577–606.
Shalhoub-Kevorkian, N. (2003) 'Re-Examining Femicide: Breaking the Silence, Crossing "Scientific" Borders', *Signs: Journal of Women in Culture and Society*, 28(2), pp. 581–608.
Shalhoub-Kevorkian, N. (2005) 'Imposition of Virginity Testing: A Life-Saver or a License to Lill?', *Social Science & Medicine*, 60(6), pp. 1187–1196.
Warraich, S. A. (2005) 'Honour Killings and the Law in Pakistan', in Welchman, L. and Hossain, S. (eds.) *'Honour': Crimes, Paradigms and Violence against Women*. London: Zed Books, pp. 78–110.
Welchman, L. and Hossain, S. (2005) *'Honour': Crimes, Paradigms and Violence against Women*. London: Zed Books.
Wikan, U. (2008) *In Honor of Fadime: Murder and Shame*. University of Chicago Press.
Yıldız Tahincioğlu, A. N. (2011) *Namusun Halleri*. İstanbul: Postiga Yayınları.

Chapter 10

A day in the life of a police officer working with male victims of HBA and forced marriages – some reflections

Mindy Mahil

Introduction

In this chapter, I hope to share some of my experiences of dealing with HBA and forced marriage cases in the United Kingdom and abroad. As a retired police detective, I often had to work at the very sharp end of difficult cases concerning HBA and forced marriages. Such cases are often very fast-paced and involve safeguarding victims both in England and transnationally in other jurisdictions. I have been involved in safeguarding victims in some very dangerous countries and in areas that do not respect the rule of law. The aim of this chapter is to provide readers with an understanding of how the police respond to HBA and forced marriage cases, how such cases are investigated and some of the positive (and negative) outcomes that can arise. In my experience, cases involving male victims are far less reported than those involving female victims; they also differ in terms of their facts, peculiarities and challenges (which I intend to highlight from a practitioner perspective). The criminalisation of forced marriages is still relatively new (see Idriss, 2015), and the government recently created a consultation in order to ascertain views about creating a 'mandatory duty to report' upon specified authorities (e.g. schools) to report instances of forced marriage as soon as a case is brought to their attention (Home Office, 2018). Academics and practitioners may have mixed responses to the criminalisation of forced marriages and the mandatory duty to report. There will also be many police forces in the United Kingdom who have never investigated HBA or forced marriage cases before, in direct contrast to West Midlands Police, who have investigated many cases in the last decade. Of course, this is influenced by the demographics of communities, but my view is that the best way to acquire knowledge of HBA and forced marriage is to be directly involved in such cases. My direct knowledge and involvement has taken several years of regular involvement, with each case that I have investigated being different. Although I am now retired, West Midlands Police are retaining my experience and knowledge in order to pass onto emerging police officers coming through the ranks. While my chapter will not be 'academic' in the traditional sense, I intend to offer some reflections on what my life was like as a police officer dealing with HBA and forced marriage victims. I will demonstrate some of the complexities of investigating such cases and what needs to be done to assist future investigations, especially in relation to male victims.

My background

My parents came to England in the late 1960s from the Punjab, India. My parents had only seen each other through photographs prior to marriage and met for the first time during their wedding ceremony. I grew up in a typical inner city street of terraced houses and most of the occupants in my street were Sikhs from the Punjab. Most of the males were uneducated and worked in local foundries, and the women were either stay-at-home mothers or worked in local factories. They spoke little English, but did immerse themselves in British culture. My dad always wore Western clothes, and my mom wore Western clothes to work and traditional clothes at home. As we got older and started school, we spoke in Punjabi and English and became natural translators for our parents. My recollection of growing up within the Asian community in the 1970s and 1980s was that most marriages were 'arranged'. Many males and females also married spouses from the Punjab, India. I can also recall a very popular Punjabi newspaper *Des Pardes*, which my Dad bought religiously every week. The paper was written in Punjabi, which I could not read at the time. I can remember flicking through it every week looking for anything written in English. The only two things in English were some adverts and the matrimonial section. The matrimonial section itself consisted of adverts placed by families in the UK and by some families of men and women in India looking for partners in the UK. One caption in an advert that has always stuck in my mind over the years is 'caste no bar', which I had no understanding of at the time, but is now very relevant in many cases of HBA and forced marriages. *Caste no bar* was placed in adverts if families, who were seeking prospective suitors, were not concerned about the caste of potential brides or grooms. Individuals from South Asian communities, particularly from India, often marry within a caste-based system. There are many different castes and in some communities, it is culturally forbidden to marry outside of one's caste. Those that do marry outside of their caste may be ostracised by their families, and in some extreme cases, even murdered in the name of honour (BBC News, 2018a). The caste system still exists within Punjabi Sikh communities in the UK and is not restricted to just Sikhs. The caste-based system also exists in other parts of South Asia. For me, the caste-based system plays an important element in forced marriages and in the cases I have dealt with; it has certainly been one of the main reasons why a forced marriage has been planned or is even carried out. Younger generations of Asians may not be as bothered about the caste system as their parents are. Some younger generations may not ask a future partner what caste they belong to before embarking on a relationship. However, the difficulties can lie when younger generations eventually tell their families of their relationships to individuals of a different caste. Problems can occur when such families hold strong beliefs on the caste-based system.

At the age of 16 years old, I left school and joined West Midlands Police as a cadet and then joined as a regular police officer in 1989. In 2000, I trained as a detective and dealt with serious criminal offences, including burglary, robbery, fraud, rape, murder/attempted murder, terrorism and domestic abuse, HBA and forced marriages. Religion, caste and culture have always played a part in every case that I have dealt with concerning HBA and forced marriages. It is common for people from the South Asian community to marry within their own religion and caste. This can still be the case in 'love marriages' (or non-'arranged' marriages), and marriages are more accepted within a community if the couple are from the same background. Many of the HBA and forced marriage victims that I have dealt with are fourth-generation Asians, born in the UK. English is their first language but many also speak their mother tongue. Many of the first and second generation Asians try to hold onto religious and cultural beliefs and this includes their views on marriage. 'Arranged' marriages still take place in the UK and for many UK nationals, travelling to South Asia and being forced into marriage is a problem. The mass migration to the UK from South Asia in the 1960s and 1970s demonstrates how some families came to the UK, while other family members remained at 'home' in South Asia to look after the family assets. Those that came to the UK were deemed as the 'fortunate ones' and were expected to financially support their families back home. Thirty to forty years on, those that remained 'back home' then expected families in the UK to help their children to migrate to the UK. In many of the cases that I have dealt with in my career as a police officer, I have frequently come across UK-born victims being forced into marriage with family members in South Asia. In some parts of Pakistan and Bangladesh, it is not uncommon to marry a first cousin. Some victims have had their marriages arranged from a very young age and when the time came to fulfil the 'promise' of an arranged marriage, this then transformed into forced marriage because the victims that I encountered were frequently subjected to threats, coercion and violence for objecting to such arrangements. Planning is often done in secret, unbeknown to victims, and deception is used to get the victim abroad. Once the victim is abroad and outside the UK jurisdiction, families can then apply pressure without the fear of reprisals from law enforcement agencies. Bribery also plays an important part in many South Asian countries because of the lack of respect for the rule of law. If a victim does decide to approach the authorities, money can be paid to the authorities by families in order to get them to turn a blind eye. This also becomes a problem if the British Embassy gets involved abroad. In my experience, rescues are extremely rare due to the danger posed in many regions of South Asia, and local authorities are rarely engaged due to heavy corruption. In some areas, British Embassies also need local permission to enter certain restricted areas, and this can be very time-consuming and costly to victims. In some cases, victims may travel to remote villages and do not have the luxury of Internet connection; furthermore, UK mobile phone networks may not work and passport and other documents may be taken away from victims. This then limits any chance of getting help. In my own personal dealings with the Forced Marriage Unit (FMU), I am not aware of any rescues in the last few years of victims from South Asia where victims had come from the West Midlands. It is impossible in many of these areas for victims to be rescued because there is no such thing as a 'snatch' or 'rescue' squad to extract victims. However, I have personally handled cases involving British females who have been forced into marriage in countries such as Afghanistan, Bangladesh, India, Iran, Iraq, Pakistan, Romania and Yemen.

Working on HBA and forced marriage cases – female victims

In early 2018, I had just completed work on a serious rape case at the Crown Court. I was then approached to assist with a case concerning forced marriage. While I had received some forced marriage awareness training beforehand, this was the first case of its kind that I was directly involved in. I became an officer involved in the case and, together with a team of experienced police officers, we prepared the case for trial. The case involved a British Pakistani female victim who was taken to Pakistan by her mother on the pretence of a family holiday. Once in Pakistan, she was forced to marry a man 20 years her senior. Although she had alerted family and friends in the UK about her forced marriage, it was too late to save her from the marriage. The victim returned to England after a Forced Marriage Protection Order (FMPO) was served upon her mother. Her mother was then arrested and the victim was safeguarded. At trial the mother pleaded 'not guilty', which resulted in a full trial. This meant that the victim had to give evidence and re-live her ordeal. The mother was found guilty of forced marriage, which resulted in the first forced marriage conviction in England and Wales since the criminalisation of forced marriages in June 2014 (Summers, 2018). The mother received a four-and-a-half year custodial sentence; this was also quite harrowing for the victim because she still loved her mother and did not want her to go to prison. Within a week, a second conviction was secured in 2018, again with a female victim who was of Bangladeshi heritage (BBC News, 2018b). To date, there have only been four convictions under forced marriage legislation in the United Kingdom, all concerning female victims (i.e. no one has yet been convicted of forcing a man into marriage; the four convictions to date also include the first conviction in June 2015 concerning a man in Cardiff who raped his victim and forced her to marry him: BBC News, 2015).

These convictions received considerable media attention in the UK and abroad, and West Midlands Police hoped that it would send out a positive message to the community that forced marriage is a criminal offence and that those responsible will be brought to justice. Over the following months in 2018, I was then inundated with reports of forced marriage, given my successful involvement in the 2018 conviction. The summer months can bring an increase in reporting of potential forced marriages because most educational establishments close for the summer period. This gives perpetrators several months to take victims out of the UK on the pretext of a holiday and force victims into marriage without arousing the suspicions of any schools, colleges and universities. Although I was already aware of the existence and benefits of FMPOs because the Pakistani victim of the forced marriage was the subject of one, I had never dealt with an FMPO on my own initiative and under my own direction. However, in 2018 I applied for multiple FMPOs for victims, the majority of whom were abroad. If an FMPO is granted for a victim who is abroad, the case is heard at the High Court, Royal Courts of Justice in London. If the victim is still residing in the UK, then the case can be heard by a designated judge at a local family court. An FMPO is not automatically a criminal matter and is initially heard at a civil court. Most of the FMPOs are applied for by the police, unless the victims are under the age of 18, in which case Social Services makes applications for FMPOs.

In my experience, the victims whom FMPOs are applied for by West Midlands Police have all been female. Once I have received a report of a victim requiring help to flee a forced marriage, I will then work closely with the Forced Marriage Unit at the Foreign and Commonwealth Office. They will then liaise with their staff at the British Embassy in that country. I then present the evidence supporting the imposition of an FMPO to a High Court judge. In most cases, the initial hearing is *ex-parte*, which means 'on behalf' of the victim – this is undertaken so that the victim's family does not interfere with proceedings in terms of moving or hiding the victim or causing serious harm to them. Once an FMPO is granted, it is then served on family members in the UK who are alleged or deemed responsible for keeping the victim abroad against their will. The FMPO will have conditions attached to it that direct the person it is served upon to provide the victim's location, to provide the police with his or her contact details and to assist that person in repatriation to the UK (or, at the very minimum, present the victim to the British Embassy in the country in which they are located). I will then liaise directly with the victim and the British High Commission to help repatriate the victim to the UK. Once the victim is in the UK, I formally apply to the court, requesting a judge to grant an FMPO for a specific period of time. The victim's family have an opportunity to dispute the FMPO. If the FMPO is disputed, the judge will then review all of the evidence, listen to the victim's views and take into account their wishes, as well as the representations of the persons the FMPO has been served upon, and then make a decision as to whether the FMPO should be discharged or granted. In some cases, a judge may instruct an expert witness to review all of the evidence and to give their opinion as to whether an FMPO should be granted.

One specific case that remains firmly imprinted in my memory involved a female who had travelled to Iraq on a pilgrimage with friends. Her parents had split when she was young and so she had travelled to the UK with her mother and younger sibling and settled here – she did not have any contact with her father. Once in Iraq her father made contact with her, stating that he was visiting from Jordan. The victim met with her father in the Iraqi capital Baghdad and everything initially went well. Shortly after this, her father asked her to visit Basra, where other extended family members were also staying. The victim went to Basra and met her father, who took her to a house. This was when she realised that her father had permanently moved to Iraq and was remarried. She now had five younger half-siblings. Her father took away her passport and mobile phone and told her she was to marry her cousin and help him get a visa to the UK. When she refused, she was threatened with violence. Her father even pointed a gun at her saying he would kill her if she 'dishonoured' him. When the victim was in Baghdad, she told her younger brother that she had met their father in Iraq. Her younger brother then travelled to Iraq and also joined her at their father's house. Her brother then joined his father in exerting pressure on her and also inflicted violence upon her. The victim had managed to hide her mobile phone and used a local Internet connection to make contact. She then alerted her mother and college friends – a report was then made to West Midlands Police and this was the start of my involvement. I managed to get a line of communication with the victim but I had to be extremely careful so as not to put her in any danger. However, the forced marriage had already taken place prior to her pleas for help, and she consequently had been raped by her husband. I then liaised closely with the FMU and British Embassy staff in Baghdad, but a rescue was out of the question for safety reasons. The victim was in Basra, which is approximately five hours by road to Baghdad ,and Baghdad itself is dangerous due to the conflict and Iraq invasion – the only safe place was the 'green zone' that had been created by the allied forces. The victim's situation became more and more desperate by the day and although I was trying my best to reassure her, there was very little that could be done to rescue her. During a secret telephone conversation with her mother, at which I was present, the victim stated that it was getting more and more dangerous for her and she was planning to escape. She was in unknown territory, and I could not support or advise her to escape. The victim's conversation was then overheard by her brother, who then told her that he was going to inform her father. The next telephone call that I received from the victim was in sheer desperation. She managed to flee the house through an insecure door and hailed a taxi. She called me from the taxi and I told her to travel to the nearest city. I then worked with the mother and the British High Commission in Iraq to eventually bring the victim to Baghdad. She stayed in a secret refuge until her flight to the UK had been arranged. This in itself had presented challenges because her visa for Iraq had expired (and so she was classed as an over-stayer and an illegal immigrant). The family had to pay a fine for this and also the victim's flight back home. I then met the victim once she returned to the UK, where she is now safe with her family. Her brother eventually returned from Baghdad after becoming disillusioned with the father, but continued to cause issues for the victim. He felt he was the 'man of the house' and had the authority to control her – perhaps an example of patriarchal control and authority. However, he eventually left the family home after his efforts were halted by his mother and from my direct intervention. When I first began to deal with repatriations from abroad for forced marriage victims, I was disappointed to discover that victims had to pay for their own emergency travel documents and flights back home. Many of the victims had already suffered a considerable amount of trauma and wanted to return back to the UK as soon as possible. Being delayed for days trying to sort out funds is not an ideal position to be in – on many occasions, I had to liaise between family members and the British Embassy to arrange for funds and payments. In some cases, victims could not obtain funds because they were escaping their families – the very people who controlled them and their finances – and so victims had to give undertakings that they would, somehow, return the money when they arrived back in the UK. In my opinion, this was unethical, and naturally I am pleased that the Home Office has amended their policies and have now scrapped charging forced marriage victims to pay for their own flights (BBC News, 2019).

Working on HBA and forced marriage cases – male victims, new challenges

Although the majority of the cases that I have dealt with have involved female victims, I have increasingly come into contact with male victims. This poses new challenges and difficulties because male victims require different approaches to intervention. Here, I discuss three cases that I recently encountered as a serving police officer at West Midlands Police, demonstrating the specific challenges that male victims pose.

Case example 1

This case was reported to the police by a girlfriend concerned that her boyfriend had been taken to Pakistan and was going to be forced into marriage against his will. Police enquiries revealed that the male's family disapproved of the girlfriend and had many times tried to keep their son away from her. I made contact with the family to ascertain the whereabouts of the male and to confirm that he was safe and well – the family stated that he had gone to Pakistan for a holiday. I then contacted the border force agency and established his travel itinerary. He had travelled on a single ticket only, and no return date had been booked with the airline. This aroused further suspicion and so I made further enquiries. Intelligence checks revealed that the family had a history of HBA which, again, added to the risk for the male. The male had ceased using his UK mobile phone and all of his social media accounts. Consideration was then given to apply for an FMPO. The male victim also had a history of drug abuse and, in my experience, concerned family members often send their children 'back home' in order to put them on 'the straight and narrow' and to rid them of their addictions. I discussed obtaining an FMPO with the girlfriend, and she said that she would continue sending him messages directly. She told him in a message that she had contacted the police. The male received a message via email, and his family had also informed him that the police had attended the family home address. I then managed to have a conversation with the male victim him, and he subsequently played down the reason for his trip to Pakistan. I then discussed an FMPO with him, but he did not support this idea. The victim was in Pakistan and I was never able to establish his true feelings. However, he made it clear that he did not want to return to the UK at that particular time. He did not want any further police intervention in Pakistan or in the UK. My initial reaction was that pressure from his girlfriend in the UK, and contact from West Midlands Police, was getting to him and it was much easier for him to cut us all off. I then liaised with the FMU and the British High Commission in Islamabad, Pakistan. I had informed the victim that unless he presented himself at the Embassy for a 'safe and well check', I would then proceed with an application for an FMPO without his support. The male victim subsequently attended the British Embassy, and they carried out a welfare interview with him. He was adamant that he was not under any pressure to marry. I had asked the Embassy staff to provide him with a safety plan in case he did get into any trouble. However, I do think it is more difficult for male victims to come forward. Men are definitely portrayed as the dominant sex and, in the cases that I have dealt with, where the father is not present, an elder brother has to take the mantle of being the 'man of the house'. While institutions like the British courts in this country *do not* treat applications from men any different to those of women, the most important thing to remember is that in order to obtain an order for a victim, you need the permission of the victim. Sadly, men do seem to be more reluctant to come forward and consequently, it can be more difficult to obtain orders for male victims of forced marriage. If a victim does not support the application for an FMPO, especially if he is an adult, it can be more difficult to obtain an FMPO via the family courts. We therefore have to think of innovative ways to encourage more male victims to come forward and access the law.

It was very clear that the victim did not want to see his family in trouble with the law or see them criminalised in any way. He did not want any police involvement or assistance, but it was important to us to carry out a 'safe and well check' upon the male victim. He was an adult who had made his own decisions, and it was important that we did not force any action upon him that could put him at any risk. It was difficult for his girlfriend to accept his decision, and she had acted in his best interests. The girlfriend was from the same religious and cultural background as the male victim, so one might have thought that marriage between the two should not have been an issue for the family; sadly, this was not the case. The male victim had suggested to his girlfriend that they could continue with their relationship, even if he was married in Pakistan. This is a common theme with male victims that I do not see with female victims – privileges and 'double standards' mean that men have more options to negotiate living with forced marriage and lead 'double lives' in comparison to women (see Chantler in this collection for further discussion of this). In all of the cases where I have dealt with female victims, female victims state that their brothers are treated differently. The brothers are given far more freedom and have more of a say in who they want marry. They are even allowed to carry on with extra-marital affairs, often with their parents' knowledge, as long as they have a wife at home and fulfil their 'family duties', such as looking after the parents and paying the bills. Some parents will turn a blind eye to their son's behaviour and illicit relationships. As a police officer, I have dealt with domestic abuse cases where the wife has had enough of the man's affair, or where the 'second partner' no longer tolerates that their partner is married and not living with them.

Case example 2

This case involved two British citizens – a male of Indian/Hindu heritage and a female of Pakistani/Muslim background. Both were in a secret relationship with each other, and neither of their families were aware of the relationship. They had met at work and continued to see each other outside work hours. Both were well educated and in professional careers. They had a sexual relationship, and the female became pregnant. She knew that her family would not accept a non-Muslim as her husband and so she suggested to the male that he convert to Islam so that they would be able to marry. He was not happy with this suggestion but said he would continue to support her and play a part in bringing up their child. The female knew that her family would not accept her having a child out of wedlock. She then told the male that if he did not convert to Islam and marry her, she would tell his family that she was his girlfriend and that she was pregnant. Furthermore, she informed him that he would never be allowed to see his child or play any part in the child's upbringing. The male knew that his family would not accept him being in a relationship with a Muslim. He was the only son and knew that they were expecting him to continue the family bloodline. The male explained that he was torn between the love of his family and his responsibility to his partner and unborn child. He said he feared his father's reaction and felt it was an easier option to leave home than tell them the truth. He left home for work and failed to return home that evening. His parents were extremely concerned as he was not answering his phone or emails, so they reported him missing. Police officers managed to locate him and informed his parents that he was safe and well but did not want any contact from his parents. The male was the victim in this case. He stated that he was under so much pressure from his partner that he had converted to Islam against his wishes. His partner then introduced him to her family; however, she did not tell them that she was pregnant. The marriage was then arranged quickly and they then rented a property together. They had an Islamic marriage ceremony and only the bride's family attended. The male victim had no family or friends at the wedding. The male victim stated that his partner also pressurised him into attending mosque and praying; however, he still held onto his Hindu religious beliefs.

After the marriage, the male victim stated that his life purely consisted of his partner's family and her social circle. He blames her for completely ostracising him from his own family and friends. She continued to make threats that if he did not do as she said, she would reveal everything to his family. In this instance, it would appear that the female with whom he was in a relationship blackmailed and emotionally coerced him into marriage. Eventually, it affected his mental well-being, and he made the decision to leave the relationship. He took the difficult step of returning home and revealing everything to his parents and siblings. His parents did not react badly towards him and were sympathetic to his situation. In their view, he was their son and they would support him no matter what – his initial fears of their reaction were unfounded. The male victim then reported the matter to police. His 'wife' was arrested on the allegation of committing forced marriage. The female pleaded her innocence, arguing the victim was not coerced in any way and converted to Islam himself and also married her according to his own free will. Although there was no prosecution or conviction in this case, it should not make a difference whether a victim is female or male. Like many other crimes, men are equally vulnerable and in this instance, the main perpetrator was a female who controlled and manipulated her male victim.

Case example 3

The victim in this case was an Indian Sikh Male. He came into police custody after his mother had reported him for an assault against her. While he was in custody, he interacted with mental health and nursing staff and disclosed to them the reasons for him being in custody. The victim lived in an inner city suburb made up of predominantly immigrant communities. He had lived within two streets throughout his life (40 years of age at the time of his arrest). He was the eldest of three siblings and the only son; he was also the only male sibling in the extended family. His father had passed away when he was 20 years old, and he had always lived with his mother. His sisters had married, leaving just him and his mother in the family home. From a young age, he knew he was different. His sisters used to dress him up in girls' clothes, and he preferred playing with girls toys. He went through junior school with no issues, but as he got older and became more sexually aware, he knew he was more attracted to men. He did not act overtly gay, but by the time he had reached 15 years of age, he started to develop feelings for boys. However, he kept his feelings hidden. He remembers some of his female cousins taunting him about being gay and he just laughed it off. Once he left school at 16, he felt more comfortable about his sexuality. He started to study and socialise away from home and felt he could live his life his way, albeit in secret. He knew that he could not 'come out' as gay – he was from a proud Sikh family where the men were 'macho' and proud of their warrior history, and so coming out was not an option for him.

Once he finished his studies, he joined a large corporate company and life was looking good for him. He had a long-term partner living in a different city, and they met up as often as they could. He had made it clear to his partner that he could not tell his family about his relationship and that he had to accept the relationship for what it was. Eventually his partner split up with him because he could not maintain the relationship and wanted more commitment. Once he had reached his late twenties, family members were pressurising him to marry. He was socialising and meeting like-minded men in the gay quarter of his home city and stated that, at that time, there were 'very few gay Asian men on the scene'. He only had relationships with white men because he could not handle a partner that was going through the same as him. All of his cousins and sisters were now married, and the pressure for him to marry was building by the day. He even contemplated marrying a woman to please his family. He thought that if he went to India and married, his wife would come to England, which would please his mother, and then he could lead his secret life alongside married life – the only concern for him was the sexual aspect of marriage, as he knew he could not have sex with a female.

He eventually decided against the idea and continued with his secret life. His mental health deteriorated and 'living the lie' was becoming increasingly more difficult for him. His mental health became so bad that he was prescribed antidepressants and was diagnosed as a having a split personality disorder. He was also diagnosed with post-traumatic stress disorder, had to leave his job and was hospitalised several times, confirming Jaspal's research (in this collection) that homosexual men in 'honour' cultures are at elevated risk of psychological harm because their sexual identity contradicts social and religious norms. His relationship at home with his mother was becoming increasingly tense as his mother could not understand why he did not want to get married. The emotional blackmail from his mother was unbearable – his mother started to control his movements and finances – if he chose not to get married then his mother was not going to allow him to do his own thing. He was in his mid-thirties by this time and she was treating him like a child. She would lock him in the house for weeks at a time. She would go out to work, lock all the doors and take the keys; she also took away the victim's bank cards and mobile phone. Throughout his victimisation, he never called out for help. The victim felt that if he reported his mother for what she was doing to him, she would be arrested, and he did not want to put her through that. The violence then started, and his mother would fly into fits of rage and attack him. He still defended her actions and, in his view, she was only doing this because he was refusing to marry. In some respects, he was playing down her violence. He confided in his sisters and was telling them of the physical violence that he was experiencing. They listened to him, but still defended their mother's actions by blaming him for not getting married. The violence continued, and eventually he fought back. While he would never hit his mother, when she did attack him he would push her away. He felt very embarrassed that he was in his thirties and was being 'chastised' by his mother – there were obvious links to masculinity here. When he did retaliate, his mother called the police and he was arrested. However, in light of his disclosure, no further action was taken by the police.

The male victim did not plan on 'coming out' to his family but he remembers his sister visiting him at the family home. He was sitting in the same room as his sister and mother and without warning, he stood up and shouted '*I'm a Gandu*', walked out of the room and went to his bedroom. The term '*Gandu*' is a very derogatory term in the Punjabi language as it is used to signify and label men as 'gay'. As a police officer, I asked him why he used this term, and he said that it was the only term that his mother would understand. The male victim explained that his mother cried for days. All the immediate family came to the house and tried to talk him out of 'being gay'. They were more concerned about what the family and community would think than how he felt, demonstrating how families are more concerned about their 'honour' and reputation. He felt an immense relief of pressure when he told his family. Although his mother was struggling to accept it, his siblings and the rest of his immediate family offered their support. His sisters told him that they had always suspected that he was gay. The immediate family knowing was one thing, but the whole community knowing was completely out of the question. On the day of his last arrest, he was at home and a male neighbour who was married with children had visited him. They were sitting in the lounge chatting. His mother came in from work and did not recognise the neighbour. She flew into a fit of rage, and the neighbour had to run out of the back door. She then attacked the male victim and in self-defence, he pushed her off him. Again, his mother then called the police and he was subsequently arrested. The male victim disclosed to the nurse what had happened to him, and although he was in custody as a suspect of a domestic assault, he was in fact the victim. This was not initially picked up by police officers when he was in custody. There is definitely something we can all learn from this. Whilst in custody, the police offer support for drugs, alcohol and mental health. Although the male victim did give his reasons for the incident, sadly it was never followed up. It would seem that, by chance, this case was referred to me in passing by a nurse who the victim had spoken to during a consultation and reached out to her. The nurse only mentioned it to me because she knew that I worked on forced marriage cases. I think there has been much positive work by police forces across the country when dealing with HBA and forced marriage cases, especially the watershed moment of Banaz Mahmod, which highlighted poor police practices (Payton, 2010). However, I still believe that, when it comes to HBA and forced marriages, the perception is that it only happens to female victims. Within West Midlands Police, our latest training and awareness promotes the existence of male victims, as well as those who do not have the mental or physical capacity to give their consent to marriage (see further, Clawson, in this collection). We are striving hard to change perceptions and attitudes within our own police force about who can be victims, but sadly, this is not necessarily reflected in all police forces as highlighted by the HMIC Report in 2015 (HMIC, 2015). Awareness still needs to improve. It is now some time since the incident and I have remained in contact with the male victim and offered him support. His home life has changed for the better and, although his mother still wants him to marry and thinks he can 'undo being gay', he is happy living at home. He would never make a formal complaint against his mother and still feels she is acting in his best interests. But he knows that he can never introduce a male partner to his family, as this would be a step too far. However, he does manage to go out socially and negotiates this around his mother being away from the house. He now wears the house key around his neck; he keeps his mobile phone close to him; and a safety plan has been created for him if ever he finds himself in danger.

Comment

The dynamics of HBA and forced marriage cases involving men differ to those concerning female victims. I have personally dealt with far more female victims than male victims. It seems apparent to me that men are allowed more freedom and can enter into relationships far more easily, whether it is an extra marital affair or having a girlfriend who is accepted in the community. Parents will also accept their sons marrying and continuing other (sexual) relationships with women. In many of the cases I have been involved with, families are content so long as they are able to have a daughter-in-law at home who will look after them, cook and clean. Female victims, on the other hand, are clearly not given the same freedom of choice. I have also discovered that male victims are more reluctant to come forward – this could come down to machoism or sheer embarrassment at the fact they are victims of HBA and forced marriages. While government figures do show that there are far more female victims than male, I do feel that HBA and forced marriages are still under-reported and that the official figures represent only the tip of the iceberg for both sexes. I also believe that the traditional belief in South Asian communities that the male is the bread winner and the female is the home-maker still exists, especially in communities that are traditional. Although we now have four generations of South Asians here in the UK, there are still large parts of the community who have come to the UK on spouse or study visas. Many of the community will live in the same area, and I have come across areas where almost all of the houses on a street are made up from people from the same village 'back home'. Parents, siblings and cousins will nearly all live on the same street. Therefore, everyone will know each other's business and 'keeping up appearances' is hugely important within honour cultures. If this means that men are to be portrayed as the 'men of the house' and the females as the housewives, then this is what will happen. Male victims will also subscribe and act in support of these norms – adding to the difficulties for men to report abuse and who do not meet to prescribed social ideals.

'Honour' and respect are extremely important within the South Asian community and anything that brings 'shame' upon the family is frowned upon. While male victims can and do get away with certain behaviour, when things go badly wrong it is my opinion that they are under the same risks as females. The most difficult challenge is to get the victim to support prosecution, and most victims are unwilling to see their parents convicted of a crime. On these occasions, this is when the civil route concerning forced marriages can be discussed with them and FMPOs utilised. Forced marriage only became a criminal offence in 2014, and it is still early – we only have four successful prosecutions. It is important as an investigating police officer that I understand the communities that forced marriage affects. Understanding the dynamics of religion, culture and the places where victims are taken to has definitely enabled me to investigate cases far better than my counterparts who lack this knowledge. Many forced marriages take place abroad, where we have no jurisdiction and obtaining evidence can be extremely challenging even for agencies based in that country. If I ever visit a country or send colleagues there on police business, then local permission has to be granted. This is common practice in South Asian countries, but permission can often take weeks and if a victim is still trapped, then little can be done. There need to be agreements with international governments on the investigation and prosecution of HBA and forced marriages committed abroad and the extraction of victims, as this will make our jobs as police officers much easier. However, corruption is also a problem and many local police forces cannot be trusted – this again can hinder investigations. Some of the regions where forced marriage victims are taken are deemed too dangerous to enter and, again, this can rule out repatriation.

A multi-agency approach is extremely important and information sharing is vital, but the most important recommendation I advocate is the promotion of awareness – for both state agencies like the police and for members of the community. Educating the community in understanding that forced marriages are illegal is a far better preventative tool than having to deal with cases where the offence has already taken place or when the victim has already left the country. As a retired police officer, I feel that forced marriage is still a taboo subject, and many communities do not see it as criminal. Many people still believe that they can choose who and where their children can marry. I have also personally come across hurdles from the community who feel we are interfering with their cultural beliefs and practices. What I do know from working on many cases and across different religious groups is that forced marriage is forbidden by most religions, and it is also a criminal offence in South Asian countries. Forced marriage is a massively under-reported phenomenon and is something that is not going to go away any time soon. Police forces that have experience with forced marriages need to share their experiences on a national and international level, and officers who are experienced in investigating HBA and forced marriages need to be retained to use their expertise to train emerging officers coming through the ranks. No UK police force has a separate HBA or forced marriage unit or a separate dedicated team. I have investigated forced marriage offences alongside other domestic abuse cases. But forced marriages cases can be very complex indeed. Investigations span partner organisations and foreign countries and many of the victims have complex needs – we need to set up and organise police forces in such a way that they have specialist police officers and specialist units to address HBA and forced marriages separately. For these reasons, I support many of the recommendations put forward by Idriss (2018) and his presentation before MPs in Parliament in January 2019.

One of the consequences of forced marriage is suicide, and victims have been murdered in so-called honour killings. One victim is too many. While the criminalisation of forced marriage is firmly established by law, my belief remains that many police forces and partner agencies still lack knowledge and experience to deal with such cases. For these reasons, there needs to be better investment on a national scale to a dedicated HBA and Forced Marriage Unit to truly investigate these crimes and to provide the victims with the service and intervention they deserve, whether female or male.

References

BBC News (2015), 'Forced Marriage Jail First as Cardiff Man Sentenced', www.bbc.co.uk/news/uk-wales-33076323 10 June (last accessed 16 August 2019).

BBC News (2018a), 'India Killing: "My Father Ordered My Husband's Murder"', www.bbc.co.uk/news/world-asia-india-45570981 20 September (last accessed 16 August 2019).

BBC News (2018b), 'Forced Marriage: Parents Guilty of Luring Daughter to Bangladesh', www.bbc.co.uk/news/uk-england-leeds-44290935 29 May (last accessed 16 August 2019).

BBC News (2019), 'Forced Marriage Victims Asked to Pay Rescue Costs', www.bbc.co.uk/news/uk-46733028 2 January (last accessed 16 August 2019).

Her Majesty's Inspectorate of Constabulary (HMIC) (2015), *The Depths of Dishonour: Hidden Voices and Shameful Crimes.* Report (8 December).

Home Office (2018) *Preventing and Tackling Forced Marriage: A Consultation*, www.gov.uk/government/consultations/preventing-and-tackling-forced-marriage (last accessed 16 August 2019).

Idriss, Mohammad Mazher (2015), 'Forced Marriages: The Need for Criminalisation?', *Criminal Law Review*, 9, 663.

Idriss, Mohammad Mazher (2018) *Recommendations from the National Honour-Based Violence Roadshow 2018* (October) www2.mmu.ac.uk/business-school/research/research-centres/national-hbv/ (last accessed 16 August 2019).

Payton, Joanne (2010), 'Collective Crimes, Collective Victims: A Case Study of the Murder of Banaz Mahmod', in Mohammad Mazher Idriss and Tahir Abbas (eds.), *Honour, Violence, Women and Islam* (London: Routledge-Cavendish, 2010), pp. 67–79.

Summers, Hannah (2018) 'Birmingham Woman Jailed for Duping Daughter into Forced Marriage', *The Guardian*, 23 May 2018, www.theguardian.com/uk-news/2018/may/23/birmingham-woman-jailed-duping-daughter-forced-marriage (last accessed 16 August 2019).

Chapter 11

The Elm Foundation

The transition from a 'women's-only' to a 'gender-neutral' domestic abuse organisation

Mohammad Mazher Idriss and Jennifer Calverley

Introduction

The Elm Foundation was established in 1985 as part of the Women's Aid Federation, directly emanating from the women's rights' movement to support female victims of domestic abuse. Specifically, it was designed and run by women for abused women and their children. During its inception, the organisation did not recognise that men could experience domestic abuse – rather, it recognised that men were the ones responsible for its perpetration. However, ten years ago the organisation changed the way it responded to domestic abuse because of an increased number of enquiries requesting support for male victims. In January 2010, The Elm Foundation conducted a pilot programme to support male victims. It still recognised that domestic abuse is gender-based and that women are its primary victims. However, it also recognised that domestic abuse occurs across all groups in society, regardless of gender and ethnicity, and that there was a serious lack of resources to support male victims, together with lack of refuge space. Following the pilot programme, The Elm Foundation formally established a male refuge in the Derbyshire area in September 2010, one of only ten male refuges in the England and Wales today. It provides refuge space for male victims, including men experiencing HBA and forced marriage. This chapter will highlight The Elm Foundation's transition from a women's-only organisation towards a gender-neutral organisation. It will chart out some of the challenges that existed at the time of its transition, including resistance from some of its own board members. In particular, it will discuss the organisation's experiences and difficulties when supporting male victims. An analysis of ten case files of men who have received support from The Elm Foundation will highlight the barriers and challenges that exist, including men not being validated as victims and not knowing where to access support. The chapter will also consider the impact that these case files have on policy development, the implications for other organisations contemplating opening up their services to both men and women and what counts as best practice when seeking to support men.

Charting the history behind The Elm Foundation

Since the 1970s, domestic abuse has gained national attention resulting in a plethora of research and literature, with radical feminists primarily focusing on women as victims and men as perpetrators (Tsui, 2014). Radical feminism has been hugely beneficial towards the recognition of VAWG, and the Women's Aid movement was part of that wider movement in the UK. Erin Pizzey was the founder of the first refuge for women (Chiswick Women's Aid) and received extensive praise for her work by Lord Hailsham in the House of Lords (see *Simmons v Pizzey* [1977] 2 All ER 432) and by legal commentators at the time (Hoath, 1978). Her refuge was set up as a centre where women could meet, talk and seek help about domestic abuse. Independent refuges for women and children were set up as part of a nation-wide movement across the UK, and many of these groups came together to share their experiences and collectively used the name 'Women's Aid'. In 1978, a group of women in the Derbyshire area came together and decided to do something for the women and children who were experiencing domestic abuse within the local area. They established the North Derbyshire Women's Aid (NDWA), using their own homes to provide emergency shelter, and offered a centre for women to receive emotional support. NDWA was heavily reliant on charitable donations for food, bedding, clothing and toys. As the years went by, the demand for their services increased, although donations were depleting. The local police force was bringing women and children to NDWA's doorstep and accommodation soon became overcrowded. In addition, NDWA was unable to support women into new accommodation because the local authority did not appreciate the difficulties surrounding domestic abuse and suggested (at the time) that victims had to return home.

NDWA was heavily involved in national campaigns and movements for the better recognition of women's rights. As a result, NDWA was able to secure funding for its first ever refuge, providing women and their children with their own bedrooms and communal living facilities. In 1985, NDWA was also able to register as a charity, which opened further doors for potential funding and provided NDWA with an even greater voice to campaign for women's rights. Over the next 25 years (1985–2010), NDWA grew and expanded further by being able to offer additional women's refuges (three in total), an advice centre, a helpline and a community service and children centre. NDWA gained important recognition within the Derbyshire area for being a leading charity that provided services and in 2009, the board of trustees decided to rebrand and change the organisation's name from 'North Derbyshire Women's Aid' to 'Derbyshire Domestic Violence and Sexual Abuse Service' (DDVSAS). Although not directly the intention, the name change was seen by the local community as a move away from providing a women's-only service towards becoming a gender-neutral organisation. DDVSAS then began to receive requests to support men who were experiencing domestic abuse, HBA and forced marriages. The organisation was perceived to be a gender-neutral service, but the problem was that this was not the case – DDVSAS still only provided a service to women and their children. DDVSAS recognised that domestic abuse was (and still is) predominantly perpetrated by men towards women, and the organisation did not want to lose any of the grassroot values upon which it was founded. However, they could not ignore the number of men coming forward. DDVSAS then made the conscientious decision to carry out a pilot service, providing a male refuge and an outreach service for male victims. This proved very controversial – when DDVSAS started working with male victims, two members of the board resigned and two support counsellors refused to support male victims. Although no members of staff from DDVSAS left employment, there was a strong resistance towards supporting men. However, after a successful trial period, from 2010 onwards the organisation developed a permanent service for men called the SAM project and secured funding for a new male refuge, which still exists today. The male refuge itself is very small – it has only three bedrooms for three single men, one communal kitchen, one adjoining dining area and one small living room. In 2016, it was felt that the name DDVSAS did not represent the organisation as a charitable third sector organisation and through a rebranding process, the organisation changed its name to The Elm Foundation.

To put The Elm Foundation's work into context, Parity (a voluntary organisation concerned with equal rights for men and women) initiated a Freedom of Information request in 2014 of a random selection of 49 city and Metropolitan Councils and 35 County Councils (i.e. 84 in total) in England and Wales in order to analyse the services provided for victims of domestic abuse for both sexes. Seventy-eight of the councils that responded provided some form of shared services generally for both male and female victims, although this extended only to outreach or support for male victims in the case of 11 authorities, while two City/Metro Councils and two County Councils appeared to provide no routine or specific services at all for male victims; in addition, only two Councils, both County, provided specific refuge accommodation for male victims and their children (Parity, 2014: 1). Furthermore, whilst 79% of Councils provided a refuge service for female victims and their children, only 28% provided emergency accommodation for male victims and their children in lieu of refuge provision; only two Councils (both County) provided actual refuge accommodation for male victims and their children (Parity, 2014: 2). Despite a gender-neutral approach in the case of some local authorities, Parity comment that the bulk of the funding for domestic abuse services by Councils is still directed at women and, in particular, dedicated refuge accommodation for women and their children. Parity conclude that the impression that this leaves is 'that the majority of Councils do not take the provision of meaningful support services for male victims of domestic abuse (and their children) as seriously as equality law might expect' (Parity, 2014: 2). They also argue that where refuge provision is provided by Councils for female victims, the least that they could do in the name of equality is to provide emergency accommodation of some form for comparable male victims and their children, as a failure to do this leads to injustice for male victims and their children (Parity, 2014: 2).

This information demonstrates just how rare The Elm Foundation is and how resources to support men are scarce in England and Wales.

The transition was a challenge for The Elm Foundation. Specialist workers were concerned that male victims might feel that their masculine identities would be questioned if they had female support workers working with them (see e.g. the discussion in Chapter 1). Initially, support workers working with men found it uncomfortable and expressed doubts about whether the men themselves were minimising their abuse in order to protect their masculinity. It was discovered very early on that The Elm Foundation needed to improve partnerships with other agencies in order to share best practice. Expert training was provided to all staff at the organisation. Male victims also (confidentially) responded that they did not find female support workers a problem, although they did acknowledge that they felt a sense of embarrassment talking to a woman. Male victims reported that they felt that female support workers were not completely confident with their approach towards addressing male victims and that this was what made them feel uncomfortable. In response, The Elm Foundation required all employees to undertake further training and embed good practice. This included a better understanding of: (a) the experiences of male victims in domestic abuse cases; (b) how to assess men's needs; (c) how to respond to male victims' needs; (d) assessing and managing risk for male victims; (e) how male victims' experiences differ from women's experiences; (f) the nature, scale and incidence of intimate partner violence against men; (g) the skills needed to identify male victims and to respond appropriately; and (h) how men are stereotyped and the effects of 'masculinity' on social constructions on who can be a 'victim'. As a result of further training, intervention and support improved dramatically as workers grew more in confidence. This also led to an improvement in feedback from male victims. Today, there is no resistance from employees and the general consensus is that The Elm Foundation needs to build upon the good work and further expand its services for men.

Methodology

To obtain data on male victims of HBA and forced marriage, the authors researched case files relating to victims who experienced intervention and support from The Elm Foundation since 2010. Case files are stored electronically on a Case Management System called OASIS. This is a specific Case Management System designed for The Elm Foundation, which tracks outcomes for service users, both male and female. The case files stored on OASIS represent a stable source of information that can be viewed by those only with access (Yin, 2003; Finnegan, 2006). It is a secure database with limited access due to confidentiality and data sensitivity. The cases retrieved were all taken from those cases where men had been staying at the male refuge, and data was extracted from the Case Management System. The files were not, and never have been, changed in any way since their creation. Case files are neither published nor available to the general public (Gillham, 2000: 42). The files are also unobtrusive – they were not created as a result of any other case study or research project and simply contained information detailing the names, references and accounts of men's experiences of victimisation, together with The Elm Foundation's subsequent intervention and support (Yin, 2003). The broad coverage and long time span (nearly nine years) of the database meant that staff with access were able to record many events within many different social settings, thus providing a rich account of experiences (Yin, 2003: 86). The authors read, analysed and interpreted a selection of the case files in order to acquire a better understanding of men's experiences and the challenges associated with intervention. The contextual nature and interpretation of case files was also enhanced by the second author having intimate knowledge of each of the male victims and having been directly involved in the support of some of the cases. HBA and forced marriages are a vastly underreported phenomenon, and it is very difficult to obtain access to participants who are willing to engage with a qualitative research design in order to draw valid conclusions. It is difficult to obtain access to victims to discuss their experiences, especially victims from minority communities because of the shame, dishonour and embarrassment involved in discussing and reliving personal and traumatic experiences (Idriss, 2018a). This includes BME women's personal experiences of sexual victimisation (Cowburn et al., 2015; Harrison and Gill, 2017). However, recent studies with survivors and stakeholders on HBA and forced marriages in the UK have been conducted, and there is a small but growing body of empirical and qualitative research highlighting women's experiences (see Begikhani et al., 2015; Aplin, 2017; Idriss, 2017a, 2017b, 2018a; Mulvihill et al., 2018; Gill et al., 2018; Chantler and McCarry, 2019). However, none of these studies explores the experiences of men, approaching research from feminist frameworks about women (see Samad, 2010). Given that one-fifth of the FMU cases annually concern male victims of forced marriages (Home Office, 2018), this small (but growing) number demonstrates the difficulties of trying to locate male victims. Chapter 1 discussed a fear on the part of some men that they will have their masculinity questioned if they come forward to discuss their abuse, so this poses a challenge with recruiting men to participate in research of this nature. This, in part, may also be due to the small number of male services and the fact that many women's organisations do not adequately cater to men. Obtaining case files was therefore considered an appropriate method for this investigation, and The Elm Foundation was able to provide case files where they had directly supported men, but which did not necessitate taking part in interviews. Furthermore, obtaining contact with previous male service users would be difficult because they had either moved on, they had dispersed to other areas, or generally their whereabouts were unknown because they had been passed on to different agencies. The authors also decided not to interview existing male service users given their existing trauma and vulnerabilities, in line with ethical research.

One of the strengths of case file analysis is that it can help to develop theory and understanding of male victimisation through an analysis of men who sought intervention from government agencies and third-sector organisations (Yin, 2003; George and Bennett, 2004). It can help to show how men experience intervention and the challenges faced when seeking to leave abusive relationships. To this end, this chapter seeks to build on the existing literature highlighted in Chapter 1, providing empirical data from a source not accessible to the general public about men who are largely hidden from HBA research, or who are silenced because of the lack of available support services that cater to men. Evidence from multiple case files is often considered compelling because it helps to offer examples where the individuals concerned share similar or conflicting experiences (Yin, 2003: 46, 53). Any data highlighting male victimisation is welcomed as part of the developing research in the field. One of the key strengths of case file analysis is the ability to examine in depth a case within its 'real-life' context (Yin, 2003). It enables stories to be illuminated about a particular situation, to obtain a close and in-depth understanding of the issues surrounding that case file by helping to make direct first-hand observations – in this case, with the assistance of the second author, who had intimate knowledge of the victims within her own natural setting of being a CEO of the charity. Furthermore, case file methods are beneficial when a research project considers both *descriptive questions* (e.g. what happened to male victims of HBA and forced marriage?) and *explanatory questions* (e.g. how and why did male victims come to experience abuse and what was their experience of intervention like?) (Yin, 2003). Undertaking case file analysis of this type also requires combining data collection and data analysis together, since the study of individual case files may produce data that conflicts with that from another case file (Yin, 2003). Reading and interpreting case files constitutes the data collection aspect of the research, but can also help to expose different conflicts, contradictions, outcomes and challenges. This potentially provides for a rich and varied account of men's experiences, and the most intriguing cases files are those that one is able to carefully compare and contrast.

There are, however, limitations with case file analysis of this type. Case files were provided and selected by The Elm Foundation and, in particular, by the second author as CEO. She decided on what she believed were 'good examples' to include of men that The Elm Foundation had supported since 2010. We therefore recognise that there could be elements of bias in the selection process by the second author (Yin, 2003: 86; George and Bennett, 2004: 22–34). The question that naturally arises is why did the second author choose particular case files for examination, but not others? The answer is because she had personally worked on some of these cases and felt that it was important to include them, given her familiarity with those male victims. Thus, the impact of bias could affect the overall data within the context of reporting and interpretation. Another limitation with the methodology relates to the accuracy of case files (and electronic storage in general), for the case files might not be accurate and may include bias in themselves (Yin, 2003: 87). This is because case files are inserted data and have been entered (and interpreted) by the relevant caseworkers at The Elm Foundation. Therefore, case files may be subject to individual bias of the (multiple) people who authored them. Case files must therefore be carefully used and should be treated with some caution (Yin, 2003: 87).

How did we overcome these issues relating to bias (either from the second author's or individual case worker's perspectives)? The authors adopted a formal case file screening procedure, where we based our screening on reviewing all available case files, reviewing documents, querying and corroborating with (multiple) knowledgeable persons within The Elm Foundation (e.g. other support workers) about each male victim who entered the refuge and why he should be chosen as a candidate for study within our sample (Yin, 2003: 87). This also included the richness of the data available, the preliminary evidence that the case file in question had the type of information that we were seeking to study and those cases that explicitly related to HBA or forced marriage. Of course, the obvious limitation of the current investigation relates to the small sample size, which may not necessarily be representative or reflective of the types of cases other support organisations are familiar with. The authors do not underestimate the significance of this, but the issues presented in the current investigation provide a 'snapshot' of the male cases that were sampled at a particular moment in history and time at The Elm Foundation. The authors are mindful that there may be other reasons, factors and explanations of why men experience HBA and forced marriages and the associated challenges for intervention. That said, the current investigation provides a glimpse into the types of cases that involve male HBA and forced marriage. It is hoped that as the research field becomes more developed, other researchers will utilise and apply other (applicable) research methods and to a larger sample in order to draw further generalisations about male HBA and forced marriages.

The case studies

The following section details the case files that were retrieved for this study. The names of the men have been anonymised to protect their identity and privacy. The Elm Foundation receives requests for refuge space from all over the country, and the case files below do not necessarily relate to specific cases in the Derbyshire area as the organisation is known to accept referrals from further afield.

Case study 1

This 22-year-old male from Pakistan had been forced into marriage against his will and had no recourse to public funds (NRPF) due to his immigration status. During his marriage, he experienced abuse from his wife and in-laws and was admitted to hospital with injuries to his spine following an attack by his brother-in-law. The hospital became suspicious of his injuries, contacted the police and he was brought into The Elm Foundation's refuge. The Elm Foundation wanted to learn why he had not the left the relationship sooner. He informed support workers that he feared deportation and was concerned that his family would disown and kill him for having abandoned his marriage and for bringing shame upon the family. He stated that he felt that no one would believe his story because of his gender. The victim was reported to be a very tall man and his wife small. The male victim believed only women could be victims of abuse (and not men) and felt too embarrassed to speak about his experiences. He did not know where to go, nor had he ever heard of a male refuge. On numerous occasions, he rang the police for help each time he was attacked, fearing that he would die. During the last three months of his relationship, he had contacted the police on five separate occasions. However, he was subsequently arrested twice as his wife made counter-allegations against him. Her family also corroborated his wife's account. No charges were brought against the victim as his wife retracted her complaints. It took a life-threatening injury for the male to leave, and when he was visited by the police in hospital, he did not want to speak to them because he feared that there would be reprisals. However, he had a very trustworthy doctor who was treating him, and for the first time he felt that he was believed and validated.

Case study 2

This 17-year-old Pakistani male was referred to The Elm Foundation as he was about to be forced into a marriage by his parents. He parents suspected that he was gay, imprisoned him in his bedroom (other than to attend school) and subjected him to numerous violent attacks from his father. The school he attended began a campaign to raise awareness on forced marriages during the summer holidays; however, this was targeted at girls and was not aimed at boys. The victim was too embarrassed to speak to staff because he believed that forced marriages only happened to girls. He felt that no one would believe him and did not seek help, nor did he reveal anything to his friends because he was ashamed, embarrassed, and felt that they would laugh at him. His family were well respected within the community and he feared that he would bring shame upon them if he refused a heterosexual marriage. He was the only son and was expected to take over the family business. He never sought help or intervention for himself and was referred to The Elm Foundation by social care after a neighbour had reported concerns of abuse towards a child (having heard screaming, shouting and crying through the walls). It took six attempts to safely remove him from the family home and bring him into refuge. The victim stated that he would never have left home had it not been for the intervention by social care. He struggled to adapt to life in the refuge and although he was 17 years of age, he was still a child living within an adult environment. Having been controlled, he did not know how to live independently and had been so disempowered that he could not function. He felt worthless, suffered severe depression and made several attempts to commit suicide whilst in refuge. Despite being abused, he missed his family and did not know how to live independently without them.

Case study 3

This 18-year-old Somalian worked for the family business. He attended private school, and his family had high academic aspirations. Throughout his childhood, he was controlled and was unable to establish his own friendships. His academic studies were heavily regulated out of school time, and he was required to undertake many hours of homework after school. His family made it very clear that he had to marry once he finished his A-levels. A bride had already been arranged when he was just 14. He initially accepted this marriage, however, he challenged this when he turned adult. The more he resisted his family's wishes, the more controlling they became, and he was forced to work in the family business at every available hour. He became withdrawn, suffered depression and idealised thoughts of suicide. The wedding date was brought forward, and the victim felt that he had no choice but to obey his family. A customer of the business regularly saw the victim and became concerned for his welfare. He addressed him about his concerns, but the victim denied that anything was wrong. The customer then raised his suspicions with the police and over a period of three months, specialist police officers built a relationship with the victim. The police felt that it was important for them to gain the victim's trust in order to provide him with an opportunity to disclose his forced marriage and to provide him with support. After three months, a plan was arranged to extract the victim from the family home and move him into refuge. When the victim arrived at the refuge, he withdrew from everybody. He did not leave his bedroom, stopped eating and became even more depressed. His depression was so severe that the mental health crisis team became involved. He was frightened that his family would find him and did not feel safe because members of the community would be looking for him. His fear was such that he refused to pursue a police investigation and withdrew all of his statements. He found it very difficult to live without control and the boundaries he had been accustomed to – he did not know how to live independently, make his own decisions and was deeply traumatised.

Case study 4

This white British male came to the refuge following a self-referral. He was gay and had kept this a secret since the age of 15. He had various relationships with males and at the time of intervention he was 20 years old. He had hidden his sexual orientation due to the fear of the reaction of his parents, who were very homophobic. In his last relationship, the victim had also experienced same-sex domestic abuse, which he had recognised early on and made a conscientious decision to leave. However, post-separation (and as an act of revenge), the victim's ex-partner announced that the victim was gay on social media. His ex-partner was aware of the fears he had about his parent's homophobia (in the case file, the victim described that his father once told him that 'he would put a bullet in his head if he was gay' and that he would 'beat the gay out of him'). The victim was very distressed by this outing. He frantically scoured the Internet for advice, but very little came up. He did, however, seek support from an LGBTQ advice centre in his local area. From there, they supported him and contacted The Elm Foundation, at which point a referral was made, and the victim stayed at the refuge.

Case study 5

This Iranian victim was 19 years old and had both learning and physical disabilities. He did not understand why he had been placed within the refuge and missed his family. He was referred to refuge via a court order specifying his removal from the family home and was subject to Safeguarding Vulnerable Adults' procedures for over three years. Whilst attending school, the victim openly talked to his teachers about his family and how he was kept indoors and that: (a) he had no friends; (b) his family verbally abused him; (c) he had to do work for the family and when he made a mistake, he would be beaten; (d) his family were embarrassed and ashamed of him; (e) his food was restricted and that he was always hungry; and (f) his mother stopped his medication, and he was having epileptic seizures more frequently. His school referred him to social care when he was 16 years old. During this time, his family engaged with social care, and things did improve as he seemed to be healthier and more relaxed. However, he did not understand that he was experiencing disability abuse and thought his experience was a 'normal' expression of love. He happily mentioned to his social worker on one of the many visits that he was going on holiday – it later transpired that he was going to be taken abroad to be married (for further discussion of forced marriage and those with learning difficulties, see Chapter 5 by Rachel Clawson). The victim would not engage with support to leave the family home, as he wanted to make his family happy. Social care classed him as not having the capacity to consent to marriage and applied to have him removed from the home. He came to the refuge with carers for two weeks, until social care found him supported housing. During this time, the victim was deeply distressed and wanted to go home – he missed his family and felt alone.

Case study 6

This 17-year-old victim was a college student who was taken to Pakistan during the summer holidays on the pretext of a family holiday. He had told friends that he had bought presents for his family and was due to return for his final A-levels. However, whilst in Pakistan he was forced into marriage. He felt that he could not say no because he did not want to upset his family. The victim then returned to the UK. There was an issue with securing entry to the UK for his wife, and the family decided that the victim should move to be with her in Pakistan until this was resolved. The victim did not want this, as he had secured a place at university and did not want to be with a woman he barely knew. The victim told his family and explained his reasons, at first believing that they understood. However, matters escalated and the victim reported that his family blackmailed and applied emotional pressure to force him to Pakistan. When he refused, he was beaten. The victim was badly injured and was admitted to A&E, where he informed hospital staff that he had fallen over and hurt himself. The victim continued to stand up to his family, but the beatings became worse. When the victim turned 18, he decided that he needed to leave. He left his family and went to seek help at the homeless department at the local council. He was later referred to the refuge. However, he did not want to make a police complaint as he feared repercussions and did not want to bring shame upon his family.

Case study 7

This victim came to the UK on a spousal visa from Pakistan. He married his wife in an arranged marriage and later joined his wife. Life deteriorated for the victim over the coming months, when his wife and her family became abusive. He was treated like a slave and experienced physical violence. He spoke no English, was reliant on his family to communicate for him and had NRPF. These issues were compounded by the control he was placed under. The victim did communicate with his own family in Pakistan that he was being abused but was unable to return home, as he needed to make the marriage work for the 'honour' of his family. However, his father spoke to his wife's father in order to try to resolve the matter. This did not work and only made the abuse worse. One evening, the victim decided to leave the family home but resorted to living in a park for three days because he had nowhere else to go. He had no clothes, food or money. Outreach workers from a local homeless charity came across him and helped him access a homeless hostel. When it became clear what he had been experiencing, they referred him to the refuge. However, there was no funding available for the victim, and so The Elm Foundation had to use its own reserves to finance his stay. The victim was reliant on donations for food and clothes. He also feared deportation to Pakistan and was concerned that he would experience HBA from his own family due to the shame and dishonour of leaving his marriage in the UK. During the application process to secure the victim some public funds under the Destitution Domestic Violence (DDV) Concession, his wife and her family contacted the police to report that he was a terrorist who was planning a terrorist attack in the UK – they attempted to get him deported from the UK. The victim was in refuge for over a year, mainly due to his immigration status. Eventually, he was granted indefinite leave to remain, and he started to learn English at his local college. He left The Elm Foundation refuge with high aspirations for his future – he wanted to support himself financially and enrolled on various courses.

Case study 8

This young victim was a Bangladeshi Muslim, and his family were prominent figures within the community. His father was a very proud man and had a number of businesses. During his teenage years, the victim exhibited challenging behaviour, became embroiled in gang culture and was subsequently convicted of assault and actual bodily harm. The victim's family made the decision that he needed to get married in order to 'put him back on the straight and narrow'. It was arranged for the victim to travel to Bangladesh to get married. The victim rebelled, and his behaviour deteriorated. He began consuming drugs and alcohol and got into more trouble with the police. His family locked him in his bedroom and refused to let him out. During this time, his family were arranging flights and his marriage, and they intended to take him to Bangladesh against his will. When the day arrived, they gave the victim his breakfast, which contained sedatives. They travelled to the airport but as the sedatives wore off, the victim began to understand what was happening to him and played along with the plan. He went to the departure lounge pretending to be in a drugged state and requested to go to the toilet, at which point he ran out of the airport. He did not go to the police because he thought that they would not believe him due to his criminal past. For a while, he stayed with a friend. During this time, he became aware that his family were looking for him and became fearful about what they might do. He approached the local authority housing department for help and was told that there was nothing that they could do. The victim contacted the men's advice helpline, whose poster he had seen in a toilet at his local gym. The men's advice line believed him. He was then referred to The Elm Foundation's refuge.

Case study 9

This British-Pakistani, age 17 at the time, was sent to Pakistan on the pretext of visiting family and attending a late cousin's funeral. Soon upon arriving in Pakistan, it was announced that he was to get married to a woman from an adjoining village. The victim protested, but his father became angry and accused him of bringing shame and dishonour to the family. The victim was scared about what would happen to him if he refused the marriage and feared that he would be killed. He then contacted the British High Commission and was supported to leave the country. Upon arriving in the UK, he was taken to The Elm Foundation's refuge. He received emotional support and was able to access education and benefits because of his nationality.

Case study 10

This Lithuanian male (age 43) was identified as a high-risk victim and was classified by agencies (including the police) as being at risk of being murdered. He disclosed physical and psychological abuse from his step-sister's husband (i.e. his brother-in-law) who he lived with after being made homeless. The victim stated that his brother-in-law attempted to strangle him on multiple occasions and made threats to shoot him, as he had access to firearms. The victim said that his 'brother-in-law is racist'. The victim was perceived to be an embarrassment to the family because of his different race and sexual orientation, since the victim identified as being gay. He saw his GP as he was struggling with his mental health, and the GP referred him to a high-risk service. The GP had undertaken specialist training to identify the issues that the victim was experiencing and was able to conduct a full risk assessment. However, though the victim received support from the high-risk service, he was reluctant to leave the family home and enter a male refuge. He was also frightened that he would be forced to return to Lithuania. He had no money, as he had worked for his brother-in-law and was concerned that he would be harmed if he made a police complaint. The victim did not file a report to the police, as he felt that he would not be believed. The violence intensified and the victim was supported to leave and accessed the refuge following a serious assault on him, causing significant injuries to his head. The victim refused to attend hospital or contact the police, believing that he would be returned to Lithuania.

Discussion

The case files presented highlight the very underlying objective of this book – to raise awareness that men are also victims of HBA and forced marriages and to provide real-life examples of men being supported by The Elm Foundation. While these files represent only ten cases, The Elm Foundation supports many more men each year. Their work is testimony to their gender-neutral approach towards helping victims flee domestic, HBA and forced marriages. An examination of the files demonstrates the point that responding to and improving service provision for men can be very challenging. Men may be forced into marriage for much of the same reasons as women, including fulfilling planned promises to marry family members abroad (to then retract a promise of marriage is perceived to bring shame and dishonour to the family: Gill and Anitha, 2011; Idriss, 2015). Actual (or potential) forced marriages and/or HBA occurred in these cases because the victims' families (mainly patriarchal figureheads in nearly all of the accounts – Case Files 1, 2, 3, 6, 7, 8, 9 and 10) wanted to control the men concerned, prevent undesirable relationships (including the sexual orientation of one victim), strengthen long-standing family commitments abroad or to assist in the claim to residency in the UK (Idriss, 2015). The men with physical, mental and learning disabilities were also targets of forced marriage, confirming the research by Rachel Clawson in this collection of essays that these vulnerable groups are also at risk of abuse. Case Studies 4 and 10 also demonstrate that HBA and risk of so-called honour killings can occur even in white Christian communities. This confirms much of the academic discussion that HBA is not specific to one community or group of individuals, but that HBA affects victims from a wide range of ethnic groups (Welchman and Hossain, 2005; Idriss and Abbas, 2010; Gill et al., 2014; Begikhani et al., 2015; Idriss, 2017a). Thus, research, policy development and the social construction of who can be a 'victim' needs to refocus and take into account groups of male victims from a variety of backgrounds (Samad, 2010). Case Studies 1, 2 and 10 in particular relate well to theoretical discussions about the social construction of victims because the men felt that no one (including the police) would believe that they were victims of abuse. This links well to essential ideas about the gendered stereotypes and expectations of men, as discussed in Chapter 1, and that state agencies and society in general must begin to recognise that men too can be victimised. Many of the male victims in this sample did not feel confident that they would be believed – Case Study 2 confirms existing research relating to 'masculine' identities, which can prevent men from coming forward because of a fear that they will be ridiculed by state agencies (Migliaccio, 2001; Grady, 2002: 91, 96; Cook, 2009). Case Study 8 also highlights the concern of the victim, who felt that he would not be believed because of his criminal past.

Furthermore, the case studies highlighted men's poor mental health, where some had even expressed suicidal thoughts. This, coupled with feelings of not being believed and not knowing what resources to access, added to the men's vulnerabilities, and it becomes even more imperative that abused men receive the right support and intervention early on. Policies on creating safe male spaces and trusting environments should be pursued in the long term if we are to successfully address male victimisation in HBA and forced marriages. It is currently a 'postcode lottery' whether there are any local services available that can cater for men, and some victims are at a distinct disadvantage because of the lack of male support organisations in their local area. In our experience, men have to travel (or move) further away to access support because it is not readily available within their locality (see e.g. Case Study 7 – the victim lived in a park for three days because there was no local male organisation that could support him). The Elm Foundation provided accommodation for the victim in Case Study 7, but can only house three men at any one time, and the next nearest male refuge is some 178 miles away.

Case Studies 3 and 6 highlight that men may be reluctant to make a police complaint for fear of wider repercussions if they report abuse, as they do not want to bring any shame to their families through police involvement. This is also true for female victims (Idriss, 2015). Male victims were deterred from coming forward as they did not want to dishonour their families by making matters public. The complex relationships that exist within the context of HBA and forced marriages can make it very difficult for victims to engage with the authorities when relationships concern parents and loved ones and which could lead to serious repercussions (Idriss, 2015). There is much work to be done in order to make *all* victims feel safe to bring complaints and to exit abusive relationships. On a more positive note however, Case Study 1 demonstrates the importance of early intervention by doctors, nurses and healthcare workers to screen male patients for signs of abuse. The victim in this case was empowered because he had a 'trustworthy' doctor who believed and validated his experiences. As stated in Chapter 1, healthcare institutions must be more willing to screen male patients for signs of domestic abuse, which is something that is largely undertaken with women in mind (Taket et al., 2003; Morgan et al., 2014). Previous studies have reported negative experiences for men when consulting with healthcare professionals (Migliaccio, 2001; Tsui, 2014), but Case Study 1 demonstrates that the doctor concerned was trained to screen male patients for abuse and was able to support intervention (Morgan et al., 2014; Hines and Douglas, 2015; Williamson et al., 2015; Entilli and Cipolletta, 2017). This is an encouraging emergence, but there are still problems with the overall complexion of male screening. In Case Study 6, the victim went to hospital after being badly beaten but declared that he had 'fallen over and hurt himself'. It is not clear whether the hospital accepted his explanation or pressed him further for disclosure, although the victim did return home and did not feel confident to disclose the real reasons behind his injuries to medical staff, suggesting that the hospital did not properly screen him or press for a disclosure.

Case Studies 2 and 3 support existing research that victims of HBA find it very difficult to adapt and move away from family homes (Idriss, 2018a; Mulvihill et al., 2018), which is also true for female victims. Thus, there needs to be better resources for victims and survivors in order to make the transition towards an independent life. This follows from what we call the 'prince ideology', where the nature and structure of (South Asian) families imposes unrealistic expectations upon men (Anwar, 1998; Cressey, 2006). There is an expectation for mothers to give birth to sons, with the ultimate aim that those sons will then look after their parents (Anwar, 1998; Cressey, 2006; Wilson, 2006). There are cultural and religious expectations that men are expected to abide by, all within a culture that idolises boys/men in preference to girls (Wilson, 2006). Men are provided with better education opportunities in comparison to women (Wilson, 2006), as well as better access to employment, property ownership and cars (Anwar, 1998). They are, in effect, treated like 'princes'. Men are also socialised to safeguard the reputation of the family, to make sure the *izzat* of the family is not tarnished, to manage shame and reduce it at all costs (Cressey, 2006; Wilson, 2006). They are also expected to accept marriage partners suggested by parents. However, when men cannot meet these expectations, they do not have or possess the right practical or emotional tools to deal with this failure (Samad, 2010). They may experience feelings of guilt and shame for failing to meet those expectations because they were given preferential access to education, property and cars. The 'prince ideology' may therefore go some way to explain why the male in Case Study 2 experienced difficulties – being South Asian and homosexual might have led to feelings of failing to meet the expectations of his parents on heterosexuality, so he felt compelled to go ahead with the planned (forced) marriage to safeguard his family's honour. He may also have felt a sense of guilt about both the privileges that he had and the shame about his sexual orientation. This highlights the difficulties related to the intersection of ethnicity, religion and cultural norms that can complicate men's ability to overcome their own victimisation and seek intervention; it is also a reminder that issues relating to intersectionality do not just apply to women in domestic abuse, HBA and forced marriage cases (Hogan et al., 2012).

Case Studies 7 and 10 also relate to immigration statuses and NRPF for those who enter the UK on a spousal visa and those whose immigration status remain uncertain. This can have a major impact on reporting and disclosure and, in line with the existing literature, there is an urgent need to amend the NRPF rules for both immigrant women and men if we are to see these categories of people successfully coming forward to disclose abuse. The current status quo and not being able to access public funding means that many migrant victims have no alternative but to stay in violent relationships (Case Study 10) or become homeless (Case Study 7), violating their dignity and human rights (Sharma and Gill, 2010). While this is also an important issue for migrant women, this is an even more difficult issue for male victims because of the lack of male support organisations and refuges in the UK that assist men. In our experience, migrant female victims may be supported by the financial reserves of the various women's charities from which they seek help, and in Case Study 7, The Elm Foundation funded the victim. However, because of the greater number of women's charities that can fund a migrant woman's accommodation despite having NRPF, the number of charities that can support men is much lower, thereby increasing men's vulnerabilities and increasing their chances of becoming homeless if they exit an abusive relationship (recall the male victim in Case Study 7 who lived in a park for three days). Case Study 7 can be contrasted with Case Study 9, where the victim, because of his British nationality, was able to access benefits with no issue. But the circumstances surrounding both cases are the same – both were victims of domestic/HBA at the hands of their families, but one was entitled to access services by virtue of being British, while the other was unable to because of his nationality (Sharma and Gill, 2010). This is untenable and undermines the safety, dignity and respect for victims of abuse who are not British nationals. There are also other issues, as Case Study 7 demonstrated that the victim's wife concocted lies and counter-allegations against him in order to get him deported back to Pakistan. In our HBV Roadshow Report 2018, support workers explained how men with NRPF are affected by HBA and highlighted that the authorities (e.g. the police and the Home Office) generally work under the assumption that men are not victims and if they do make applications for indefinite leave to remain, then their applications are not genuine. On the other hand, the process for female victims with NRPF can be much quicker (Idriss, 2018b, para. 26). Furthermore, NGO organisations noted that obtaining support for male victims on spousal visas with NRPF can be extremely hard and that the amount of evidence required to support male victims (e.g. to secure support from the Home Office under the current DDV Concession) can take double the work and can take even longer to process in comparison to female victims with NRPF. There still seems to be an element of non-acceptance within government departments and the police that migrant men can be victims of abuse (Idriss, 2018b, para. 26). And to compound male victims' sense of injustice, when investigating complaints of abuse by men with NRPF, the police treat male victims with suspicion, acting as border control agencies by making enquiries about the victim's immigration status and suspecting that the male victim is fabricating stories in order to secure permanent stay. Support organisations during our HBV Roadshow 2018 advised that police forces should not turn into the 'immigration police' since this is not their primary function, but that they should investigate complaints about abuse regardless of who might be the victim or perpetrator (Idriss, 2018b, para 27).

Conclusion

This chapter is a contribution to the academic debate surrounding male victimisation in HBA and forced marriage cases. An analysis of the case files provided demonstrate that men can be abused in the name of 'honour' and face similar risks as women. However, as an organisation that supports both women and men, The Elm Foundation have come to realise that the general support mechanisms available for men in the UK are not the same as they are for women. While we recognise the gendered nature of domestic abuse, we cannot ignore the increasing number of men that walk through our doors seeking refuge from HBA and forced marriages. Men bring their own unique challenges to intervention, and more awareness campaigns are needed to encourage men to recognise and identify their ordeals as abuse. Raising awareness and improved training for professionals is also imperative so that male victims are correctly identified by the agencies they approach. This includes school teachers, healthcare professionals, the police and social workers, to name but a few – it is imperative that all professionals in this area are provided with the necessary skills to identify the signs of male abuse and to have the confidence to provide intervention in such cases (Idriss, 2018a; Mulvihill et al., 2018). The next generation of children and young adults also needs to be educated, as a matter of prevention, to understand that victims can be from either gender (and so too perpetrators), to ensure that a more gender-neutral approach to talking about HBA and forced marriages takes place (Idriss, 2018a; Mulvihill et al., 2018).

We are mindful that we provide a very important service to both female and male victims, but there is clearly a need to expand our male services to support men experiencing abuse. To this end, we support a separate Ending Intimate Violence Against Men and Boys Strategy and Violence Against Men and Boys Transformation Fund to really put male victims on the map and to recognise, validate and support male victims in their own right. In this way, we hope to expand our services and support more men and not (as is currently the case) refuse refuge space because our three rooms are all occupied by male victims exiting abusive relationships. As noted in Chapter 1, the government in their report 'Transforming the Response to Domestic Abuse – Consultation Response and Draft Bill' have earmarked only £500,000 'to improve support to male victims of domestic abuse' (HM Government, 2019: 47). This pledge does not go far enough. There is no discussion of a separate Male Strategy or Transformation Fund (HM Government, 2019: 46–48) since the response itself largely focuses on VAWG, nor is there any discussion about amending the current NRPF policy for both male and female migrants wishing to exit abusive relationships. We believe that the Domestic Abuse Bill represents a missed opportunity for the government to support other vulnerable (and minority) groups who experience domestic abuse within the context of the issues raised in this chapter. We also hope that this chapter can encourage other women's organisations to open up their services to abused men, for we can certainly testify that the men we have supported over the last ten years have been very grateful for our intervention and support. It is important to promote awareness to ensure that men know that there are services available to support them and receive intervention of equal proportion to women (where there is a demand for male services). We believe that charities, including ourselves, should not be turning *any* victim away, regardless of gender.

References

Anwar, Muhammad (1998) *Between Cultures: Continuity and Change in the Lives of Young Asians*, London: Routledge.

Aplin, Rachael (2017) 'Exploring the Role of Mothers in "Honour" Based Abuse Perpetration and the Impact on the Policing Response', *Women's Studies International Forum*, Vol. 60, 1.

Begikhani, Nazand, Aisha K. Gill and Gill Hague (2015) *Honour-Based Violence: Experiences and Counter-Strategies in Iraqi Kurdistan and the UK Kurdish Diaspora*, London: Ashgate.

Chantler, Khatidja and Melanie McCarry (2019) 'Forced Marriage, Coercive Control and Conducive Contexts: The Experiences of Women in Scotland', *Violence Against Women*, 1 [Online First], available at https://journals.sagepub.com/doi/full/10.1177/1077801219830234 (last accessed 1 March 2019).

Cook, Phillip W. (2009) *Abused Men: The Hidden Side of Domestic Violence*, Westport, CT: Praeger, 2nd Edition.

Cowburn, Malcolm, Aisha K. Gill and Karen Harrison (2015) 'Speaking about Sexual Abuse in British South Asian Communities: Offenders, Victims and the Challenges of Shame and Reintegration', *Journal of Sexual Aggression*, Vol. 21, No. 1, 4.

Cressey, Gill (2006) *Disapora Youth and Ancestral Homeland: British Pakistani/Kashmiri Youth Visiting Kin in Pakistan and Kashmir*, Ledien: Brill.

Entilli, Lorenza and Sabrina Cipolletta (2017) 'When the Woman Gets Violent: The Construction of Domestic Abuse Experience from Heterosexual Men's Perspective', *Journal of Clinical Nursing*, Vol. 26, No. 15–16, 2328.

Finnegan, Ruth (2006) 'Using Documents', in Roger Sapsford and Victor Jupp (eds.) *Data Collection and Analysis*, London: Sage Publications, 2nd Edition, pp. 139–152.

George, Alexander L. and Andrew Bennett (2004) *Case Studies and Theory Development in Social Sciences*, Cambridge, MA: MIT Press.

Gill, Aisha K., Pamela Cox and Ruth Weir (2018) 'Shaping Priority Services for UK Victims of Honour-Based Violence/Abuse, Forced Marriage and Female Genital Mutilation', *The Howard Journal of Crime and Justice*, Vol. 57, No. 4, 576.

Gill, Aisha K., Caroline Strange and Karl Roberts (eds.) (2014) *Honour Killing and Violence: Theory, Policy and Practice*, Hampshire: Palgrave MacMillan.

Gillham, Bill (2000) *Case Study Research Methods*, London: Continuum.

Grady, Ann (2002) 'Female-on-Male Domestic Violence: Uncommon or Ignored?', in Carolyn Hoyle and Richard Young (eds.) *New Visions of Crime Victims*, Oxford: Hart Publishing, pp. 71–96.

Harrison, Karen and Aisha K. Gill (2017) 'Breaking Down Barriers: Recommendations for Improving Sexual Abuse Reporting Rates in British South Asian Communities', *British Journal of Criminology*, Vol. 58, No. 2, 273.

Her Majesty's Government (2019) *Transforming the Response to Domestic Abuse: Consultation Response and Draft Bill*, January, CP 15.

Hines, Denise A. and Emily M. Douglas (2015) 'Health Problems of Partner Violence Victims: Comparing Help-Seeking Men to a Population Sample', *American Journal of Preventative Medicine*, Vol. 48, No. 2, 136.

Hoath, David C. (1978) 'A Charitable Crime', *Modern Law Review*, Vol. 41, 195.

Hogan, Kevin F., John R. Hegarty, Tony Ward and Lorna J. Dodd (2012) 'Counsellor's Experiences of Working with Male Victims of Female Perpetrated Domestic Abuse', *Counselling and Psychotherapy Research*, Vol. 12, No. 1, 44.

Home Office (2018) *Forced Marriage Unit Statistics 2017*, 16 March.

Idriss, Mohammad Mazher (2015) 'Forced Marriages: The Need for Criminalisation?', *Criminal Law Review*, No. 9, 663.

Idriss, Mohammad Mazher (2017a) 'Not Domestic Violence or Cultural Tradition: Is HBV Distinct From Domestic Violence?', *Journal of Social Welfare and Family Law*, Vol. 39, No. 1, 3.

Idriss, Mohammad Mazher (2017b) '"The Mosques Are the Biggest Problem We've Got Right Now": Key Agent and Survivor Accounts of Engaging Mosques with Domestic and Honour-Based Violence in the United Kingdom', *Journal of Interpersonal Violence*, 1 [ONLINE FIRST], available at https://journals.sagepub.com/doi/abs/10.1177/0886260517703376 (last accessed 18 February 2019).

Idriss, Mohammad Mazher (2018a) 'Key Agent and Survivor Recommendations for Intervention in Honour-Based Violence in the UK', *International Journal of Comparative and Applied Criminal Justice*, Vol. 42, No. 4, 321.

Idriss, Mohammad Mazher (2018b) *Recommendations from the National Honour-Based Violence Roadshow 2018*, October, available at www2.mmu.ac.uk/business-school/research/research-centres/national-hbv/ (last accessed 18 February 2019).

Idriss, Mohammad Mazher and Tahir Abbas (eds.) (2010) *Honour, Violence, Women and Islam*, London: Routledge-Cavendish.

Migliaccio, Todd A. (2001) 'Marginalizing the Battered Male', *Journal of Men's Studies*, Vol. 9, No. 2, 205.

Morgan, Karen, Emma Williamson, Marianne Hester, Susan Jones and Gene Feder (2014) 'Asking Men About Domestic Violence and Abuse in a Family Medicine Context: Help Seeking and Views on the General Practitioner Role', *Aggression and Violent Behavior*, Vol. 19, No. 6, 637.

Mulvihill, Natasha, Geetanjali Gangoli, Aisha K. Gill and Marianne Hester (2018) 'The Experience If Interactional Justice for Victims of "Honour"-Based Violence and Abuse Reporting to the Police in England and Wales', *Policing and Society*, 1 [ONLINE FIRST], available at www.tandfonline.com/doi/full/10.1080/10439463.2018.1427745 (last accessed 18 February 2019).

Parity (2014) *Services Provided for Domestic Abuse Victims by Councils in England and Wales: Survey by PARITY of 78 City/Metropolitan and County Councils in Autumn 2014*, December, available at www.parity-uk.org/Briefing/FOISummaryAllAuthorites%20Jan15Rev4%20Complete.pdf (last accessed 18 February 2019).

Samad, Yunas (2010) 'Forced Marriage among Men: An Unrecognized Problem', *Critical Social Policy*, Vol. 30, No. 2, 189.

Sharma, Kaveri and Aisha K. Gill (2010) 'Protection for All? The Failures of the Domestic Violence Rule for (Im)migrant Women', in Ravi. K. Thiara and Aisha K. Gill (eds.) *Violence against Women in South Asian Communities: Issues for Policy and Practice*, London: Jessica Kingsley, pp. 211–237.

Simmons v Pizzey [1977] 2 All ER 432.

Taket, Ann, Jo Nurse, Katrina Smith, Judy Watson, Judy Shakespeare, Vicky Lavis, Katie Cosgrove, Kate Mulley and Gene Feder (2003) 'Routinely Asking Women about Domestic Violence in Health Settings', *British Medical Journal*, Vol. 327, No. 7416, 673.

Tsui, Venus (2014) 'Male Victims of Intimate Partner Abuse: Use and Helpfulness of Services', *Social Work*, Vol. 59, No. 2, 121.

Welchman, Lynn and Sara Hossain (eds.) (2005) *'Honour': Crimes, Paradigms and Violence against Women*, London: Zed Books.

Williamson, Emma, Sue K. Jones, Giulia Ferrari, Thangam Debbonaire, Gene Feder and Marianne Hester (2015) 'Health Professionals Responding to Men for Safety (HERMES): Feasibility of a General Practice Training Intervention to Improve the Response to Male Patients Who Have Experienced or Perpetrated Domestic Violence and Abuse', *Primary Health Care Research and Development*, Vol. 16, 281.

Wilson, Amrit (2006) *Dreams, Questions, Struggles: South Asian Women in Britain*, London: Pluto Press.

Yin, Robert K. (2003) *Case Study Research: Design and Methods*, Thousand Oaks, CA: Sage Publications, 3rd Edition.

Index

Note: Page numbers in *italics* indicate a figure and page numbers in **bold** indicate a table.

For Product Safety Concerns and Information please contact our EU representative GPSR@taylorandfrancis.com
Taylor & Francis Verlag GmbH, Kaufingerstraße 24, 80331 München, Germany

www.ingramcontent.com/pod-product-compliance
Lightning Source LLC
LaVergne TN
LVHW011128300926
849160LV00008B/555

9781032082561